The Undetected Enemy

TEXAS A&M UNIVERSITY ☆ ☆ MILITARY HISTORY SERIES 39

The

Undetected

Enemy

French and American Miscalculations
at Dien Bien Phu, 1953

by

John R. Nordell, Jr.

TEXAS A&M UNIVERSITY PRESS
COLLEGE STATION

Library of Congress Cataloging-in-Publication Data

Nordell, John R. (John Robert), 1947–
    The undetected enemy : French and American miscalculations at Dien
Bien Phu, 1953 by John Nordell, Jr.—1st ed.
    p. cm.—(Texas A&M University military history series ; 39)
Includes bibliographical references and index.
ISBN 0-89096-645-1
1. Diên Biên Phú (Vietnam), Battle of, 1954. I. Title
II. Series.
DS553.3.D5N67 1995
959.704′2—dc20   94-37073
                                                              CIP

To my mother, Dorothy Nordell,
for her love and support,
and to my late father, John Nordell,
whose humor and warmth
will always be with us.

Contents

Illustrations

MAPS

Preface

The French Indo-China war of 1946–54 was one of the longest and bloodiest conflicts of the twentieth century. It grew out of France's attempt in 1945–46 to restore its former colonial rule over Viet-Nam, Laos, and Cambodia, which had been lost to Japan during World War II. In December 1946 full-scale fighting broke out between France and the Viet-Minh, a communist-led opposition movement that had grown in power in northern Viet-Nam during the war years and had established its own government over most of Viet-Nam by V-J Day. A virtual stalemate existed during the first three years of the war, with France managing to reestablish its control over the urban areas of Viet-Nam while the Viet-Minh waged a guerrilla war throughout the vast rural areas of that country.

This situation ended in 1949–50 when Communist Chinese forces—who were victorious over their Nationalist adversaries in the Chinese civil war of 1946–49—reached the border of northern Viet-Nam. The Chinese were now able to provide the Viet-Minh with sanctuary, training bases, and arms. The French were driven back from the Sino-Vietnamese border in late 1950 and, despite some significant victories in 1951, were slowly losing the war to the Viet-Minh by 1952–53. It was clear that the fighting that would take place in 1953–54 would be crucial to the outcome of the war. Against this backdrop the French occupied the strategic valley of Dien Bien Phu, located in northwestern Viet-Nam, in November 1953.

Dien Bien Phu would become the site for the decisive battle of the French Indo-China war from March to May, 1954. Indeed, the French defeat at Dien Bien Phu set the stage for America's own military involvement in Viet-Nam a decade later. Yet, despite the historic importance of this military engagement, there remains to this day a great deal of uncertainty, contradictory testimony, and outright mythology as to why the French chose to make a stand at a location that, with hindsight, held such apparent risks. This book addresses that question and, with the aid of a wide array of recently declassifed U.S. documents on Indo-China, tells the full story of the strategic, tactical, logistical, and intelligence considerations by the French High Command during November–December 1953 that underlay their final decision to fight at Dien Bien Phu.

Most studies of the battle of Dien Bien Phu, especially by American historians, have focused on the climactic Viet-Minh siege of the French position in the spring of 1954. The issue of U.S. intervention hung in the balance during this period and American officials, in their memoirs and subsequent recollections, have universally condemned the French decision to fight there. This book offers evidence that, in fact, these same officials, including President Eisenhower, initially reacted to the French seizure of Dien Bien Phu with little or no concern and displayed a continued willingness to trust in French military judgment. In addition to my use of declassified documents, some of which I obtained through the Freedom of Information Act, I have looked closely at older primary sources, particularly Gen. Henri Navarre's wartime account, *Agonie de l'Indochine, 1953–1954,* and his autobiography, *Le Temps des Vérités.* Also valuable was the large collection of secondary sources that are available on Dien Bien Phu, including the two standard works on the subject, Bernard Fall's *Hell in a Very Small Place* and Jules Roy's *The Battle of Dienbienphu.*

The text of this story is written as a narrative chronology in order to allow the reader to see, and vicariously experience, the rapidly unfolding developments from the "ground level" perspective of the participants themselves. To enhance the realism and provide additional insight, I have included quotations from contemporaneous press coverage and from previously classified government documents from that period. Necessary background and information supplementary to the text appear in the footnotes and appendices. In the epilogue I pull together the threads of the story and present my answer to the decades-old question, "Pourquoi Dien Bien Phu?"

Acknowledgments

I want to express my thanks to those who assisted me in my research on *The Undetected Enemy*. Included are the staffs at the Military Reference Branch and the Civil Reference Branch of the National Archives in Washington, D.C. as well as the staffs at the Dwight D. Eisenhower Library in Abilene, Kansas, the Office of Air Force History at Bolling Air Force Base in Washington, D.C., the U.S. Army Center of Military History in Washington, D.C., and the U.S. Army Military History Institute at Carlisle Barracks, Pennsylvania. Their wide knowledge and unfailing courtesy are greatly appreciated.

Nearer home, I wish to acknowledge the friendly assistance of the Penn State staffs at both Pattee Library and the Center for Academic Computing. Members of the interlibrary loan department at Pattee fielded (and found) an unending stream of requests. Tom Minsker at CAC was especially helpful in solving technical problems with the layout of the manuscript. My thanks also to Darcy Wertz, a former Penn State graduate student in French, for carefully reviewing my translations, to John Beck and his associates at The Bookmakers, Inc. in Wilkes-Barre, Pennsylvania, for their thoroughly professional work on my maps, and to Richard Ross of Wilkes-Barre, for his excellent work on nineteen of my photographs. My sincerest thanks go to Dr. Ira Brown, professor emeritus of American history at Penn State, for his help in obtaining research support for this project.

The following publishers have generously given permission to use extended quotations from copyrighted works:

From *The Ten Thousand Day War*, by Michael Maclear. Reprinted with permission from St. Martin's Press, Inc., New York, N.Y. Copyright © 1981 by Michael Maclear. From an article in the *Times* (London). Reprinted by permission. Copyright © Times Newspapers Ltd., 1953. From *Eisenhower: Captive Hero*, by Marquis Childs. Reprinted by permission of Brandt & Brandt Literary Agents, Inc. Copyright © estate of

Marquis Childs, 1958. From *The First Vietnam Crisis,* by Melvin Gurtov. Copyright © 1967 Columbia University Press, New York. Reprinted by permission of the publisher. From an article in *Time* magazine. Copyright © Time, Inc., 1953. Reprinted by permission. From *Communist Revolutionary Warfare,* by George K. Tanham (Praeger, 1967); *The Smaller Dragon,* by Joseph Buttinger (Praeger, 1958); *Modern Warfare,* by Roger Trinquier (Praeger, 1964); and *End of a War,* by Philippe Devillers and Jean Lacouture (Praeger, 1969). Copyright © by Greenwood Publishing Group, Inc., Westport, Conn. Reprinted by permission. From *The Endless War: Fifty Years of Struggle in Vietnam,* by James P. Harrison. Copyright © 1982 by the Free Press, a division of Macmillan, Inc. Reprinted by permission. From "The War in Indo-China," in *Brassey's Annual: The Armed Forces Year-Book, 1954,* (Macmillan, 1954). Copyright © by Brassey's, Inc. Reprinted by permission. From *The Face of South Vietnam,* by Dean Brelis and Jill Krementz. Text copyright © by Dean Brelis, 1967. Reprinted by permission of Houghton Mifflin Co. All rights reserved. From articles in the *New York Times, Atlanta Constitution, Washington Post,* and *Los Angeles Times.* Copyright © 1953. Reprinted by permission of United Press International, Inc. From *From Pearl Harbor,* by Stephen Jirika. Reprinted by permission of Hoover Institution Press. Copyright © 1976 by the Board of Trustees of the Leland Stanford Junior University. From *Hell in a Very Small Place,* by Bernard Fall. Copyright © 1966 by Bernard B. Fall. Reprinted by permission of HarperCollins Publishers, Inc. From *The Battle of Dienbienphu,* by Jules Roy. Copyright © 1965 by Harper and Row Publishers, Inc. Reprinted by permission of HarperCollins Publishers, Inc.

Note on Vietnamese Names

In writing this book, it was necessary for me to determine the correct spelling and word placement for certain Vietnamese proper names. On the spelling of the name "Viet-Nam," I was guided by the earlier judgments of Allan Cameron and Bernard Fall.

Cameron writes: "Vietnam, Viet Nam, and Viet-nam are variant spellings in current use, but Viet-Nam is the form most in accord with the Vietnamese language" (Allan W. Cameron, ed., *Viet-Nam Crisis: A Documentary History,* vol. 1 [1940–56], p. xxiii).

Fall elaborates on this point as follows:

> The word "Viet" has always designated the people of Viet-Nam, with the additional word "Nam" ("south") indicating that they were located to the south of their Chinese-dominated kinsmen. Therefore, the term is properly divided into two words, with a separation between place (or ethnic) name and location. . . . The hyphen between the words is dictated by Vietnamese grammar and pronunciation. (Bernard B. Fall, *The Two Viet-Nams: A Political and Military Analysis,* 2nd ed., rev., p. 9, n.)

I also sought to present the names of individual persons in a manner that would conform with traditional Vietnamese usage. On this I have adopted the practice that was used by James Pinckney Harrison.

> When Vietnamese names are given in full, the surname or family name is traditionally put first and the given name last. When shortened names are used, Vietnamese are normally called by their given names. Thus Vo Nguyen Giap is universally referred to as Giap or General Giap . . . [although his surname is Vo]. Certain historical figures, however, like Ho Chi Minh, are addressed by their surnames, as Ho or Uncle Ho. The bibliography . . . [is] organized by

surname, so that the writings of Giap, for example, are listed under Vo Nguyen Giap. (James Pinckney Harrison, *The Endless War: Fifty Years of Struggle in Vietnam,* p. xi.)

In all cases, the spelling of words and names from quoted material is presented as it appears in the original sources.

The Undetected Enemy

1
Operation Castor

The American-built C-47 took off from Hanoi's Bach-Mai military airport at approximately 5:00 A.M. on November 20, 1953. It carried enough fuel for eight hours of flying and was outfitted with sufficient radio communications equipment to enable it to maintain contact with the entire command.

The purpose of this military mission was to evaluate the weather conditions over the valley of Dien Bien Phu. If the results were favorable, the twin-engine Dakota would drop the pathfinders—an elite group of paratroopers—whose task was to jump a few minutes before the bulk of the troops and to earmark the designated drop zones with smoke markers.[1]

The aircraft also contained three French generals: Lt. Gen. Pierre Bodet, French Air Force, the deputy commander in chief in Indo-China; Brig. Gen. Jean Dechaux, French Air Force, the commander of Gatac Nord, the tactical air group that controlled all French air operations in northern Indo-China; and Brig. Gen. Jean Gilles, the commander of French airborne forces in Indo-China.[2] The responsibility for deciding whether or not to proceed with the airdrop belonged to General Dechaux.

Dien Bien Phu was located 187 miles west of Hanoi. The transport arrived over its destination at 6:30 A.M. and its occupants observed that the valley was covered by the *crachin*, the dry fog that was characteristic of the weather in Viet-Nam's northwestern region. By 7:00 A.M. General Dechaux had made a decision. He gave a brief message to the radio operator who was specially assigned to handle direct communications between the aircraft and headquarters at Hanoi.

At 7:20 A.M. the message reached Maj. Gen. René Cogny, the commander of ground forces in northern Viet-Nam and the overall commander of the operation. He immediately relayed the information to Col. Jean Louis Nicot, the commander of the transport air force for

Indo-China, who was waiting at the airport at Bach-Mai. By 7:30 A.M the news reached the assembled transport aircraft where it created considerable excitement among the paratroopers who had been gathered there since 6:30 A.M. The mission was "on."[3]

The sixty-five lumbering C-47s were to take off in two serials: the first serial of thirty-three aircraft would depart from Bach-Mai Airport; the second serial of thirty-two aircraft would leave from Gia-Lom Airport.

At shortly before 8:00 A.M. the airplane engines began to turn over in the cold air and red signal flares rose above the control towers at the two airports. One after another the heavily loaded Dakotas became airborne, each carrying about twenty-five paratroopers. The aircraft flew in slow circles until all had formed up in groups of three (their noses painted blue, yellow, or red). When they had taken their proper places in the flight pattern, the transports made up a column that extended over seven miles.

By 8:15 A.M. the entire armada, flanked by B-26 Invaders, was slowly heading westward toward Dien Bien Phu. Operation Castor had begun.

General Gilles already knew that there were communist troops at Dien Bien Phu and that his airborne forces would therefore meet with at least initial resistance. He had decided to drop two battalions in the first phase of the operation and, for this hazardous mission, he had chosen the most able units and commanders that were available in all of Indo-China: the 6th Colonial Parachute Battalion (Bataillon de Parachutistes Coloniaux, or BPC) of Maj. Marcel Bigeard and the 2nd Battalion of the 1st Parachute Light Infantry Regiment (II/1 RCP) of Maj. Jean Bréchignac. The 6th BPC and the II/1 RCP had 651 and 569 men, respectively. Together with the 1st Colonial Parachute Battalion (1st BPC), another elite unit which was commanded by Maj. Jean Souquet, these two battalions formed Airborne Battle Group No. 1 (Groupement Aeroporte), or GAP 1.[4]

Three drop zones (DZ) had been selected in the valley of Dien Bien Phu, two of them for the paratroopers and one for their equipment (see map 1). The most important drop zone, dubbed "Natasha," had a total length of 4,268 feet and a total width of 1,478 feet. Aligned almost north-south, it was covered with semidry rice fields, had considerable brush at its lower end, and was crossed by a small creek at its middle. It was located 657 feet northwest of the village of Dien Bien Phu and 985 feet to the west of its airfield. DZ Natasha had been assigned to the 6th BPC. DZ "Simone," extending over rice fields and hillocks, was situated 4,597 feet to the southeast of Dien Bien Phu. It had been chosen for the II/1 RCP. The material drop zone, DZ "Octavie," was located to the southwest

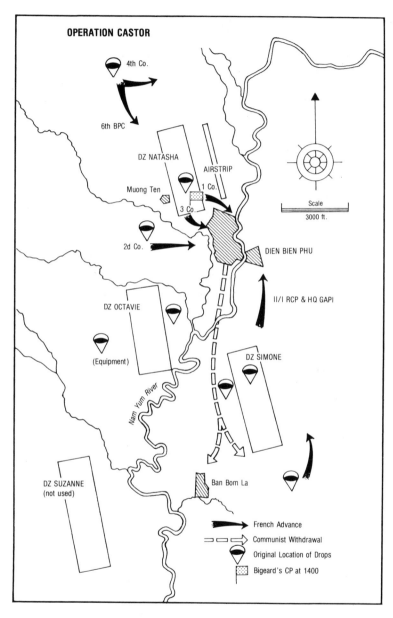

1. The map of battle at Dien Bien Phu.

of Dien Bien Phu and was well away from the personnel drop zones so as to avoid the serious injuries that could occur from free-falling equipment.

The 6th BPC was to be reinforced by the 17th Company of Airborne Combat Engineers and two batteries from the 35th Airborne Artillery Regiment. The II/1 RCP would give cover to the Headquarters Group of GAP 1 that was to jump with it. In pushing northwestward from DZ Simone in the direction of Dien Bien Phu, the II/1 RCP would also insure that no major communist elements would escape to the south.

The paratroop commanders had two objectives in this operation. The first was to secure the airfield as quickly as possible and the second was to capture the headquarters of Trung-Doan Doc-Lap (Independent Regiment) 148. The 148th specialized in mountain warfare and was an old elite regiment of the communist Viet-Nam People's Army, or "Viet-Minh" as it was popularly called.[5] It had made Dien Bien Phu its main base of operations for nearly a year.

Three of the 148th Regiment's four battalions—the 900th, the 920th, and the 930th—were away from Dien Bien Phu and in jungle garrisons along the Vietnamese-Laotian frontier. The 910th Battalion and the regimental headquarters had remained behind. French intelligence knew this but what it did not know was that Heavy Weapons Company 226 of Battalion 920, equipped with mortars and recoilless rifles, had also remained at Dien Bien Phu. It had been joined there by another heavy weapons company, this one from the 675th Artillery Regiment of Heavy Division 351, the Viet-Minh's Soviet-patterned artillery division. In addition, there was one infantry company of the 48th Regiment of the 320th Infantry Division.[6]

At 9:00 A.M. Rear Adm. Georges-Etienne Cabanier, assistant secretary general of the Permanent Secretariat of France's Committee of National Defense, was shown into the Saigon office of Gen. Henri Navarre, the commander in chief of French forces in Indo-China.[7]

After the customary courtesies, Admiral Cabanier came to the point of his trip: the president of France, Vincent Auriol, and the prime minister, Joseph Laniel, wanted some information directly from General Navarre. With the signing of the armistice in Korea (on July 27, 1953) and the consequences this might have on increased Communist Chinese aid to the Viet-Minh, and in light of the favorable situation created by recent French military successes in the Red River Delta, was the time not right, they inquired, to open negotiations for the purpose of obtaining a cease-fire in Indo-China?[8]

Gen. Henri Navarre. From John Keegan, *Dien Bien Phu.*

Smiling, Navarre pushed a tray toward the admiral in which were piled the dispatches on Operation Castor.

"Read that," he said.[9]

Cabanier then learned of the vast airborne mission that would shortly be carried out at Dien Bien Phu.

It would take some time, Navarre estimated, for Chinese aid to increase and when it did, he would be alerted by his intelligence sources. Furthermore, he expected the military situation to be even better by the spring of 1954. Therefore, as far as he was concerned, this new operation provided his answer to Paris on the proposed negotiations: an unqualified "No."[10]

Admiral Cabanier had news of his own that morning. The government, Cabanier told Navarre, wished to inform him of the decisions that had been made by the Committee of National Defense at its meeting of November 13. The committee asked that the commander in chief "adjust his plans to the means at his disposal" and limit his ambitions to containing the enemy. It confirmed to him that "the objective of our action in Indochina is to make the enemy realize that it is impossible for him to win a military victory."[11]

The committee gave substance to these instructions by its handling of General Navarre's demands for reinforcements: it decided not to fulfill them.

Dien Bien Phu was a large village that sat in an oblong valley, the major valley axis lying on a north-south line and measuring approximately ten miles in length. The valley's width ranged from a narrow waist of about three and a half miles to a maximum of around five miles across the northern sector where the village was located.[12]

The valley was composed mainly of rice paddies and was the biggest and richest of the four plains in this mountainous region. Although flat, it contained a few scattered hillocks as well as several streams and canals. A small river, the Nam Yum, flowed through the village from north to south. The valley also had the unique natural feature of being in a saucer-shaped basin that was dominated by hills and mountains on all sides. The proximity of these slopes, with their dark jungle tree cover, gave them a forbidding-looking appearance.[13]

Throughout the region there were a hundred or so villages and tiny hamlets that were occupied by about ten thousand inhabitants of various ethnic minorities. Most belonged to the Thais who lived in the valley and were distinguished by the color or style of dress that was worn by the women of the different communities. Dour-looking Meo tribesmen were

Dien Bien Phu: The valley. From Pierre Langlais, *Dien Bien Phu*.

Dien Bien Phu: The mountains. From Pierre Langlais, *Dien Bien Phu.*

located high up on the surrounding mountains. Halfway up the slopes were the Xas, who served both the Thais and the Meos as slaves.[14]

Dien Bien Phu was in the middle of a fertile and prosperous opium growing district. The Meo tribesmen specialized in growing opium poppies and the Thais, with their control of the valley, were the middlemen who marketed the poppies to the Vietnamese.

The valley, located in the Thai Highlands of northwestern Viet-Nam, was only eight miles from the Laotian border and was situated about equidistant from the Red River Delta to the east, from the Sino-Vietnamese border to the north, and from Luang Prabang to the southwest. It was thus a center of communications and at the junction of many important routes: north to China and to Lai Chau (Viet-Nam); northeast to Tuan Giao (Viet-Nam); east toward Son La (Viet-Nam), Na-San (Viet-Nam), and Hoa-Binh (Viet-Nam); southeast to Sam Neua (Laos); south to the Plain of Jars (Laos); and southwest toward Luang Prabang (Laos) (see map 2).[15]

The paratroop transport armada reached the valley of Dien Bien Phu at 10:30 A.M. The sun had burned away the last particles of fog as the Dakotas appeared from behind the crests. The headquarters aircraft with the three generals was still flying high above the valley.

As the first wave of aircraft neared DZ Natasha, the pilots could see tiny human figures running away. They were peasants frantically seeking the safety of the villages or the mountains.

The peasants were not the only ones who were surprised that morning. A Viet-Minh mortar unit and several rifle companies were carrying out exercises and field problems near the airstrip at the moment when the airdrop was about to commence. They comprised the bulk of the one and a half battalions of approximately eight hundred communist troops who were then in the valley. Furthermore, most of their mortars and machine guns were deployed in firing positions all over Natasha.

The jump buzzers in the vanguard of the C-47s began to ring at 10:35 A.M. Suddenly the sky was full of parachutes. The communists opened fire on the paratroopers of the 6th BPC while they were still swinging helplessly in the air. Two men were killed before landing. One of them was the doctor of the battalion, Captain André, who died from a bullet that hit him squarely in the forehead. A third paratrooper was killed by accident when his main parachute failed to open and his backup chute became entangled in the folds of the first chute.

The first men to land on Natasha were fallen upon by the Viet-Minh unit that was undergoing mortar training. The communists fought hard.

2. Dien Bien Phu. Its location in northwestern Viet-Nam and northern Indo-China.

Some of the paratroopers were knifed to death before they could unbuckle their parachutes.[16]

Fortunately for the 6th BPC, the fighting was confusing as well as deadly. The tall elephant grass hid friend and foe alike and, in addition, both the paratroopers and the communists were wearing the French paratroop camouflage uniform.[17] As the men continued to land, they shed their parachutes, loaded their weapons, and either made for cover or joined up with others and advanced toward the clouds of colored smoke that marked the rallying points.

Many of the paratroopers did not land where they were supposed to. The whole 4th Company of the 6th BPC was dropped much too far to the north of Natasha and landed in thick brush. The same thing happened to part of 2nd Company. The rest of the battalion—1st Company and 3rd Company as well as the 17th Engineers and the 35th Artillery—

French paratroopers await the order to descend on Dien Bien Phu during Operation Castor. From John Keegan, *Dien Bien Phu.*

landed more or less within the general area of the drop zone but were immediately pinned down under small arms and mortar fire.

At DZ Simone, the airdrop was also off target because of poor communications between the air formations. The II/1 RCP landed too far to the south and was spread over too wide an area. However, Simone was deserted and the troops met with no resistance.[18]

The commander of the 6th BPC, Major Bigeard, set up his command post at the southern end of his drop zone. By 10:40 A.M. part of the 1st Company was deployed around him and by 11:00 A.M. two more platoons from that company had regrouped and faced westward toward the village of Muong Ten.

At 11:30 A.M. the Viet-Minh fired a heavy barrage of mortars into the center of Natasha. Bigeard could not call for help because his command set's aerial had been shot up by communist fire. However, the major was able to make contact with all of his companies and to take command of the battle with the aid of U.S. Army ANPRC-10 radio sets. First Company remained under heavy enemy fire but was being reinforced by 3rd Company. Second Company was holding its own to the west and 4th Company was assembling in the north (see map 1).

At 12:15 P.M. a Morane-500 Cricket French Army observation plane arrived over Dien Bien Phu. With its radio equipment, the tiny aircraft was able to relay Bigeard's request for air strikes from B-26s that had been standing by to support the paratroopers since the beginning of the operation. Bigeard himself directed as the fighters successfully carried out their attacks.[19] The intensity of enemy fire began to taper off substantially.

The 1st BPC of Maj. Jean Souquet had also been ready since 6:30 A.M. that day. With the Dakotas having returned to their bases in Hanoi for refueling, the battalion of 722 paratroopers embarked on thirty of the transport aircraft and jumped over DZ Natasha in mid-afternoon.[20]

At 3:30 P.M. 1st Company of the 6th BPC attempted to encircle Dien Bien Phu from the north and came under heavy automatic weapons fire. Bigeard again called for air support and the resulting strike destroyed the whole center of the village. The major also used his mortars to begin to hit the enemy's probable line of retreat to the south.

Third Company and part of 1st Company, supported by the 1st BPC, were now able to penetrate Dien Bien Phu. First Company advanced along the town's main road as it closed in on the headquarters of the Viet-Minh's 148th Regiment. There was brutal house-to-house fighting and the headquarters company of the Viet-Minh 910th Battalion made a

The 1st BPC lands at Dien Bien Phu on November 20. From Pierre Langlais, *Dien Bien Phu.*

suicidal, last-ditch counterattack in order to shield a successful withdrawal by the regimental staff.

The communist troops pulled out of Dien Bien Phu about 4:00 P.M. and traveled south along the right bank of the Nam Yum River. The terrain was heavily overgrown along this section of the river and not sufficiently sealed off to bar the enemy's way, with the result that the bulk of the Viet-Minh forces escaped in this direction (see map 1).

The II/1 RCP was hampered in its efforts to assist the other two battalions by its assignment to protect GAP 1 Headquarters. Poor radio communications with the other units also undermined its effectiveness and thus prevented any successful maneuvering by the II/1 RCP against the enemy.

An air force liaison team, which had jumped with the 6th BPC that morning, set up quarters near Bigeard's command post at the southern end of Natasha. At 4:02 P.M. two American-built H19-B helicopters arrived from Lai Chau, fifty-five miles to the north, carrying one high-frequency and two VHF transmitters. With these, the forward air controllers had the means for direct communications with the B-26s and with the radio sets of the paratroop battalions. The two helicopters took the most seriously wounded with them on their return trip.

The equipment drops on DZ Octavie began that afternoon. Losses of equipment were minimal and due mostly to scattered parachutes.

At 4:15 P.M. General Navarre sent an official dispatch from Saigon to Paris in order to inform the French government of Operation Castor. Encoded and marked urgent, it was addressed to Marc Jacquet, Secretary of State for Relations with the Associated States.[21] It read as follows:

> From the General Commander-in-Chief. The veering off toward the north-west of the [Viet-Minh] 316th Division constitutes a serious menace for Lai-Chau and will bring about within a short time the destruction of our guerrilla forces in the [Thai] highlands.[22] I have, therefore, decided upon a thrust on Dien-Bien-Phu which is to be the base of operations for the 316th, and whose reoccupation will, furthermore, cover the approaches to Luang-Prabang which, without this, would be in grave danger within a few weeks. The operation began this morning at 1030 hours by the drop of a first wave of two paratroop battalions. A second wave composed of a battalion reinforced by elements of 75-mm. guns jumped at 1500 hours [3:00 P.M.]. An engagement in the center of the village was indicated at the beginning of the afternoon and was terminated to our advantage.

The airborne operation will be continued tomorrow by the parachuting of three new battalions. An operation by Laotion forces is anticipated shortly in order to establish a link between Luang-Prabang and Dien-Bien-Phu. Once this connection is realized, Dien-Bien-Phu will be occupied by a mixed detachment of forces from North-Vietnam and from Laos. Respectfully—NAVARRE[23]

After being decoded, General Navarre's dispatch was sent by Jacquet's chief private secretary to Prime Minister Laniel who, in turn, transmitted its contents to President Auriol and to René Pleven, the minister of national defense, as well as to the other ministers, and to the chiefs of staff. The news caused enormous surprise. Why, it was wondered, was Navarre launching such a large-scale operation so far from his bases?

Later that day in Saigon, Maurice Dejean, the French commissioner general in Indo-China, gave a dinner at the Norodom Palace to which both General Navarre and Admiral Cabanier were invited. Neither Navarre nor Cabanier said anything about the real nature of the admiral's trip and Cabanier limited his remarks to noting the optimism that was being displayed by the High Command at the start of a new campaign.

By 5:30 P.M., as night fell, Major Bigeard had established his command post inside Dien Bien Phu and was covering the approaches to the village with the four companies of the 6th BPC. The II/1 RCP had come up along the left bank of the Nam Yum and installed itself on the first hills along the southeastern edge of Dien Bien Phu. The 1st BPC, reinforced by two batteries of 75-mm. airborne artillery and a company of 120-mm. heavy mortars, protected DZ Natasha. An airborne surgical unit, dropped during the afternoon, was set up in the drop zone and a Father Chevalier comforted the wounded and administered the last rites to the dead and the dying.[24]

At least ninety Viet-Minh troops had died in the battle.[25] In addition, the French captured four enemy wounded and found one automatic rifle, ten submachine guns, and the one hundred field packs of Heavy Weapons Company 226 of Battalion 920. Also, most of the 148th Regiment's document files were abandoned at its headquarters.

Operation Castor offered fresh evidence of the power and strategic mobility of the Expeditionary Corps. There was satisfaction and confidence about the future in both civilian and military circles. Most important, as the first day of battle ended, the French had Dien Bien Phu.

2
Digging In

The news of Operation Castor came too late to make the Paris newspapers that Friday but most of the papers carried banner headlines on Saturday, November 21.

Typical was the headline of *Paris Presse,* which boldly announced: "Lightning-like Operation in Tonking [Tonkin]—Parachuted from 150 Dakotas, Thousands of French-Vietnamese Paratroopers Conquer Dien Bien Phu . . . 'This is not a raid. We've taken the place and we shall stay there,' declares General Cogny."[1]

The United Press (UP) sent a more acccurate account from Hanoi early that day:

> More than 1,000 French Union paratroopers dropped in a mass jump at dawn yesterday to attack a Communist stronghold 125 miles west of here.
>
> The paratroopers jumped from a fleet of more than sixty planes that roared out of Hanoi under cover of twenty B-26's in a top secret operation. General Rene Cogny, French northern commander in Indo-China, supervised the take-off.
>
> Little resistance was encountered at the Red stronghold, Dienbienphu, the reports said.[2]

The Associated Press (AP) also sent an early dispatch from Hanoi that gave this report:

> The French High Command said today that the French and Vietnamese paratroopers dropped at Dienbienphu had fully occupied that rebel center. . . .
>
> The French said their paratroopers were dropped early yesterday in a surprise attack on the broad plain around Dienbienphu and quickly captured the town and its airfield. They claim to have in-

flicted heavy losses on the rebels. Gen. Rene Cogny said the paratroopers involved in the operation would remain in Dienbienphu. He said the main object of the attack was to give assistance to partisans among the Thai tribesmen and to build them into a strong striking force so they could, by stages, take back much of the Thai territory the Vietminh captured in a sweeping offensive last winter.[3]

The AP pointed to two additional benefits resulting from the capture of Dien Bien Phu: "Fall of the town ended a long-standing threat to Lai-chau, capital of the pro-French Thai mountain tribes fifty miles north of Dienbienphu.

It also put the French in a strong position to block any new attempt by the Communist-led Vietminh to invade the Kingdom of Laos, one of three associated Indo-Chinese states."[4]

Airborne Battle Group No. 2 (GAP 2) arrived at Dien Bien Phu on November 21. Its lead element was the 1st Foreign Legion Parachute Battalion (1st BEP) which jumped at 8:00 A.M. and parachuted through a blue morning haze and low clouds to land on DZ Natasha.[5]

General Gilles and his command headquarters were also dropped in this first wave. Their arrival meant that Operation Castor was now being commanded from Dien Bien Phu itself.[6] The forty-nine-year-old general landed correctly and uneventfully in a rice field. The glass eye that he always took out before a drop was carefully placed in the breast pocket of his jump suit.

A ceremony was held that morning in which the 6th BPC's fatalities of the day before were buried. The parachutes that had carried the paratroopers into the valley served as their shrouds. Before the end of the day the graves were marked by a small row of white wooden crosses and wreaths of flowers. The burial site was surrounded by a hand rope and behind it stood a newly raised flagpole for the French tricolor.

The 656 men of the 8th Parachute Assault Battalion (8e Bataillon de Parachutistes de Choc, or 8th BPC) dropped on Natasha at 1:05 P.M. From there they left for Dien Bien Phu's airfield to help with its rebuilding; the communists had guarded against the possible use of airplanes by the French by putting twelve hundred deep holes in the airstrip.

Other French platoons were in pursuit of retreating elements of Viet-Minh Regiment 148. They were assisted by circling B-26s and Bearcats that were guided by Major Bigeard. Larger and slower four-engine Privateers, with a longer range, bombed communist approach routes to the valley.

Lumbering transport aircraft, assisted by civilian crews, began to disgorge tons of airdropped freight over DZ Octavie. Among the rain of provisions were rolls of barbed wire, known as "fakir's pillows," that bounced when they hit the ground.

That afternoon the American ambassador in Saigon, Donald R. Heath, sent the following cable to the State Department in Washington:

> SECRET   SAIGON, November 21, 1953—4 P.M.
>
> 897. Repeated [for] information [to] Paris 258, Hanoi unnumbered. General Navarre told me last night he was much encouraged over [the] success of [the] three-battalion parachute drop at Dien Bien Phu. He had absolute intelligence that [the] Viet Minh planned to take Lai Chau. He must resist this not because of [the] importance in itself of Lai Chau but because it was [a] necessary case for expanding [the] guerrilla operations which were harassing [the] Viet Minh rear with increasing success. He could not defend Lai Chau by increasing [the] garrison because by reason of its cuplike situation he would need 12 battalions to hold it. His battalions at Dien Bien Phu aided by [the Thai] guerrillas, should be able to thwart Viet Minh operations against Lai Chau.
>
> Navarre told me that he had hesitated to make [the] Dien Bien Phu parachute operation since with [a] limited number of transport planes he could only drop two battalions at a time in an area where they would be opposed by two Viet Minh battalions. Fortunately [the] latter had not reacted promptly and he had sent [the] planes back for [an] additional battalion. He had had some 40 casualties but [the] Viet Minh had had double that number. . . .HEATH[7]

General Cogny met with the press that evening in Hanoi and did nothing to conceal his joy over the newly won French position. "This is a point from which we can extend offensives as we see fit, along with aid from the [Thai] partisans,"[8] he declared. He added that he intended to use as many troops as necessary to hold Dien Bien Phu until such time as he no longer found it profitable.

Cogny also talked at length about guerrillas and the *maquis,*[9] and his most memorable remark was made to a UP correspondent. "If I had been able to," he said, "I would have moved Na-San en masse to Dien Bien Phu."[10]

Cogny's intention to "hold Dienbienphu," observed the Associated Press, "reverses the recent French strategy of striking, wrecking rebel bases and withdrawing quickly."[11]

The Indo-China war and the future of Southeast Asia. From the *New York Herald Tribune*, Nov. 20, 1953, p. 18. Courtesy of the *International Herald Tribune*.

The AP had the following additonal information to report on the previous day's seizure of Dien Bien Phu: "French pilots flying American-
built B-26 bombers wrecked the key Viet Minh fortress here and forced
most of the garrison, estimated up to 3,000 men, to head for the hills
before the first paratroopers were dropped yesterday.

Small detachments of the rebels, disguised in paratroopers' uniforms,
stayed behind to fight. Eighty of them were killed. The French and Vietnamese losses were described as light."[12]

The news service brought the story up to date with this report on that
day's arrival of GAP 2: "The French dropped 1,000 more paratroopers
on the broad plain about this newly captured Viet Minh stronghold today
and dug in to hold it indefinitely.

French and Vietnamese troopers jumped from American-supplied
Dakotas to the rice paddies and grazing land around Dienbienphu, 180
miles west of Hanoi."[13] The latest paratroopers were dropped, said the
AP, "to reinforce the thousands of others—'many battalions,' the French
said—who captured the town yesterday." The plain, it was added, was
"dotted" by the cast-off parachutes of the soldiers.[14]

The AP did not overlook the reaction of the Thais, both in Dien Bien
Phu and throughout the tribal zone, to the turn of events:

> Thai peasants gathering rice or tending to their herds were smil-
> ing. The arrival of the French Union forces meant an end to the Viet
> Minh control of their town, made up of clusters of straw-thatched
> clay huts. The Red control was established when the rebels overran
> most of the pro-French Thai country a year ago. . . .
>
> Armed tribesmen were already rallying to the French. The
> 300,000 Thai have long feared that the Viet Minh would try to com-
> plete the conquest of their region by taking the palm-lined regional
> capital of Laichau, on the upper Black River fifty miles north of Dien-
> bienphu.[15]

The 5th Vietnamese Parachute Battalion (5e Bataillon de Parachutistes Vietnamiens, or 5th BPVN) parachuted into Dien Bien Phu on the
morning of November 22. It was the last of the paratroop battalions that
would make up the initial garrison and, with its arrival, there were now
4,560 troops in the valley.

Everywhere there was the joyful hum of a successful operation. The
men were digging holes, filling sacks with earth, putting up barbed wire,
erecting bivouacs and field kitchens, bathing in the river, opening crates,
and piling up parachutes. Telephones rang and radios crackled in Gen-

eral Gilles's headquarters. Officers rode about on bicycles and a few made use of mountain ponies that they had found tethered to Thai peasant houses. Gilles, for his part, traveled to the various battalion command posts on his paratroop scooter.

Adding to this air of fantasy was the multinational character of the French Union forces. French soldiers cooked over small camp fires and slept in pup tents along with Vietnamese, Arabs, Africans, and Foreign Legionnaires.[16]

Amid the hustle and bustle, the verdant valley was slowly being transformed by the preparations for war: several of the native houses were dismantled by the 17th Engineers in order to build emergency bridges across the Nam Yum River; new tent cities for the paratroopers covered formerly empty hillocks; and shells were fired off into the hills in order to get the range. The dust that was kicked up by the continuing rain of cargo added to the smoke from large brush fires, some of which were set by the paratroopers in order to clear away vegetation from prospective fields of fire and future strongpoints. Other fires were intended to clear approaches to the airfield which, thanks to intensive spade work, had been partly opened to receive small aircraft. Meanwhile, the engineers began to put in place long rows of prefabricated pierced steel plates for a planned 3,500 foot long runway.

The new airfield received its first outside visitor early that afternoon when General Cogny arrived in a Canadian-built Beaver. The giant Cogny laboriously emerged from the small aircraft, which was otherwise filled with bicycles. Gilles was there to greet his commander, with whom he exchanged salutes and shook hands. The two then went to the combat post where Gilles explained to Cogny what measures he had taken to protect the camp from attack, indicated the siting and purpose of his gun batteries, and gave a detailed account of the reconnoitering expeditions that had been carried out.

Cogny was already aware that many senior officers in his command, including Gilles, had been opposed to establishing a new airhead behind communist lines. Despite his optimistic statements of the night before, Cogny himself could not help thinking about the implications of a new Na-San. Gilles had personally conducted the difficult defense of Na-San for six long months and, although he had earned his brigadier general's stars there, he did not want to go through the same sort of experience again. He had been assured that—after seizing Dien Bien Phu—he would turn over his command to someone else.

"I'll feel happier," Gilles said privately to Cogny that afternoon, "when you've found a successor for me."

Gen. René Cogny (*left*) and Gen. Jean Gilles at Dien Bien Phu on November 22. From Jules Roy, *The Battle of Dienbienphu.*

"We're thinking about that," Cogny replied.

"At Na-San I spent six months of my life like a rat," Gilles continued. "Use me in the open air."

"That's a promise," said Cogny. "It will only be a matter of days."[17]

As the two men were talking, the first flight of three Morane-500 observation aircraft of the 21st Aerial Artillery Observation Group (21e Groupe Aerion d'Observation d'Artillerie, or 21st GAOA) touched down on the airstrip. The Thais continued to watch these strange events from the nearby mountains. However, because of their long association with the French, they were cautiously beginning to return to their homes.

The Associated Press summed up that day's developments with this report:

> French [and] Viet Namese paratroop patrols fanned out ten miles around Dien Bien Phu today in search of Viet Minh rebels after consolidating their newly captured offensive position on the broad plain here.
>
> Simultaneously, thousands of Thai partisans joined other loyal troops in sweeping a wide area south of their capital of Lai Chau, 200 miles northwest of Hanoi.
>
> The attackers failed to contact troops of an estimated one regiment with which the Communist-led Viet Minh had held the plain of Dien Bien Phu and its airstrip since October 1952.
>
> One hundred more airborne troops were poured into Dien Bien Phu from Hanoi today.[18]

The AP repeated its assertion of the previous day by observing that "the paratroopers' assault appeared today to have blocked a Viet Minh attack upon the Thai capital [Lai Chau] and any fresh invasion of Laos."[19]

A French Army spokesman, however, had some news to report as well: Viet-Minh Division 316 was still advancing in the direction of Lai Chau and the Laotian frontier. It was moving, he said, from the Hoa-Binh sector on the Black River, forty miles southwest of Hanoi, when the paratroopers landed in Dien Bien Phu two days earlier. The division was now reported to be near Na-San, 117 miles west of Hanoi (see map 2).

The Paris correspondent for the *Times* (London) sent the following account of Operation Castor that day:

> Several thousand French and Viet Namese parachute troops, dropped in the course of Friday in the neighbourhood of Dien Bien

Gen. Vo Nguyen Giap (*standing*) meets with his staff officers. From Edgar O'Ballance, *The Indo-China War, 1945–1954*.

Phu, have occupied this important Viet-minh base almost without re-sistance and are now consolidating their hold on the surrounding country.

According to General Cogny, the French commander in northern Indo-China, the aim of this operation is not merely to effect demoli-tions, or even to set up another "entrenched camp," but to dislodge the Viet-minh permanently from a rich tract of country by rallying the Thai population and putting its defences on a self-supporting ba-sis. With this in view, the occupying troops are now working with parachuted implements to restore the town's airstrip, which it is hoped will be in working order before the nearest regular Viet-minh forces, believed to be five days' march away, around Nasan, can reach the scene.[20]

Gen. Vo Nguyen Giap, the commander of the Viet-Nam People's Army, sat in a hut near a road along which were moving the columns of troops and porters of the 316th Division. By now Giap had learned of the details of Operation Castor and he was trying to evaluate this action from the messages that were reaching him. He questioned his staff officers as he studied a big map. Was this operation intended to counter his initial movement of the 316th Division toward the northwest or was it part of a plan to prevent him from invading Laos?

The general sensed both danger and opportunity in this latest turn of events. The 316th Division, he realized, would now have to increase its precautions to avoid discovery and attack by the fighters and bombers that could be based at this new enemy position. However, if Navarre intended to install himself permanently at Dien Bien Phu, then Giap's staff officers agreed with their chief's conclusion: the French were trapped.

3
Main Front: The Northwest

At 6:30 A.M. on November 23 General Gilles ordered Major Bréchignac's II/1 RCP to head north from Dien Bien Phu in order to link up with the 1st Thai Partisan Mobile Group (GMPT 1), which had set out from Lai Chau. The paratroopers met the Thai partisans at the village of Ban Na Ten, located 4.3 miles north of the garrison, without meeting any communist resistance.[1]

The GMPT 1 was led by Captain Bordier, the Eurasian son-in-law of Deo Van Long, the chieftain of the Thai Federation. The Thai officers made their men assume a kind of military order as they entered the valley and the II/1 RCP presented arms as the tribesmen filed past.

The GMPT 1 carried the French flag and that of the Thai Federation. The Thai flag consisted of three vertical stripes of blue, white, and blue, with a sixteen-pointed red star (representing the sixteen *chau,* or feudal baronies, of the Thai Federation) in the center of a white field. The Vietnamese flag was nowhere to be seen.[2]

A hail of "fakir's pillows," drums of gasoline, and cases of everything from ammunition to food and frozen wine continued to land on the outskirts of Dien Bien Phu, sometimes lodging in trees and on straw roofs.

Among the heavy equipment drops that Monday was a seventeen-thousand-pound bulldozer that was urgently needed by the engineers at Dien Bien Phu. First, the bulldozer's small extracting parachute appeared between the tail booms of a U.S. C-119 transport aircraft, followed by the main chute. The close to nine thousand square feet of canopy opened properly but the bulldozer somehow worked its way loose from the parachute on the opening shock and promptly nosedived toward an open rice field. It landed with a tremendous crash and buried itself under ten feet of earth.[3]

The smell of smoke continued to fill the entire camp as brushwood was burned in front of the first strongpoints. Trees were also chopped down and cut up to make beams and supports.

Morane-500s took off from the airstrip and flew over the approaches to the basin in order to monitor the reconnaissance parties that were still searching the villages and climbing the lower slopes in quest of enemy troops. At the same time, French fighters and bombers from other bases in Indo-China struck at the advancing 316th Division.

American diplomatic and military officials in Viet-Nam were supplying Washington with updated information on Operation Castor and its aftermath. The American consul in Hanoi, Paul J. Sturm, sent the following cable to the State Department:

SECRET SECURITY INFORMATION

FROM: Hanoi
TO: Secretary of State
NO: 310, November 23, 6 p.m.

SENT DEPARTMENT 310, REPEATED INFORMATION SAIGON 229, PARIS 142

[A] Spokesman for General Cogny today gave [the] following information on operation CASTOR (BEAVER):

Five battalions parachuted into Dine-Bien-Phu [*sic*] and environs [on] November 20 and 21. [A] Second wave of parachutists, dropped on [the] town itself, met some opposition. Viet Minh casualties to date are 92 killed and 15 prisoners; French Union casualties [are] described as 12 wounded.

[The] Purpose of [the] operation is to establish [a] base in [the] Thai country.
(1) To serve as [the] northern anchor of Laos defenses, [the] southern anchor being [the] Plaine des Jarres [Plain of Jars];
(2) To send out scout in hand attack parties in all directions to seek out [the] enemy and engage him;
(3) To foster [the] development of Thai guerrilla and partisan forces to supplement those already formed and based on Lai Chau.

Viet Minh division 316, which has for some time had elements deployed from [its] Thanh-Hoa base [see map 3] toward [the] Thai country, has not offered [a] special threat recently, but [the French]

3. The approximate positions of the seven Viet-Minh divisions in northern and north-central Viet-Nam on November 23.

High Command feared that it might be acting as [a] precursor of other major Viet Minh elements for [an] eventual attack on Laos.

[The] Spokesman insisted that there is no intent [to] establish a new Nasan at Dien-Bien-Phu, but only a base for positive and offensive operations. Forces will be maintained there only as long as proves expeditious.

Units based on Lai Chau have descended [the] mountain trail leading due south from Lai Chau to Dien-Bien-Phu to make contact with [the] parachute battalions. [The] Informant said this trail is now in French Union hands over its full length.

STURM[4]

A more detailed account of the Dien Bien Phu operation was sent by the U.S. Army attaché in Saigon, Col. Leo W. H. Shaughnessey, to the chiefs of staff of the Army, the Air Force, and the Navy in Washington. His report contained a more somber assessment of the potential enemy threat to the new French position.[5] It read as follows:

SECRET SECURITY INFORMATION

DEPARTMENT OF THE ARMY

PRIORITY
FROM: USARMA SAIGON VIETNAM
TO: CSUSA WASH DC FOR G2, CSUSAF WASH DC,
CNO WASH DC
NR: OARMA MC 319–53   231330Z NOV 53

Release to British only

Weekly SITREP IC [Situation Report, Indo-China] for 15–21 Nov and late details on Dien Bien Phu Opn [Operation].

[The] French launched airborne opn "CASTOR" [on] 20 Nov to destroy VM [Viet-Minh] rice stocks in Oien Bien Phu [sic] Area and [to] harass VM units [that were] moving to NW Tonkin. BPC 1, BPC 6, 2/1 BPC [2/1 RCP], 1 Engr Co [Engineer Company] and 2 Btrys [Batteries] (8875 MM recoilless rifles) [were] dropped in 2 serials starting [in the] late morning [of] 20 Nov. . . . BEP 1 and GCP 8 [BPC 8] plus General Gille [Gilles], [the] Commander of [the] opn, were parachuted in two serials starting [on the] morning [of] 21 Nov. BPVN 5 and 1 heavy mortar co (4–120 MM and 4–81 MM) [were] dropped [on] 22 Nov. 20 FTVN and 17 VM [were] killed during [the] first days fighting.[6] Elements [of] VM Bn [Battalion] 910 [were] contacted in [the] area during [the] first day. No contact since [the] first day. [It is] Estimated [that the] air strip will be ready for C47 [transports] on 25 Nov. EMIFT G2 estimates [that the] VM can have seven bns in [the] Dien Bien Phu area by 27 Nov; Bns 910 and 920 of Regt [Regiment] 148 and 5 bns from Div 316.[7] RP 41 is in good condition from Moc Chau to Son La and VM have adequate trucks available to transport one bn at [a] time. . . .[8]

[The] French continued long range patrolling out of Lai Chau. Patrols operated from 40 to 50 kms [25–31 miles] North, NE, SE, and

SW [of] Lai Chau. Minor contacts [with the Viet-Minh were] reported. . . .

Comment: This infor[mation] [was] given by [the] sqdn [squadron] briefing officer on 23 Nov. . . .

VM situation: [There is] Little change [in] VM troop dispositions North of [the Red River] Delta. [The] French state [that] some elements [of] Div 308 [are] moving slightly to [the] East possibly to [a] new assembly area. Div 312 [is] reported ready for action and Regt 45 of Div 351 [is] still in training between Yen Bay and Tuyen Quang.

On [the] South[ern] periphery of [the] Delta, Regt 48 [of] Div 320 moved to Thanu Hoa [Thanh Hoa] followed by [the] Hq [Headquarters of] Div 320. During [the] period [of] 21–22 Nov Regt 66 [of] Div 304 moved Southward to join Div 325 [in the] vicinity [of] Vinh.

Comment: [The] Southward movement [of] elements [of] Div 320 and 304 and [the] Northward movement [of] Regt 95 with [the] resultant concentration [of] troops [in the] Vinh Area would put [the] VM in [an] excellent position to attack to [the] West along [the] Vinh/Nape axis [thereby] threatening [the] French loc[ations] along [the] Mekong [River].

Div 316 started [its] movement to [the] NW [on] 14 Nov.[9] Regt 174 with one company [of] mortar 120 [mm.], and advanced elements [of] Div Hq [are] moving along RP 41 between Moc Chau and Son La. [The] Bulk of [the 316th] div [is] on RP 1 between Vinh Loc and Suyut. [A] Co. of VM troops on RP 41 called [a] meeting of subordinates in Chien Dong [on] 21–22 Nov for [a] conference with representatives [of the] VM high command.[10]

Lt. Gen. Harold R. Bull, U.S. Army, Retired, was accorded an interview with General Navarre in Saigon that day. A former Commandant of the National War College and Gen. Dwight D. Eisenhower's G-3 (Chief of Operations) in Europe, General Bull was the current deputy chief of the Office of National Estimates in Washington. He was accompanied by Dr. J. R. Smith of the Office of National Estimates and Robert McClintock, the counselor of the American embassy in Saigon, who served as an interpreter.

General Navarre began by expressing satisfaction with his recent air drop of six battalions at Dien Bien Phu. The motivation for this spoiling action, he said, was the fact that the 316th Division had been found moving northwest toward Lai Chau, an important French base for the expanding maquis movement in northwest Tonkin. The 316th, he added, was stretched out over an area of perhaps one hundred miles.

Navarre briefly reviewed for his visitor how Operation Castor had been conducted. The first two airborne battalions, he explained, were dropped near Dien Bien Phu on November 20. They met resistance from one Viet-Minh battalion, but the enemy was dispersed and the area was in French hands when a third battalion was dropped late that same day. Subsequently, three more parachute battalions were dropped on this important center.[11]

As a result of this thrust, in Navarre's view, he had a strong base with which to provide protection to Lai Chau and Luang Prabang. He had also denied the Viet-Minh the rice crop now being harvested in the Dien Bien Phu area.[12]

Navarre did not intend, however, to keep his parachutists at Dien Bien Phu. Once the airfield had been restored, he said, the parachutists would be relieved by regular forces and moved into the reserve striking force. He estimated that the airfield would be able to take C-47s by December 1.

General Bull questioned the commander in chief about the overall Viet-Minh plan of campaign in the current fighting season.

Navarre replied that the enemy's original plan had been to launch a coordinated attack on the Red River Delta: two divisions, the 308th and the 312th, pressing from the north and northwest, and two other divisions, the 304th and 316th, from the southwest. Meanwhile, the 320th Division would have infiltrated the delta and assisted the regional battalions in a general uprising at the French rear. This communist plan had been frustrated, Navarre asserted, by his Operation Mouette and second, by the current air drop on Dien Bien Phu which had put the 316th Division in an awkward spot. He estimated that his spoiling attack on the 320th, which was launched on October 15 in Operation Mouette, had caused enemy losses of between twenty and thirty percent of his effectives, with the result that the 320th had now withdrawn to a regroupment area in order to build up its strength.[13] He expected the 320th Division to be ready for action by December 15.

In all, said Navarre, thanks to the French having gained the initiative this season, the Viet-Minh plans had been postponed by at least two months. He conceded, however, that he was in for some stern fighting in the delta. Despite the success of his immediate efforts, the Viet-Minh still had the capacity to launch a four-division attack on the delta, assisted by interior sabotage and skirmishing from Viet-Minh elements on permanent station inside the delta.

Turning to the other Viet-Minh divisions, Navarre told Bull that the

351st, the so-called "heavy" division, was not a division in the occidental sense of the word, but rather a conglomeration of artillery, signal, and engineer battalions. According to his information, he said, the 351st Division had a regiment of 75-mm. pack artillery and a regiment of 105s. They also had heavy mortars and bazookas to a lesser degree. The motive power in moving the artillery was human labor. In fact, Navarre continued, this was one of the gravest disadvantages the enemy suffered, since to move even a battalion of infantry required the services of between one thousand and fifteen hundred coolies. Furthermore, each artillery piece required a minimum of 150 men for transport and servicing.

Bull inquired about the armament of the regular Viet-Minh battalions and divisions.

The commander in chief told him that there were rifles, made up of approximately one-third each of American, Japanese, and Czech origin, along with light machine guns and machine pistols. In a heavy weapons company, there were also heavy machine guns, 50-mm. and 81-mm. mortars, plus grenade throwers.

Navarre added that along with the five regular Viet-Minh infantry divisions and one heavy division which he had described, there was one of lesser value, the 325th, which was located in the Vinh area. There was also the equivalent—in independent regiments—of one division in the area between Nha Trang and Tourane.[14]

Bull asked about Viet-Minh fighting tactics.

Navarre told him that the enemy invariably chose action at night, attacking in wave after wave of banzai (suicide) charges. Once an attack was repulsed or even if a given objective was not achieved within a specified time, perhaps thirty-five to forty minutes, the Viet-Minh soldiers would retire, sometimes in a very demoralized condition.

Communist training was meticulous and planning was methodical, said the commander in chief. Before an attack was launched on any major French or Vietnamese outpost, he explained, a *maquette,* or exact model, of the post was erected at a training zone in the rear, and the task force practiced their attack perhaps fifteen times, memorizing details of terrain and fortification so that when at last the night assault began, each man knew automatically where he was.

Viet-Minh tactics in such onslaughts, Navarre continued, were to attack an isolated post in perhaps two-battalion strength, detaching other battalions to engage nearby posts, and sending skirmishers to the rear to plant mines and booby traps and establish ambushes in order to prevent the sending up of reinforcements to the beleaguered post.

These enemy tactics, said Navarre, although stiff and lacking in imagination, had proven effective. Nevertheless, he concluded, with his air, armor, and artillery superiority, increasing numerical strength, and the improved training of his troops, he could confront this prospect with a certain equanimity.

General Bull came away from the interview impressed by the lucidity of General Navarre's thoughts and by the dispassionate and objective manner in which he appeared to be confronting a task of enormous difficulty.

Despite the confidence that he displayed to his American visitor that day, the commander in chief was disturbed by news from the home front. In reviewing a summary of Paris press reports, supplied by his aide-de-camp, Navarre noticed among them a huge headline that had appeared in *France-Soir*. It read: "TONKIN PARATROOPERS RAIN DOWN ON DIENBIEN-PHU." Also, spread across the first two columns, in heavy type, was Cogny's bold announcement: "This is not a raid as at Lang Son, but the beginning of an offensive."[15]

Navarre saw Cogny, France's youngest major general, as already having skillfully taken credit for the Lang Son operation for himself. And it was he, Navarre, who had now decided on Dien Bien Phu, not Cogny. Furthermore, declarations about "the beginning of an offensive" would enlighten the enemy and might risk alarming both French public opinion and the government. The commander in chief and his staff had remained silent about this new operation except for Navarre's November 20 dispatch to Marc Jacquet. Who had given Cogny permission to speak and what was he trying to do?[16]

The latest edition of *Time* contained Cogny's remarks about Dien Bien Phu, although they were not directly attributed to him. The magazine also praised Navarre's performance in the opening weeks of the fall campaign. "The great Communist offensive in Indo-China, which had been expected since the monsoons ended in October, has not materialized," observed *Time,*

> probably because General Henri Navarre's aggressive spoiling operations have kept the Viet Minh off balance. Last week Navarre launched the biggest airborne attack since the Langson border raid in July, this time against the Communist base at Dienbienphu, between the Black River and Laos. This time it was not a hit and run raid; the French meant to seize Dienbienphu and hold on.
>
> The enemy in Dienbienphu had been threatening the isolated French base at Laichau, a hedgehog supplied by air,[17] which the French have been using to build up anti-Communist guerrilla forces

among the friendly Thai tribesmen. Dienbienphu was also important to the enemy supply, especially for rice raids.[18]

The Viet-Minh's stake in Dien Bien Phu's other homegrown crop, opium, was pointed out that day by both the *Times* (London) and the French newspaper *Le Monde*. Dien Bien Phu, said the *Times*, was "the centre of a fertile opium growing district which has been one of the Viet-Minh's most important sources of revenue." [19] "The whole area of Dien Bien Phu, and the whole T'ai [Thai] country in general," said *Le Monde*, "is a major opium-producing area, from which the Viet-Minh draws many of its resources and particularly the means of paying the deliveries in material, arms and ammunition from Communist China. [Viet-Minh leader] Ho Chi Minh also uses clandestine sales of opium in all of Indochina to finance his intelligence services and his propaganda and to pay his troops."[20]

Le Monde was much less hopeful about the Dien Bien Phu operation than were most other French newspapers. Given the economic importance of Dien Bien Phu to the Viet-Minh, warned the *Le Monde*, "it is not certain . . . [that the enemy] will not soon react."[21]

Time, in spite of its optimistic assessment of recent French military successes, also sounded a wary note: "The Viet-Minh were reported to be moving up their 316th Division, and it seemed possible that the Communists might break their own tactical rules by fighting a pitched battle for Dienbienphu, rather than let Navarre's men stay in possession."[22]

In a forest near Thai Nguyen, just north of the Red River Delta (see map 5), a senior officers' conference of the Viet-Nam People's Army was in its fifth day of talks with the Central Military Committee of the communist Lao-Dong (Workers) party. Under discussion was the winter–spring campaign for 1953–54.[23]

General Giap began his closing report to the conference by discussing the new French operation at Dien-Bien-Phu. "We are not yet precisely informed on what places were occupied by the enemy and for how long," explained Giap,

> but we have nonetheless foreseen this operation—if the northwest is threatened, the enemy will bring reinforcements there. Thus, faced with our initiative, the enemy has been reduced to the defensive and compelled to scatter part of his mobile forces, by bringing

troops to Dien Bien Phu to protect the northwest and upper Laos and to check our offensive.[24]

What will he do in the days to come?

He may try to keep both Lai Chau and Dien Bien Phu, with Dien Bien Phu as the main position and Lai Chau as the secondary one. If our threat becomes more serious, he may fall back on one single position and bring reinforcements there; we don't know yet what his choice will be, but it will probably be Dien Bien Phu. If he is pressed, he may reinforce this position considerably and turn it into an entrenched camp, but he may also withdraw.

At present we cannot judge whether the enemy will entrench himself or will withdraw, whether he will occupy one or two positions, and for how long, how many reinforcements he will bring, etc., because precise information is still lacking and also because the enemy is meeting with many difficulties. If he withdraws his troops, he will lose territory; if he reinforces his positions, he will scatter his mobile forces. It may well be that he has not yet taken any decision, or that having taken a decision, he has changed his mind on account of our action.

At any rate, whatever changes may happen inside the enemy camp, the dropping of his troops on Dien Bien Phu has created a situation in the main favorable to us. It lays bare the contradiction in which the enemy finds himself entangled, namely, that between the occupation of territories and the regrouping [of] forces; between the occupation of mountain regions and the reinforcement of the delta fronts.[25]

Giap then announced the operational plans for the winter–spring campaign:

The northwest is the main front. Our task consists in wiping out enemy forces, intensifying political work among the population, and liberating the Lai Chau region so as to consolidate and widen our resistance base in the northwest and threaten upper Laos, which will scatter the enemy forces even further and create favorable conditions for future campaigns.

Forces to be employed: two to three divisions.

Part of our troops must move rapidly there so as to prevent the enemy from withdrawing from or bringing reinforcements to Lai Chau, and to annihilate part of his forces should he try to withdraw them.

Gen. Vo Nguyen Giap. From Edgar O'Ballance, *The Indo-China War,*
1945–1954.

The main body of our troops will follow suit. If the enemy seeks to re-inforce himself, we must be ready to bring to this front three divisions or even more if necessary.[26]

4

Portents

In Hanoi on November 25 General Cogny listened as his chief intelligence officer, Major Levain, explained the latest information that had been gathered by his listening posts. It was already known that Viet-Minh Division 316 was on its way toward the northwestern mountain areas. Now, according to Levain, there was strong evidence that the enemy was shifting other key divisions of its battle force in the same direction. This was not a certainty, in the major's opinion, but it was an extremely serious probability.

The Viet-Minh 308th, 312th, and 351st divisions—currently stationed in the Phu-Tho/Yen Bay/Thai Nguyen triangle, north of the Red River Delta (see map 3)—were constantly being tracked by the French. During the night French radio intelligence had intercepted the orders that General Giap had issued to the command posts of these big units.[1] Among the intercepted messages were orders for communist engineering units to build bridges on the Black River, west of the delta, and to prepare ferry facilities at Yen Bay sufficient for six thousand troops per night as of December 3.

Levain calculated that the 316th Division would reach Dien Bien Phu about December 6, the 308th Division around December 24, the 351st Heavy Division about December 26, and the 312th Division on approximately December 28.

At Dien Bien Phu the paratroopers kept up their search of the surrounding areas as Morane-500s observed from above. The picnic-like aura at the camp continued as the men cooked their rations over hearths hollowed out of the earth, slept in scores of little tents, and spread washed clothing out to dry on barbed wire.

Parachutes drifted down with packages that added to the growing stocks. At one point a cheer went up from the paratroopers as a huge mass floated toward the ground. A new bulldozer, under the support of twenty-one multicolored parachutes all tied to one another, landed gently in a rice field, upright on its tracks.[2]

At 11:30 A.M. the first Dakota cargo plane landed at Dien Bien Phu's rebuilt airfield. The airstrip was approximately 3,940 feet in length, 230 feet in width, and capable of receiving seventy to eighty cargo planes each day. Material that was too fragile to be dropped by parachute could now be brought in by transports and the wounded could be evacuated to Hanoi.

Admiral Cabanier returned to Paris that day to give a report of his mission to President Auriol and Prime Minister Laniel. The admiral described the optimism of the High Command and this was noted with cautious satisfaction by the government.

In one of the heaviest air attacks of the seven-year-old Indo-China war, French Bearcat fighter bombers sprayed Viet-Minh Division 316 with machine-gun fire and napalm on November 26.

The High Command announced that more than a week of constant attack by land and air had crippled the 316th. The enemy division had been hit so hard, it was said, that it had not been able to move from its position for the last forty-eight hours.[3]

Despite such pronouncements, there was growing concern in Hanoi about the new French position in the northwest. As soon as the previous day's intelligence report was fully confirmed, General Cogny immediately sent a radio message to General Navarre suggesting a diversionary stab into the communist base area north of the Red River Delta in order to slow down the apparent enemy build-up aimed at Dien Bien Phu.

Cogny's dispatch was received in Saigon with doubts tinged by suspicion. Navarre and his staff were responsible for analyzing information from listening posts throughout Indo-China. Cogny's staff, however well informed, was responsible only for those listening posts within its jurisdiction. Mistakes of both analysis and synthesis, it was thought, could not be ruled out. Neither could the possibility that the northern command was deliberately exaggerating the danger in order to empahasize Hanoi's importance and to warn against encroachments by Saigon.

Furthermore, Henri Eugène Navarre had first served with French Army Intelligence sixteen years earlier, in 1937, and had spent nearly all of his career in that field. Obtaining and exploiting information were jobs that the commander in chief knew well and he was not inclined to rely on the interpretations of others.

The Associated Press sent the following dispatch from Dien Bien Phu on November 27:

A Vietminh division—perhaps 10,000 men—was reported moving from the east today upon the Thai tribal town which French Union forces captured a week ago. The French were hoping the division intended to fight.

Thousands of French and Vietnamese troops were waiting on the broad plain of Dien Bien Phu, strategically placed between the border of Laos, eight miles to the south, and the French-held Thai capital of Lai Chau, fifty miles to the north.[4]

The AP went on to describe the preparations that were being made by the Franco-Vietnamese forces:

In the past week they have converted the 10-square mile plain base for both defensive and offensive operations against the Communist-led rebels.

Smoking bonfires bound the plain, fed by brush cut as the soldiers cleared their field of fire. Barbed wire barricades ring more than six miles of defense perimeter. An air strip, originally built by the French and used by the Japanese in World War II, has been cleared of debris. A hundred holes with which the Vietminh packed it have been filled.

American-supplied transport planes daily are bringing in men and supplies further to bolster the French-Vietnamese positions. The French aren't saying just how many thousands of troops are on hand.

Friendly Thai guerrillas show up almost hourly to help military patrols hunt through the surrounding hills for elements of a Vietminh regiment that yielded Dien Bien Phu to French Union parachute troopers after a brief fight, then lingered for harassment work.[5]

The wire service concluded with additional details on the approaching enemy force: "The westbound rebel division was identified as No. 316. Presumably pulled out of the line menacing the French-held Red River Delta, it was reported less than 50 miles from this town, a collection of mud-caked, straw-thatched villages. Mountainous country intervenes, however, and French Gen. Rene Cogny said the division would require several days to complete the march."[6]

In Washington Philip W. Bonsal, the State Department's director of the Office of Philippine and Southeast Asian Affairs (PSA), was also keeping track of the 316th Division as well as the other six Viet-Minh divisions, all of which were located in northern and north-central Viet-Nam. That Friday Bonsal addressed the following memorandum on the

Philip Bonsal, director of the Office of Philippine and Southeast Asian Affairs in the State Department. Courtesy National Archives, Still Picture Branch, Washington, D.C.

Walter Robertson, assistant secretary of state for Far Eastern affairs. Courtesy National Archives, Still Picture Branch, Washington, D.C.

subject to Walter S. Robertson, the assistant secretary of state for Far Eastern affairs:

SECRET SECURITY INFORMATION

OFFICE MEMORANDUM
UNITED STATES GOVERNMENT
TO: FE-Mr. Robertson   DATE: November 27, 1953
FROM: PSA-Philip W. Bonsal

SUBJECT: Westward movement of Viet Minh units

Army G-2 [Army Intelligence] tells us that four of the six Viet Minh infantry divisions in North and Central Viet Nam are now moving westward.[7] Two divisions [308 and 316], plus elements of a third [304] are moving from their recent positions North and West of the Hanoi-Haiphong perimeter in the direction of Son-La/Lai-Chau.[8] One division [325] reinforced with half of another [304] is moving from Central Viet Nam, south of the perimeter, in the direction of Central Laos.

Two divisions, one near the Northern edge of the perimeter (312) and one on the Southern edge (320) remain in place apparently as a threat to penetration of the perimeter defenses and to force defensive units to remain [see map 4].

We do not know how far the Viet Minh troops have advanced, but French Intelligence estimates that the movement discloses an intent to occupy the area between the Red River to the North and the Black River to the South which is the stronghold of the Thai tribesmen who harass the Viet Minh, through guerrilla activity under French leadership, in the general area Lai-Chau/Son-La.

Perhaps in anticipation of this movement, the French Commander, General Cogny, dropped six parachute battalions at Dien Bien Phu on November 20, and has sent patrols from there North to Lai-Chau. An airstrip has been rehabilitated and some heavy equipment dropped. This operation was the largest air force exercise so far executed in the war.

Continued occupation of Dien Bien Phu will block Viet Minh use of one of the two principal East-West roads leading into Northern Laos. Viet Minh attacks against Franco-Vietnamese installations in that area may be an indication of renewed Viet Minh incursions against Laos, or else an effort to clear away forces having a harassing capacity against the Viet Minh.

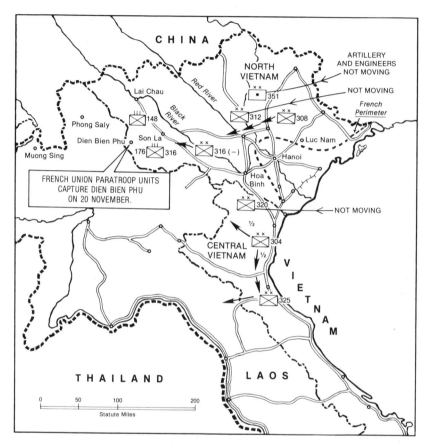

4. PSA Director Philip Bonsal's map of November 27 on Viet-Minh troop movements in northern and north-central Indo-China. Courtesy National Archives, Still Picture Branch, Washington, D.C.

If the movement of the 325 division from its present location in central Viet Nam is continued in the direction of central Laos it would support the hypothesis that [an] invasion of Laos is the principal Viet Minh plan for the time being.

We have insufficient information of the enemy movements or of the French plans to arrive at any firm conclusion as to the importance of this development. The enemy movement may not take its final form for several weeks. Nevertheless, the Viet Minh are moving some forty to fifty thousand troops away from the perimeter for a still undisclosed purpose.[9]

5
Command Decision

On November 28 General Navarre flew the eight hundred miles from Saigon to Hanoi to meet personally with General Cogny at the northern front.

Cogny, as he had indicated in his November 26 telegram to Navarre, wanted to launch a raid from his base in the Red River Delta against the enemy's rear. The plan was to spread disorder, disrupt lines of communication, make contact with part of the Viet-Minh battle corps, and possibly force it to turn around. The French Air Force would also conduct full-scale strikes from its bases around Hanoi and Haiphong, which would involve two or three bombing and machine-gun attacks on the communist columns every day.

Several alternatives for carrying out this offensive stab were given serious consideration.

The first was a large-scale operation against the major communist supply and communications center at Yen Bay, located almost one hundred miles to the northwest of Hanoi (see map 5).[1] Cogny, who would command the operation, estimated that the following forces would be necessary: six motorized regimental combat teams (mobile groups), two armored regimental combat teams, and two airborne regimental battle groups; in addition, three to four mobile groups for guarding the lines of communication; and two to three mobile groups, two armored groups, and one airborne group to keep in reserve inside the Red River Delta. To these forces, five to six battalions were added in order to occupy the upper region of Indo-China against the light enemy units that already operated there and against those that the enemy was able to send there in a state of readiness.

Available to the French throughout the entire Indo-China theater at that time were eight mobile groups, two armored groups, and three airborne groups. The forces being requested, therefore, required the use of

General Cogny (*left*) and General Navarre in August, 1953. From Jules Roy, *The Battle of Dienbienphu.*

all airborne groups and exceeded by about one-third the available mobile groups, and by one hundred percent the total number of armored units.[2]

There were other considerations as well. French capabilities only permitted the restoration and maintenance of a single axis of roads, which Navarre regarded as totally insufficient for an undertaking of this breadth. Furthermore, the operation could cause a considerable strain

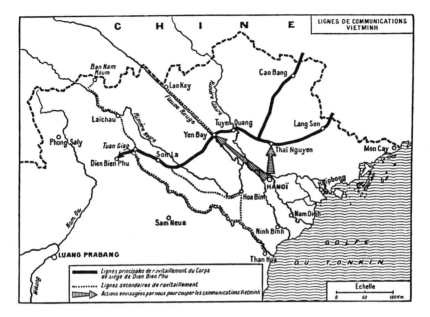

5. Proposed operations against Yen Bay and Thai Nguyen. From Henri Navarre, *Agonie de l'Indochine.*

on the already greatly overworked French air potential in Indo-China. On that Saturday French fighters and bombers were attacking Viet-Minh offensive concentrations north and northwest of Hanoi for the eighteenth successive day.

For all of these reasons, the commander in chief rejected an attack against Yen Bay as absolutely impossible.

The second alternative was an operation against the important Viet-Minh administrative headquarters at Thai Nguyen, where limestone caves housed Ho Chi Minh and his war cabinet as well as being the home base of General Giap and his staff. This target, located fifty miles north of Hanoi, involved a more economical operation than that against Yen Bay (see map 5). However, in Navarre's judgment, it would be less efficient than the first and would still require means considerably greater than were available.

A third alternative was likewise deemed unsuitable, and, therefore, with all possible actions having been studied in detail and rejected, the commander in chief decided to turn down General Cogny's proposal for a diversionary attack from the Delta.[3]

Navarre's disagreement with Cogny went deeper, though, than the issue of what military action, if any, should be taken to relieve the growing pressure on Dien Bien Phu. It involved the very nature of the Viet-Minh threat to the newly won French position. Cogny was concerned that the enemy might now be able to concentrate the overwhelming bulk of its battle force against a lightly defended airhead. Navarre disputed this assessment. He believed, as did his deputy chief of operations, Col. Louis Berteil, that it was elements of Viet-Minh divisions, not entire divisions, that were on the move. Nor did Navarre rule out the possibility of fake orders. In any case, he felt, no conclusions could be drawn for the moment.

The commander in chief also expressed the view that the logistical capabilities of the Viet-Minh divisions were being overestimated. He had been assured by his predecessor, Gen. Raoul Salan, that the enemy did not have the means to sustain as many as four divisions for very long at such a great distance from its natural bases. Among those who shared that judgment were Navarre's chief of staff, his operational deputy, and his technicians and specialists. In fact, most of the staffs of the Expeditionary Corps regarded the concentration of four communist divisions as a utopian project.

The Viet-Minh was an army that both moved and was supplied on foot. To keep fifty thousand troops alive, the French assumed, fifty thousand coolies would have to carry rice constantly. Even if such an effort were possible, it was thought, its very size and volume would confine it to a rather limited period of time. In the event of a general attack on Dien Bien Phu, the High Command was confident that the strain on communist logistics would increase at a tempo that could not be sustained for more than a week.

Furthermore, the French believed, material and ammunition for the Viet-Minh would have to be transported along vulnerable communications lines where the convoys would be subject to surprise attack by the French Air Force. Heavy support for the communists would have to be brought up unprotected and would, it was felt, be especially open to air assault.[4]

Some of the officers in Navarre's group were unabashedly delighted by the impending developments. They claimed that the Air Force would smash the enemy divisions on the march and administer such a severe pounding to their communications lines as to render them unusable.

The commander in chief's only real worry was Communist China's aid to the Viet-Minh since, four months after the signing of the Korean armistice, the success of his operational plans still hinged on no increase in the level of Chinese assistance. Despite the risks, he "wagered" that Chinese aid would remain the same.[5]

Navarre's judgment on this matter was contradicted by an article in the latest issue of *U.S. News & World Report:*

> Near French Indochina where French and native forces are fighting desperately to hold their own against Communist-led rebels, Chinese Communists are active. The French, always up against the fear that Chinese Communists will invade Indochina, Korea-style, have reports of new arms shipments, new concentrations of Chinese forces, just north of the Indochina border.
>
> Such activity was not possible when the Chinese Communists were fully engaged with [a] shooting war in Korea. Now, however, [the] Communists are free to concentrate elsewhere.[6]

General Navarre's Command Dakota took off from Hanoi for Dien Bien Phu on November 29. Nine days after Operation Castor had been launched, the commander in chief, accompanied by General Cogny, was about to get his first look at the new French base. During the flight Navarre reminded Cogny of the latter's promise to relieve General Gilles of his command at Dien Bien Phu. Gilles, as both men knew, wished to resume his regular duties as the commander of French airborne forces in Indo-China and somebody would have to be found to take his place.

"Who is your candidate?" Navarre asked Cogny.

"There's a man I'd like to suggest," replied Cogny.

"Perhaps we've both got the same man in mind," said Navarre. "Let's see."

"[Colonel] Vanuxem isn't inspiring enough," answered Cogny, adding, "I'm thinking of [Colonel de] Castries. A cavalryman would be ideal at Dien Bien Phu, where the situation will be mobile. We need somebody who can harry and harass the Viets [Viet-Minh]."

"He's my choice also," said Navarre. "You can appoint him whenever you like."

"I would rather you told him yourself," replied Cogny.[7]

The aircraft landed at Dien Bien Phu at 1:15 P.M. Navarre got out with Cogny and, together, they decorated those paratroopers who had distinguished themselves during Operation Castor with *Croix de guerre* (crosses of war). Some of the crosses were given posthumously.

Making the trip with the two French generals that Sunday was Maj. Gen. Thomas Trapnell, the chief of the U.S. Military Assistance Advisory Group (MAAG) in Indo-China. On the previous day Trapnell had flown in a MAAG aircraft from Saigon to Hanoi where he had called upon Navarre and Cogny in order to discuss operations. At Dien Bien Phu the MAAG chief conferred further with Navarre and Cogny, along with Gilles, on the status of ammunition.

Gilles, who agreed with the selection of de Castries, drove Navarre along the dusty tracks of the valley in a jeep. During the lurching ride, Navarre pondered the need to keep the approaches to these stretches open and one advantage of choosing de Castries became clearer to him. This was, he felt certain, a job for a cavalryman.

As Navarre saw it, armored cars would be brought to Dien Bien Phu in dismantled parts and, with them, de Castries could traverse the basin and cover the crests. Should the Viet-Minh venture onto the plain, the colonel could sweep it with the fire of his guns and automatic weapons. And if the enemy were installed on the high crests that surrounded the valley on all sides, de Castries could both use his artillery and call upon the French Air Force to deliver a mighty blow.[8]

At 4:50 P.M. the commander in chief and his traveling party departed from Dien Bien Phu.

On November 30 General Cogny's headquarters issued Directive No. 739/FTVN/3TS to the Dien Bien Phu command. The new directive contained orders to (1) "guarantee at the very least the free usage of the airfield," (2) "gather intelligence from as far away as possible," and (3) proceed with the withdrawal to Dien Bien Phu of the units from Lai Chau.[9]

Specific and detailed instructions were given as to how each of these missions was to be carried out.

The "free use" of the Dien Bien Phu airfield was explained to mean that the entire "defensive position" of Dien Bien Phu was to be held *sans esprit de recul* ("without any thought of withdrawal").[10] The troops, as a result, were now responsible for maintaining freedom of movement within a radius of eight kilometers (five miles) around the airfield. On this point, Cogny's headquarters forecast that the major enemy effort against the garrison would come from the east or northeast and, accordingly, the commander at Dien Bien Phu was ordered to concentrate his defenses in that direction.

The directive's second point involved offensive stabs from Dien Bien Phu toward Ban Tau to the north and Tuan Giao to the northeast, and it required the garrison to use "at least one half of its strength" in operations intended to inflict heavy losses on the enemy and to delay his laying a tight siege ring around the valley. In addition, the Dien Bien Phu command was ordered to conduct a link-up operation to the southwest

General Cogny (*holding cane*), Colonel de Castries (*hatless*), and General Navarre (*center*). From Georges Boudarel, *Giap.*

toward Muong Khoua, Laos. French-Laotian troops under Col. Boucher de Crèvecoeur, the commander of all French forces in Laos, were advancing toward Dien Bien Phu from this direction.[11]

Concerning the evacuation of Lai Chau, the directive said that this would take place at General Cogny's order. The operation would be covered by French-led guerrillas who would continue their activities in the Lai Chau area after the regular French units had been withdrawn.

That day General Navarre and General Cogny flew in a Beaver aircraft to Thai Binh, located at the mouth of the Red River in the southern part of the delta. Standing at the foot of the small plane when it landed and saluting his commander in chief was Col. Christian de Castries.[12] Navarre's face reflected his joy at being reunited with his former subordinate. It was an important promotion that he was bringing for de Castries: the command of Dien Bien Phu.

The colonel exhibited no great delight at the news. Besides, he had already been promised that he would receive his brigadier general's stars in the spring.

"If you're thinking of establishing an entrenched camp," said de Castries, "this isn't my line. I'd rather you picked somebody else."

"Gilles would like to have another Na-San," replied Navarre. "I don't agree with him. Dien Bien Phu must become an offensive base. That's why I've picked you."

To help persuade de Castries, Cogny interjected by saying: "We need a mountain cavalryman out there. You will be that cavalryman, and roam the wide-open spaces of the highlands."[13]

De Castries was given a copy of the directive that presented Cogny's plan for waging a defensive-offensive battle in the geographic triangle of Dien Bien Phu/Lai Chau/Tuan Giao, based on Dien Bien Phu (see map 3).

The colonel was puzzled by the idea of mobile warfare in such a mountainous area. It was true that he did not know the region as well as he knew the delta, but, even so, it seemed to him that only very light units would have any real latitude to maneuver. Furthermore, the proposed triangle of battle measured nearly five hundred square miles in area and was crossed by only a handful of mediocre trails, a few mule paths, and one road—the paved Route 41—which was known to be held by the Viet-Minh along its entire span.

In the end, however, de Castries put aside his hesitation. He would examine everything, including the terrain, once he assumed command.

Washington received ambiguous information that day concerning the possibility that the French military position in northwestern Viet-Nam might be more vulnerable than previously thought. The news came circuitously, in a report from the U.S. Army liaison officer in Singapore who was over one thousand miles away from the developing battlefront. The report was sent to both Army Intelligence and the chief of naval operations in Washington. It was also sent, for information, to the commander in chief, Pacific, at Pearl Harbor, and to the U.S. Army attaché in Saigon. It read as follows:

SECRET SECURITY INFORMATION

DEPARTMENT OF THE ARMY
STAFF COMMUNICATIONS OFFICE

FROM: USARMLO SINGAPORE SGD YORK
TO: DEPTAR WASH DC FOR ACOFS G2,
        CNO DEPT OF THE NAVY WASH DC

INFO: CINCPAC PEARL HARBOR TH,
         USARMA SAIGON VIETNAM
NR: REH 63   300430Z NOV 53

Weekly signal significant developments. This report [is] for [the] period ending 28 Nov. 53.

Indochina (present situation)

There is conflicting evidence on the weight of the Vietminh threat in [the] Lai Chau Area. [The] French capture of Dien Bien Phu may be [a] defensive move to counter what may be [an] initial Vietminh major effort, or, it may be [a] prelude to French offensive operations in [the] area . . . .[14]

6
First Sortie

At Dien Bien Phu the French Union forces launched a stab deep into the surrounding jungle as soon as they received General Cogny's Directive 739 of November 30.

The small force chosen for this first sortie was made up of components of the 8th BPC, commanded by Capt. Pierre Tourret, and was reinforced by a company of Thai mountaineers from the 3rd BT (Bataillon T'ai, or Thai Battalion) under Captain Guilleminot. Captain Tourret was the overall commander of the operation and Captain Guilleminot was in charge of the lead element of the group. To take maximum advantage of the Thai company's knowledge of local conditions, the force was organized so that each of the paratroop companies had one mountaineer platoon attached to it.

The objective of the mission was to make contact with the French-trained and French-led tribesmen, particularly the Meo tribesmen at Ban Phathong, who operated as guerrillas throughout the steep mountainous area. The force also intended to press as far as Tuan Giao, located twenty-five miles northeast of Dien Bien Phu, which was the site of an important road junction.[1]

The guerrillas and their French cadres were commanded by Maj. Roger Trinquier and they operated directly under the supervision of the French Central Intelligence services. These commando units had the responsibility of setting up native maquis deep inside Viet-Minh areas in order to create insecurity for the enemy by accentuating pressure on rear communications lines, just as the communists did behind French lines. The commandos also reported back as much intelligence as possible.[2]

On December 1 the chief of the American Military Assistance Advisory Group (MAAG), General Trapnell, sent a progress report on the overall French military campaign to the commander in chief, Pacific (CINCPAC) at Pearl Harbor, Hawaii. It was repeated for information to the commanding general, U.S. Army, Pacific, at Fort Shafter, Hawaii,

Capt. Pierre Tourret. From Bernard B. Fall, *Hell in a Very Small Place.*

and to the chief of staff of the U.S. Army in Washington. The report read as follows:

TOP SECRET

DEPARTMENT OF THE ARMY
STAFF COMMUNICATIONS OFFICE

FROM: CHIEF MAAG (INDOCHINA) SAIGON VIETNAM
SGD TRAPNELL

Maj. Marcel Bigeard (*left*), Capt. Pierre Tourret (*center*), and Col. Pierre Langlais (*right*). From Pierre Langlais, *Dien Bien Phu.*

TO:	CINCPAC PEARL HARBOR TH	
	INFO:	
	CGUSARPAC FT SHAFTER TH,	
	CSUSA WASH DC	
NR:	MG1925 A	010400Z DEC 53

[The] Fol[lowing] is [the] 1 Dec rept [report] on [the] status of French actions designed [to] fulfill [the] principles for [the] conduct [of the] war [in] IndoChina [sic] as rqst [requested]:

Part 1.A. [French] Fall offensive: Navarre informed me yesterday [that] his strategic plan will be developed without change with [a] Jan[uary 1954] offensive [in the] Cantho area [of] South Vietnam,[3] amphib[ious] and clearing opns [operations] in cent[ral] Vietnam in [the] spring, concurrent vigorous action inside and outside [of the] Tonkin [Red River]

Delta with [the] present forces to keep [the] enemy off balance and finally [a] gen[eral] offensive from [the] Tonkin Delta in Oct[ober] 1954.[4] Navarre has revised [his] estimate of enemy intentions. He considers [the] Vietminh [to] presently [be] incapable of launching [its] original [Red River] Delta campaign.[5] He believes [the] enemy [is] executing [an] alternate plan. However, because of [the] inability of French intel[ligence] to produce accurate info[rmation] on [the] size of [the] Vietminh tp [troop] movement, Navarre is uncertain whether [the] enemy threat will develop in Cent Annam [central Viet-Nam], [in] Laos or [in the] triangle [of] Lai Chau/ Dien Bien Phu/Son La. In the meantime, and in lieu of [a] projected [French] limited atk [attack] in [a] northerly direction from [the] Delta in [the] absence [of] enemy offensive action after 10 Nov, [the] maj[or] French effort since [Operation] Mouette has been shifted to [the] Dien Lien Phu [sic] area of NW Tonkin. Here [an] air head [was] established [on] 20 Nov (Opn CASTOR) [and] subsequently built up to [a] gp [group of] 6 prcht [parachute] bns [battalions] and supporting arms and services. Concurrently in Laos, a Fr[ench] Union task force of aprx [approximately] 5 in[fantry] bns has advanced along [the] Nam River NE of Luang Prabang in [the] direction of posts recently lost to [the] Vietminh.[6] Navarre states [that the] Fr intention is to regain control of [the] Thai country, stimulate [a] friendly guerrilla effort in [the] region and invite [the] enemy [to] atk [the] Dien Bien Phu area. He plans to develop Dien Bien Phu as [a] permanent defensive base astride [the] gateway to Luang Prabang. Navarre while not admitting [the] resemblance [of] this air head to Na San, has pointed to [the] similarity and strategical relationship to [the] Plain Des Jarres [Plain of Jars] base [in Laos] with [the] probability in each instance for supporting long range recon[naissance] and clearing opns. Navarre admits uncertainty as to [the] real enemy intentions, considering that [the] present enemy movements up [the] Black River Valley [toward the Lai Chau/Dien Bien Phu/Son La triangle] and in [the] Vinh area [in north-central Viet-Nam] may be part of [an] enemy cover plan [for] inducing [a] Fr dispersal of forces from [the] Delta thereby enabling [the] Vietminh to atk [the] Delta from [the] north and NW, formerly rated as [the] number one capability. MAAG

comment: While [it is] too early to assess the effect of
CASTOR upon [the] enemy, the fact that [a] conservative
[French] move has been followed by [a] base development
scheme [at Dien Bien Phu] in [the] sparsely populated hinterland leads to [a] reasonable doubt [that the] Fr have [the]
will to seize [the] initiative by opns threatening enemy supply
lines from China in [the] northern Delta area where maj enemy concentrations now exist. [It is] Apparent [that the] Viet-
minh still have [the] initiative as evidenced additionally by Fr
sensitivity to [the] enemy threat to lower Laos along [the]
axis Vinh-Savannakhet.[7] As an example, one [French] Foreign Legion Bn [was] shifted from [the] Delta to Paksane [in
Laos] with [the] mission of improving [the] road to [the] Plain
Des Jarres area, with [the] probable objective of enabling rapid
movement of reinforcements south in [the] event of [an] enemy
atk on [the French] Seno [air] base [near Savannakhet]. . . .

. . . Part 2. Additional info:
A. [The] Fr have revised [their] estimate [of the] casualties
inflicted upon enemy Div 320 by [the French] Mouette
forces. [The French] Originally stated [that the] Div would
not be combat eff[ective] until Jun[e] 1954. [They] Currently
realistically express [the] capability of [the enemy] force for
eff[ective] opns by mid-Dec.[8]

On the same day that General Trapnell was reporting the French
downgrading of their claims for Operation Mouette, the State Department received an even more disquieting assessment of that operation's
effectiveness.

PSA Director Philip Bonsal was visited that Tuesday by F. S. Tomlinson, the counselor of the British Embassy in Washington. Tomlinson had
asked to come to the State Department in order to discuss Bonsal's recent trip to the Far East as the State Department's representative on the
U.S. Joint Military Mission to Indo-China of November 6–15, 1953,
which was headed by Lt. Gen. John W. ("Iron Mike") O'Daniel, commander, U.S. Army, Pacific. Bonsal gave Tomlinson a general report on
the favorable impressions of the French war effort that General O'Daniel
and the mission had brought back. Tomlinson, in turn, presented information to Bonsal that was based on a report prepared by the British military attaché in Saigon, Brigadier Pierce.

It was the attaché's view, said Tomlinson, that Operation Mouette had failed to dislodge the Viet-Minh from strongly held positions along the perimeter of the Red River Delta and, to that extent, it had not succeeded in its objective of throwing the enemy off balance or in crippling Viet-Minh offensive capabilities.

After Tomlinson had left, Bonsal wrote a memorandum of conversation in which he observed that "Brigadier Pierce's impression of the Mouette Operation was less optimistic than that obtained by our own Military Attache or from French briefings."[9]

Future French moves in Indo-China were the subject of several paragraphs in a new U.S. National Intelligence Estimate (NIE) that day.[10] The paragraphs relating to the military situation read as follows:

NATIONAL INTELLIGENCE ESTIMATE

SECRET   WASHINGTON, I December 1953
NIE 63/1 . . .

PROBABLE FRENCH POLICIES IN INDOCHINA

37. The gradual deterioration of French will to continue the Indo-China war had been checked at least temporarily by the Laniel-Navarre Plan and by the greatly increased US financial assistance.[11] The French are reinforcing their own units, accelerating the buildup of Indochinese [Associated States] armies, and seeking to regain the military and political initiative. Despite strong parliamentary opposition, the French are likely to implement their promises of independence for the three states, on the basis of voluntary association with France in the French Union.[12] No French government could continue the war outside of this French Union framework.

38. However, the implementation of the Laniel-Navarre Plan will probably be the last major French offensive effort in Indochina. We believe that even if the Laniel-Navarre Plan is successful, the French do not expect to achieve a complete military victory in Indochina. They probably aim at improving their position sufficiently to negotiate a settlement which would eliminate the drain of the Indochina war on France, while maintaining non-Communist governments in the Associated States and preserving a position for France in the Far East.[13]

Two high U.S. officials commented publicly the next day on the military situation in Indo-China.

Adm. Arthur Radford, chairman of the Joint Chiefs of Staff. From Eisenhower, *Mandate for Change* (Garden City, N.Y.: Doubleday, 1963). Courtesy Doubleday & Co., a division of Bantam, Doubleday, Dell Publishing Group, Inc.

In an address entitled "The Communist Threat in the Far East," which was delivered before the Women's National Republican Club in New York City on December 2, the Assistant Secretary of State for Far Eastern Affairs, Walter Robertson, sounded a confident note: "Everywhere [in the Far East]," said Robertson, "the military attacks launched by the communists since 1948 have been decisively repelled—except in Indo-China, where, however, we believe the tide is now turning."[14]

In his first public remarks since becoming the Chairman of the Joint Chiefs of Staff nearly five months earlier, Adm. Arthur W. Radford addressed a U.S. Military Academy student conference at West Point, New York.

Admiral Radford's assessment of the situation in Indo-China was also upbeat but his views were tempered by the ever-present threat of Communist China:

Indochina . . . is a very real part of the overall conflict between the free world and communism. Today, I am happy to say that there is reason to be optimistic about its eventual outcome. Militarily, the forces of freedom can win. And politically, sound and just arrangements have been promised.

In the past, the efforts to win the war in Indo-China have been limited. General Navarre, however, has sparked his entire military command with a fighting spirit. This fact, combined with the planned augmentation and improved training of the military forces, should rapidly improve the military position of the French and the Associated States.

The United States is providing military assistance to this area. With our programs of assistance, we hope that increased military operations in Indo-China will defeat the communist military forces of Ho Chi Minh.

Of course, the entire outlook on the war in Indo-China could change if Red China chose to intervene overtly with military forces. In that event, the war would no longer be localized. The free world could not permit Indo-China to go under the communist yoke.[15]

7
Commitment to Battle

On December 3 General Navarre issued his final operational instructions concerning the future defense of Dien Bien Phu. These secret orders were formally designated as "IPS 949/EMIFT/3/TS," and were transmitted to General Cogny that same day.

The commander in chief began by stating that this new directive emanated from the fact that an enemy menace was putting pressure on Lai Chau. This menace, he explained, was being carried on by one communist division which might be reinforced by the end of December. Navarre then made the following declaration:

> . . . I have decided to accept battle in the Northwest under the following general conditions.
>
> 1. The defense of the Northwest shall be centered on the air land base of Dien Bien Phu which must be held at all costs.
>
> 2. Our occupation at Lai Chau shall be maintained only inasmuch as our present forces there shall permit its defense. . . .
>
> 3. Ground communications between Dien Bien Phu and Lai Chau (until we eventually evacuate our forces from there) and with Laos via Muong-Khoua shall be maintained as long as possible.
>
> In view of the remoteness of the northwestern theater of operations [from the enemy's main bases] and the logistical obligations of the Viet-Minh, it is probable that the battle will be fought according to the following scenario:

> The *movement phase*, [italics here and following in original] characterized by the arrival of the Viet-Minh units and their supplies in the Northwest; whose duration may extend over several weeks.
>
> An *approach and reconnaissance phase*, in the course of which enemy intelligence units will make efforts to determine the quality and

the weaknesses of our defenses and where the [enemy's] combat units will proceed with the positioning of their means of attack. That phase may last between six and ten days.

An *attack phase* lasting several days (according to the means employed) and which must end with the failure of the Viet-Minh offensive.

MISSION OF THE AIR FORCE

1. The mission of the Air Force shall be, until further orders, given priority and with the maximum of means at its disposal, to the support of our forces in the Northwest.

2. The Commanding General of the Air Force in the Far East will, to that effect, reinforce the Northern Tactical Air Group. . . .[1]

The coming battle would be conducted by General Cogny who would set up three headquarters to carry out operational, mobile group, and airborne group functions, respectively, for the units at Lai Chau and Dien Bien Phu.

The forces at Dien Bien Phu were to be increased to a total strength of nine battalions, including three airborne battalions. Providing support for the garrison would be five batteries of 105-mm. howitzers (a total of twenty field pieces), divided into two groups of two and three batteries, respectively; one group of two batteries (eight pieces) of 75-mm. recoilless rifles; and one company of heavy mortars.

According to General Navarre's plan, the mission of this defensive corps would be tailored to the four-phase scenario of battle (movement, approach and reconnaissance, attack, and fall back) that he foresaw for the Viet-Minh.

The defense would be carried out as follows: in the first phase, retard Viet-Minh movements by conducting ground and air actions; in the second, perform raids to divert the enemy from Lai Chau; in the third, stop the enemy attacks and render them costly for the communists by executing counteroffensive operations; and in the fourth, exploit the enemy's retreat. The specific mission of the airborne forces would be: in the movement and approach phases, harass Viet-Minh communications; in the preparations for the enemy's attack and during the attack, support the defense; and, during all phases, provide intelligence.

The success of this entire plan rested on the underlying assumption, stated by General Navarre at the outset of his instructions, that the French would, in fact, be faced with only one communist division at Dien

Bien Phu by the end of December. Even if this division was, as expected, considerably reinforced, it would still have only about a dozen battalions and a few heavy guns.

Another prerequisite for successfully defending Dien Bien Phu was that the garrison's landing strip would always be available. On this matter, however, the French had to contend with another adversary: the weather. Thursday, December 3, was the third straight day that Dien Bien Phu had been buried under a fog that did not lift until late in the morning. During the periods of zero visibility, the French had not yet found a way to continue to drop supplies, let alone to land aircraft.

On the same day that General Navarre made his final decision to accept battle at Dien Bien Phu, General Giap's staff officers reached the same conclusion. Despite the formidable obstacles presented by the mountains, the jungle, and the poor lines of communication, it was essential, they felt, to engage the enemy at the new French stronghold in the Thai Highlands.

One final question remained, however, involving an issue on which Navarre and his staff were already in full agreement. It was simply this: once the Viet-Minh battle corps was brought to the site of the engagement, could it be maintained there? The French High Command was convinced that it could not.

When that matter was put to the Viet-Minh director general of supplies, he replied without hesitation that it would be a difficult task but one for which he felt himself capable. Such an effort, he explained, would require the following means of transport: trucks to pull the guns; hundreds of sampans that would go up and down the rivers with tons of food and supplies[2]; and an enormous number of Peugeot bicycles, bought years before in the shops of Hanoi, which could now be converted to carry up to five hundred pounds each, and would be used to move tons of rice and munitions over their designated routes.

Human labor would be a vital component in this undertaking and, to that end, said the supplies director, a mass appeal would have to be made in order to mobilize the entire population. Thirty, forty, and, if necessary, fifty thousand porters—men and women—would be assembled. Thousands of horses, each of them equivalent to four porters, would also be used.

That day General Giap and his aides went to the government headquarters of the Democratic Republic of Viet-Nam in order to present the plans for this new military campaign to D.R.V. President Ho Chi Minh,

D.R.V. President Ho Chi Minh. From John Keegan, *Dien Bien Phu.*

Prime Minister Pham van Dong, and Political Commisar Truong Chinh.[3]

The Viet-Minh commander began by explaining the situation. The movement of the 316th Division, he said, had already led to a scattering of the French Expeditionary Corps, and it was now a matter of deciding on future operations. In his judgment, declared Giap, a threat to Dien

General Giap (*far right*) presents his plan for attacking Dien Bien Phu to D.R.V. Prime Minister Pham Van Dong (*far left*), Ho Chi Minh (*left center*), and Lao Dong party member Truong Chinh (*right center*). From Georges Boudarel, *Giap.*

Bien Phu would oblige General Navarre to reinforce the garrison, which could then be destroyed.

After a careful study of the details, the operation was approved by the government and Giap was directed to take the necessary measures.

In Saigon the next day Ambassador Heath presented Sen. Edward J. Thye (Rep., Minn.) to General Navarre. Senator Thye was visiting Indo-China as a member of the Senate Appropriations Committee.

Navarre continued to be greatly encouraged by the military situation. There was no doubt, said the commander in chief, that the Viet-Minh had planned a serious attack on the Red River Delta beginning on October 15. Operation Mouette and the present taking of Dien Bien Phu, in his judgment, had spoiled that plan. Navarre thought that the Viet-Minh might still attack the delta but, if so, this would come later since it no longer seemed to be a "must" operation in the current campaign.[4] In fact, during Mouette, he added, the 320th Division had been hit so hard that it would take until the end of December until it could be utilized.

Communist troops were now moving into the Thai country, said the commander in chief, both because of the French operation at Dien Bien Phu and because of the French promotion of counterguerrilla activity among the Thai mountain people.[5] The recent development of the Thai counterguerrilla units, in his view, was a most hopeful one. Navarre concluded by saying that France might have to take some very hard knocks in the next few months but he was confident that they would stand these.

That day the U.S. Army attaché in Saigon, Colonel Shaughnessey, sent a new report to Army Intelligence in Washington concerning Viet-Minh troop movements. It was repeated for information to the commanders of U.S. forces in the Far East and the Pacific. The attaché's report, which reflected continued French uncertainty about enemy plans, read as follows:

SECRET SECURITY INFORMATION

DEPARTMENT OF THE ARMY

ROUTINE
FROM: USARMA SAIGON VIETNAM
TO: CSUSA DEPTAR WASH DC FOR G2
INFO: CINCFE TOKYO JAPAN, CINCPAC PEARL HARBOR TH
NR: MC 331–53   040800Z DEC 53
Div 304 (minus) [is] now confirmed [to be] moving NW towards
      Cho Bo.[6] Cas has info[rmation that] Div 312 [is] moving in
      [a] westerly direction.[7]

      G2 [Army Intelligence] states [that] info[rmation] of [on
      the] VM [Viet-Minh] [is] sparse and conflicting. VM
      counter[-]intelligence always tightens before major opera-
      tions. This fact, coupled with [the] usual problem of getting
      timely accurate info on moving troop units, results in [a] tem-
      porary "blind spot" in French intelligence. G2 believes [the]
      picture will clarify by 10 December.

      Lead elements [of] Div 316 [are] now closed in Tuan
      Giao.[8] Expect [the entire] Div [to be] close by 8 Dec. . . .[9]

As Viet-Minh Division 316 was rapidly approaching Tuan Giao, the 8th BPC and 3rd BT continued their mission toward the same objective, clawing and hacking their way through the hills to the north of Dien Bien Phu. Their route was by way of Ban Tau and Muong Pan and over the six-thousand-foot-high Phanthong Mountain ridge.

Aside from the physical exertion of the operation, Captain Tourret's paratroopers and Captain Guilleminot's Thai mountaineers had neither encountered any difficulties nor made any contact with enemy troops. The small force was, however, in need of silver coins for the partisans and also maps for the push on to Tuan Giao. Tourret, accordingly, radioed back to Dien Bien Phu to set up a rendezvous with a Cricket aircraft (Morane-500) and that appointment was kept at 10:00 A.M. on December 5.

8
Strongpoint Beatrice

While visiting Dien Bien Phu on December 5, General Cogny decided to establish the garrison's first fortified position, or strongpoint, on Hill 506, which was located three miles northeast of Dien Bien Phu's center. The strongpoint, officially baptized "Beatrice" five days later, would have the twin tasks of helping to cover the central position as well as enhancing the security of the airspace above the airfield.[1]

At 509 meters (1,671 feet) in height, Beatrice would be the highest French postion at Dien Bien Phu. From its escarpments the view to the southwest extended over the entire valley. The hill also controlled Provincial Route 41 which passed along the base of the slope on the way from Hanoi (see map 6).[2]

Looking to the northeast, Beatrice would also command a wide view. Here, however, the strongpoint would be faced with both numerous ravines and wild, wooded cone-shaped peaks (see fig. 19). Among the latter were Hills 781 and 1066, looming on the horizon, which were even higher than Hill 506. This, clearly, was terrain that lent itself to infiltration and it was the direction from which to expect attack. If provided with cover by other hillocks, Beatrice could still be a strong position but, isolated as it was from the center of French resistance, it would be at the mercy of an enemy who was determined to take it at all costs.

General Gilles was not too happy about the decision to fortify Hill 506 because of its being overshadowed by Hills 781 and 1066. These hills, however, were located in the middle of the jungle and could be immediately cut off from Dien Bien Phu's main position. Hill 506, it seemed, offered the best communication lines to the garrison.

There was also the hope that the communists would never be able to bring their artillery in close enough to take advantage of the controlling hill line. However, in the event that the Viet-Minh did place artillery pieces on these heights, it was expected that the French fighter bombers

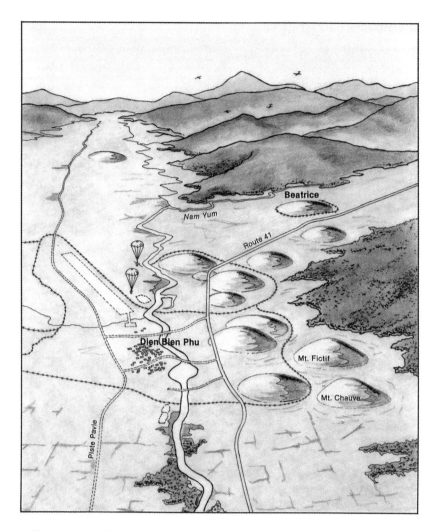

6. The location of Strongpoint Beatrice in relation to the central position at Dien Bien Phu.

and the heavy 155-mm. howitzers that General Cogny had decided to have brought to Dien Bien Phu would put them out of action in short order.

Cogny's choice of Hill 506, therefore, prevailed. He was, after all, not only the northern commander but an artillery general as well.

Strongpoint Beatrice and other nearby peaks. From Pierre Langlais, *Dien Bien Phu.*

Maj. Jean Souquet's 1st BPC and parts of Maj. Jean Bréchignac's II/1 RCP set out from Dien Bien Phu that day on a reconnaissance mission that pushed directly along Route 41.

At a point along the road three miles northeast of the center of Dien Bien Phu, the paratroopers approached a small Thai tribal village named Ban Him Lam. Here Route 41 twisted through a narrow valley that was overshadowed on both sides by hills in the twelve-hundred-foot range. The site of Ban Him Lam itself was located only three hundred yards to the east of Hill 506, across rice fields.

While still advancing toward the village, 1st Company of the 1st BPC radioed back to the rest of the reconnaissance party that it saw suspicious signs of enemy troops nearby. The message had hardly been transmitted when deadly accurate Viet-Minh mortar and grenade-launcher fire completely enveloped 1st Company. The paratroopers had not expected enemy forces to be operating this close to Dien Bien Phu so soon and had, therefore, been pressing ahead without taking any particular precautionary measures. The lead platoon of 1st Company was virtually wiped out within a matter of seconds.

The remainder of 1st Company, with the sound discipline of well-trained regulars, immediately formed a hedgehog position as screaming waves of communist infantrymen emerged from the bush. The two sides were soon engaged in bitter hand-to-hand fighting, using machetes, commando daggers, and hand grenades.

Over the din of the battle, the Viet-Minh troops could be distinctly heard appealing to the Vietnamese members of the paratroop battalion not to lay down their lives for the "French imperialists."[3] For a brief moment, the communist appeals caused a few of the Vietnamese paratroopers to cease firing and to begin to look for a way to crawl out of the fight.

First Company was finally saved from destruction by the arrival of the rest of the task force and by artillery fire that was laid down by the main position's howitzers. Nevertheless, the paratroopers had taken heavy losses—forty casualties overall, with fourteen dead, and twenty-six lying wounded and bleeding.

As usual, the communists had disappeared as suddenly as they had come and had taken almost all of their casualties with them. The identity of the attackers was quickly established, however, by searching the quilted mountain uniforms of those who were left behind. They were members of Battalion 888 of the 176th Regiment of Viet-Minh Division 316.

The Associated Press in Saigon sent the following same-day report on the battle after receiving a news briefing from the French High

Command: "French and Viet Namese troops fanning out from their newly established position in the Northwestern Indo-China's Thai country clashed today with Viet Minh forces and inflicted heavy losses. A French army spokesman said strong French Union units engaged the Viet Minh in battalion strength 7 miles northeast of Dien Bien Phu. He did not give the exact losses for either side."[4]

The military situation in Indo-China was the subject of a report to the State Department on December 5 by Paul Sturm, the U.S. consul in Hanoi. It read as follows:

SECRET SECURITY INFORMATION

FROM: Hanoi
TO: Secretary of State
NO: 327, December 5, 10 a.m.

SENT DEPARTMENT 327 REPEATED INFORMATION SAIGON 244, PARIS 145

In [a] series of conversations officers of [the French] Delegation Generale have indicated that recent operations initiated by [the] French Command along [the] northern perimeter of [the Red River] Delta . . . although not spectacular have been profitable in permitting [the] destruction of [a] series of caches which Viet Minh Divisons 308 and 312 would need in order [to] execute large-scale incursions into [the] North Delta.

It is too early to affirm [a] basic change in Viet Minh fall campaign plans, which have been generally assumed to hinge on [a] major effort against [the] Delta by regular forces now outside [the Delta]. Such an attempt, from the north, would probably not have been made under any circumstances before about November 20, after completion of [the] fall rice harvest. However, chances of Viet Minh success in any such move appear to have been lessened by General Cogny's timely operations.

Some sources assume (and hope) that Diem-Bien-Phu [sic], seized in operation "Castor," will in time become the focus of Thai partisan and guerrilla activities, in effect replacing Lai Chau militarily, and will not be transformed into another Nasan, tying down French Union battalions in static positions. Political problems which must be solved before this military objective can be realized are considerable in that many among [the] Thais must be decontaminated of Viet Minh indoctrination received over [the] last year, and

actual and potential frictions among Thai leaders must be objects of
constant attention on [the] part of French military and political authorities.

Informants comment that [the] signature of [the] new Franco-
Laotian accord on October 22 was not without its part in [the] decision to undertake "Castor," which offers concrete evidence of [the]
military benefits [for the three Associated States] deriving from membership in [the] French Union.

STURM[5]

That day the Reuters news service carried the following in-depth analysis of the war between France and the Viet-Minh, written by reporter
Corley Smith in Hanoi:

Normal military methods are as useless against the Viet-Minh rebels in Indo-China as a cannon ball against a horde of mosquitoes.

In the steamy jungles and red mud rice paddies of Indo-China,
the Communist-led Viet-Minh attack in swarms suddenly, and usually by night.

As soon as the modern military machine of the French Union
forces rumbles into action against them, they just disappear, to strike
another day.

Soldiers here get aggravated and frustrated, like men vainly slap-
ping their necks and arms to keep off mosquitoes—killing one or
two and always being bitten.

Gen. Henri Navarre, [the] French commander in chief here, real-
izes that if the Viet Minh are to be defeated, they must be dealt with
like swarms of gnats. They must be kept away from food and other
supplies. Whenever possible, they also must be cornered and scien-
tifically swatted.

The coming months will show whether the "mosquitoes" of Indo-
China can be controlled, or whether they will spread and multiply to
dominate the entire country.

The campaign against them will soon begin in real earnest and
will probably reach its peak by the second half of next year. United
States aid in the next 12 months will increase from $400,000,000 to
$785,000,000 in addition to the huge sums being found by France.

More regiments of French and North African troops have begun
to arrive here, and a big training program, aimed at expanding the
Viet-Namese army by the middle of 1954 from just over 200,000 to
350,000 men, has begun.

Even with limitless supplies and troops, Gen. Navarre would have a difficult job before him. During the eight years of war here, since the Japanese left Indo-China, the Communist-inspired Viet-Minh rebels have developed their power mainly in Viet-Nam, the eastern most [sic] of the three Associated States of Indo-China.

They now control about one-half of Viet-Nam, though the richest regions are held by French Union forces and the Viet-Namese army.

The Viet-Minh also operates on a smaller scale in the other two States—Laos and Cambodia.

But most of the fighting takes place in and around the rich Red River delta in North Viet-Nam. This is a huge rice field more than 150 miles long and capable of feeding tens of millions of people.

The main French Union fighting strength is concentrated in the delta. Around them in the hills which stretch to Communist China are six divisions of regular Viet-Minh troops under their commander, Gen. Vo Nguyen Giap. Each division has between 10,000 and 15,000 highly trained troops who form a permanent threat to the delta and prevent Navarre [from] taking his troops elsewhere.

Until Gen. Rene Cogny cleared out their main strongholds early this fall [Operation Mouette] there was also a division of Viet-Minh regulars within the delta [Division 320], though it was split up into smaller units.

Also there, and much more elusive, are hundreds of small bands of Viet-Minh irregulars, whose job it is to threaten villages into handing over food and recruits for the Communist-led armies.[6]

By December 6 French Union forces at Dien Bien Phu had reached a total of 4,907 troops.[7]

The continuing movement of Viet-Minh Division 316 toward the garrison was the subject of the following report that day from the Reuters news service in Hanoi:

French Union parachutists holding the important mountain and valley stronghold of Dien Bien Phu, on the Tonking [Tonkin]-Laos border, today dug in for a Viet-Minh Communist attack expected this week.

A French High Command spokesman said today that a 12,000-strong Viet-Minh division had reached the area of Sonla, 65 miles east of Dien Bien Phu (see map 3), after a three-week march from the rim of the Red River Delta. A spearhead of the division is believed to be less than 30 miles from the stonghold.

The spokesman said the rebel division's advance had been slowed by heavy bombing attacks by French air force planes.[8]

Another newspaper story on Indo-China contained a less favorable account of the December 5 battle near Ban Him Lam than that released by the AP the day before.[9] The Paris correspondent for the *Times* (London) sent the following report:

> Violent fighting has been reported for the first time near Dien Bien Phu, where the Franco-Viet Namese parachute troops who occupied the town a fortnight ago were ambushed by units of the former Viet-Minh garrison on the mountain road which links it with the main highway from Hanoi to the Thai resistance centre at Lai Chau. Regular troops of the Viet-minh 316th division advancing along this highway are reported to be two days' march from either of the two French Union centres.[10]

In preparing to lay siege to Dien Bien Phu, General Giap now began to direct his Chinese-supplied trucks, heavy artillery, and anti-aircraft guns toward the Thai country. This equipment would have to be carried a considerable distance since it was a journey of over two hundred miles along the mountains that led from the Viet-Minh divisional bases to the hills surrounding the French garrison.

Such an undertaking would require a vast army of porters and, to this end, Giap issued an order of the day on December 6 mobilizing the population, in accordance with the Central Committee decision of three days earlier. In this order the Viet-Minh commander spoke of "developing the victories of the winter campaign of 1952" and he called upon the people to do everything in their power to keep the French from reoccupying the northwest.[11]

The order also contained the following exhortation: "You must repair the roads, overcome all obstacles, surmount all difficulties, fight unflinchingly, defeat cold and hunger, carry heavy loads across mountains and valleys, and strike right into the enemy's camp to destroy him and free our fellow countrymen. . . . Comrades, forward!"[12]

Giap also decided to augment the forces that were already being moved into the Thai country. In the rice granery of Thanh Hoa, south of the Red River Delta, the chief of staff of the 57th Regiment of the Viet-Minh 304th Division received word that his group was to take part in the Dien Bien Phu campaign.[13]

On the evening of the day that Giap issued his mobilization order, General Navarre's directive of December 3 to hold Dien Bien Phu "at all costs" arrived at French headquarters in Hanoi.

9

Pollux and Atlante

The coverage given to Operation Castor by American photojournalists received dramatic display in the weekly magazines (both news and picture) that came out on December 7. Large photo layouts of French Union paratroopers descending onto the plain of Dien Bien Phu and later carrying out patrols were accompanied by articles that credited the French military move with surprising the enemy.

Life said General Navarre's capture of Dien Bien Phu would disrupt the communists' annual food raids, bolster the defenses of Laos and Lai Chau, and boost the morale of the pro-French Vietnamese troops.[1]

Newsweek pointed out that the French move was staged in order to seize and hold a base in enemy territory and that this would not only provide food but serve as a center for increased partisan activity against the communists by Thai and Meo tribesmen.[2]

General Cogny had been aware since December 5 that the airhead at Lai Chau would soon become untenable. Since the French Command had already determined that no attempt would be made to defend the position against the entire 316th Division, Cogny decided on December 7 to launch "Operation Pollux," which would involve a high-speed airborne pullout of all regular units and civilians from the little valley town. The operation would be covered by GCMA units and the remaining subgroupments of the GMPT 1.

Cogny flew to Lai Chau that day for the last time, accompanied by his wife and daughter, and by General Gilles. His mission was to speak to Deo Van Long, the federal president of the Thai Federation, and personally to inform the Thai leader of his decision. Deo Van Long accepted the news stoically.

Cogny also notified General Navarre about Pollux since the commander in chief had issued instructions in his battle directive of December 3 ordering that ground communications between Dien Bien Phu and Lai Chau be held "as long as possible." In a long dispatch, Cogny acknowledged the belated receipt of Navarre's directive and explained his reasons for hurriedly evacuating the Lai Chau garrison. The Viet-Minh, wrote Cogny, had established itself strongly on the Pavie Trail, completely cutting off land communications between Lai Chau and Dien Bien Phu, on which two regiments from the 308th and 312th Divisions were marching.[3] He added that the enemy had also cut the paved road, Route 41.[4]

The garrison at Dien Bien Phu was already feeling the pressure. With Lai Chau about to go, the original concept of maneuvers in the Dien Bien Phu/Lai Chau/Tuan Giao triangle had collapsed. It was now thought impossible to venture as far as six miles to the east, thus putting in jeopardy the mission of maintaining freedom of movement within a radius of five miles around the airfield.

The French would have to be able to maneuver and they were finding it difficult to do so. As soon as they reached the first slopes that surrounded the valley, they had to hack their way through creepers, tall grass, and undergrowth. It looked as though neither horses nor tanks could ever be useful in such a jungle.

Major Bigeard, who was a paratrooper and not a cavalryman, had tried to move around and had found himself hemmed in on all sides. He told this to Colonel de Castries, who took over the command of Dien Bien Phu from General Gilles on December 7.

De Castries believed that Bigeard was exaggerating but the new commander did not complain. He remained confident that light patrols, with artillery and air protection; patrols in strength; and powerful raids would be able to destroy the enemy's weapons.

That day, in fact, a new offensive stab was launched from Dien Bien Phu along Route 41 in the direction of Ban Him Lam in order to disrupt communist road traffic that was near the garrison. This time the French had sufficient strength to discourage the kind of ambush that had occurred two days before. The force was composed of two battalions, the 1st BPC and the 6th BPC, reinforced with recoilless rifles and mortars, and covered by fighter bombers. By the end of the day the group had pushed forward to Ban Na Loi, four miles beyond Hill 506.

General Gilles was happy to be getting out of the hot seat by turning over his command to Colonel de Castries. He could look forward to being reunited with the battalions of Operation Castor, which were due to be relieved one by one with three other parachute battalions that would

General Gilles (*left*) and Colonel de Castries. From Bernard B. Fall, *Hell in a Very Small Place*.

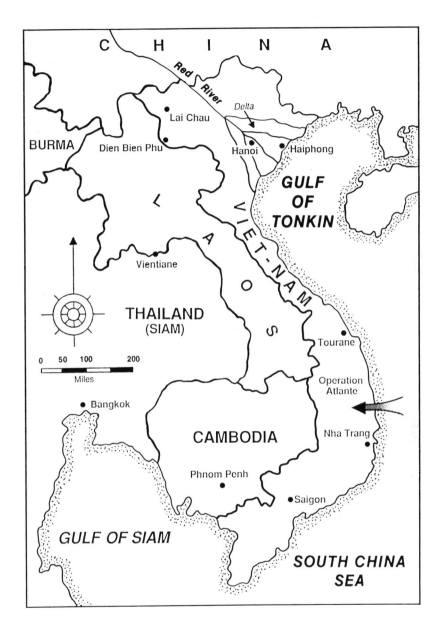

7. The projected location for Operation Atlante in south-central Viet-Nam.

then constitute the camp's general reserve.[5] De Castries had struck Gilles as being full of confidence in the future, which prompted the general to give him some advice.

"Watch out," he told his successor, adding: "If you lose an inch of ground, you are done for."[6]

On December 7 General Navarre issued Instruction No. 964 in which he notified his subordinate commanders of his decision to launch Operation Atlante, his long-planned offensive in south-central Viet-Nam, 650 miles away from the northern theater (see map 7).[7]

The complete battle plan covered ten full pages but the gist of the operation was contained in the following lines:

> The essential objective which I expect to reach [in the 1953–1954 campaign season] is the disappearance of the Viet-Minh zone which spreads from south of Tourane to the north of Nha Trang and eastward to the Southern Mountain Plateau; that is, the destruction of the military forces of Lien-Khu V [Viet-Minh Fifth Interzone]. . . .
>
> In view of the considerable strategic and political results which one is entitled to expect from the complete execution of that operation, I have decided to subordinate to it the conduct of the whole Indochina campaign during the first semester of 1954.[8]

According to the details and appendices that were attached to the instruction, Atlante was to be subdivided into three phases. In the first phase, code-named "Arethuse," Navarre expected that the troop requirements would be twenty-five infantry battalions, three artillery battalions, and two engineering battalions. In the second phase, code-named "Axelle," these requirements would be increased to thirty-four infantry battalions and five artillery battalions. Finally, in the third phase, code-named "Attila," the plan called for up to forty-five infantry battalions and eight artillery battalions.

The fifth military region of the Viet-Minh and its three million inhabitants had been in communist hands since 1945 and, as a result, this area had been transformed into a strongly defended bastion. The French would face thirty thousand enemy troops, including twelve good regular battalions and six well-trained regional battalions.

In Washington that day the Pentagon's Joint Strategic Plans Group circulated for consideration a draft report on the O'Daniel mission, which it had been directed to draw up by the Joint Strategic Plans Committee.

Gen. John "Iron Mike" O'Daniel. From Al Santoli, *To Bear Any Burden.*

Copies were sent to both the Joint Strategic Plans Committee and the Joint Logistics Plans Committee.[9] The draft report read as follows:

J.S.P.C. 958/136
7 December 1953

REPORT BY THE JOINT STRATEGIC PLANS COMMITTEE
(In collaboration with the Joint Logistics Plans Committee)
to the
JOINT CHIEFS OF STAFF
on
REPORT OF U.S. JOINT MILITARY MISSION TO INDOCHINA

THE PROBLEM

1. To submit comment and recommendations on a progress report dated 19 November 1953, submitted by the U.S. Joint Military Mission to Indochina, and comments thereon by CINCPAC [Commander-in-Chief, Pacific].

FACTS BEARING ON THE PROBLEM

2. In response to an invitation extended by the French, and with the concurrence of the JCS [Joint Chiefs of Staff], Lieutenant General John W. O'Daniel, USA [United States Army], and his assigned mission returned to Indo-China on 6 November 1953 to survey the military progress made since [the first O'Daniel mission in] June–July 1953.

3. The Mission progress report and CINCPAC comments thereon, are summarized in the Appendix to Enclosure "A" hereto.

4. For further facts bearing on the problem and discussion, see Enclosure "C" and "D" respectively hereto.

CONCLUSIONS

5. Real military progress in implementation of the "Navarre Plan" is evident. To a limited extent, the French and Associated States have succeeded in regaining the initiative in the conflict. As a result, prospects for victory appear increasingly encouraging. . . .

RECOMMENDATIONS

12. It is recommended that:

a. The report of the Mission be accepted as a basis for further planning in connection with operations in Indochina. . . .

g. The memorandum in Enclosure "A," together with its Appendix, be forwarded to the Secretary of Defense to inform him of the action taken by the JCS in connection herewith.

h. The message in Enclosure "B" be dispatched to CINCPAC for information of JCS action on the subject report.

ENCLOSURE "A"
DRAFT
MEMORANDUM FOR THE SECRETARY OF DEFENSE
Subject: Report of the U.S. Joint Military Mission to Indochina

1. The Joint Chiefs of Staff have reviewed and accepted for further planning purposes a progress report submitted by the Chief of the U.S. Joint Military Mission to Indochina, a summary of which is appended hereto.

2. . . . This current memorandum is to advise you of the action taken by the Joint Chiefs of Staff as a result of their review of the subject progress report. . . .

APPENDIX TO ENCLOSURE "A"
DRAFT
SUMMARY OF PROGRESS REPORT OF U.S. JOINT
MILITARY MISSION TO INDOCHINA

1. A summary of the subject report, the comments and recommendations of the Mission, together with the comments of Commander in Chief, Pacific, is given below:

a. The Joint Mission, consisting of Lieutenant General John W. O'Daniel, USA, as Chief, nine officers from each of the three services and one representative from the State Department [Philip Bonsal], arrived in Saigon on 6 November 1953, for a nine-day survey of the progress made since the previous visit of the Mission in June–July 1953 and [to] render assistance when indicated with respect to the military situation in Indochina.

b. Conferences were held with Bao Dai, the Chief of State of Vietnam, President [Prime Minister] [Nguyen Van] Tam of Vietnam, Governor [Nguyen Hu] Tri of North Vietnam and King Norodom [Sihanouk] of Cambodia, as well as numerous conferences with General Navarre, Commander in Chief of the French Union Forces, General [Nguyen Van] Hinh, Chief of Staff of the Vietnamese Armed Forces and members of their staffs and American military and diplomatic representatives to the Associated States. Visits were also made to the subordinate commands of the French Union Forces in Cochin China [southern Viet-Nam], Tonkin [northern Viet-Nam], Cambodia and Laos.

c. Real military progress in [the] implementation of the "Navarre Plan" is evident. The French have established a far better situation than existed during the previous dry season [the fall of 1952 to the spring of 1953]. . . .

m. Although the political situation has shown little change, an increase in confidence in General Navarre by both military and civilian people was noted. . . .

n. Positive action taken since July to organize and expand the action of [the] Associated States guerrilla forces has met with considerable success. . . .

ENCLOSURE "B"
DRAFT
MESSAGE FOR COMMANDER IN CHIEF, PACIFIC
INFORMATION FOR: CG USARPAC
CHIEF, MAAG, INDOCHINA[10]

1. The Joint Chiefs of Staff have reviewed and accepted for further planning purposes the progress report of the U.S. Joint Military Mission to Indochina dated 19 November 1953. . . .

ENCLOSURE "C"
FACTS BEARING ON THE PROBLEM

1. This visit of the Mission, a follow-up to that made in June-July 1953, was for the purpose of surveying the progress made by the French and Associated States with respect to the military situation in Indochina. Particular attention was directed to the implementation of the "Navarre Plan." . . .

3. By American standards the French continue to be overcautious in the conduct of the war as well as less effective in the utilization of available means. Much remains to be done prior to achieving victory over the Viet Minh. However, real military progress since the previous visit of the Mission is evident and French Union forces have wrested the military initiative from the enemy during the past four months. Although all of the operations scheduled by the French for this period were not completed, the operations that were executed definitely kept the enemy off balance, forced a redeployment of a portion of the enemy forces,[11] and in general established a far better situation for the French than existed during the previous dry season. . . .

13. There has been little change in the political situation in Vietnam since July 1953, although it was noted that there is an increasing growth of confidence in General Navarre. Also, the Mission found no evidence of a disposition on the part of French or Vietnamese officials to envisage negotiations with the Viet Minh. However, this was conditioned by concern in some quarters lest a seemingly

plausible offer from the enemy might at a later date prove damaging, particularly if made in the absence of any real military progress by the French. . . .

14. Positive action taken since July 1953 to organize and expand the action of [the] Associated States guerrilla forces has met with considerable success. Presently, French Union guerrilla forces operating in the northwest section of Indochina have forced the Viet Minh to deploy one regiment plus one battalion to counteract this guerrilla action.[12] Approximately 6,000 guerrillas are now being directed by the para-military organization and the prospects for the future appear good. . . .

16. . . . His [General Navarre's] strategic plan for the coming year involves an offensive in Cochin China to start in early January 1954 to clear the enemy from that area; an offensive [Operation Atlante] to start about 15 January 1954, involving a series of operations, many of them amphibious, to clear the enemy from the area between Cape Varella [south of Nha Trang] north to Tourane; simultaneously, limited objectives in the [Red River] Delta area to keep the enemy off balance and prevent massing of his forces for attack; and about 1 October 1954, a final all out offensive in the north, the details of which General Navarre was not ready to discuss.

17. The report of the mission states that "a revitalized French leadership is well on its way to the creation of a military force believed capable of forcing the enemy regular forces either to give battle or to break up and withdraw into inaccessible areas" from which no serious coordinated offensive could be sustained. The report emphasizes that the total military effort is designed to obtain a decision within a period of eighteen months, a period beyond which it is anticipated that essential political support in France and Vietnam for the hostilities would be withdrawn or non-effective. General O'Daniel therefore concludes that U.S. assistance should be concentrated on those items which will make a definite contribution within the next twelve to eighteen months. He reiterated his belief that the "Navarre Plan" offers a means of obtaining a decisive victory, that it will continue to be in general effectively carried out by the French High Command in Indochina, and that prospects for victory appear increasingly encouraging. Therefore he heartily recommends not only continuation but also intensification of U.S. support.

18. In a message dated 2 December 1953, CINCPAC[13] concurred in general and stated that, although his own views were less optimistic than those of General O'Daniel, considerable progress has been made under General Navarre's leadership, with the most notable

improvements occurring in the development of the potential of the French Union Forces. However, the establishment of the training and amphibious commands has lagged. CINCPAC believed further that all U.S. effort should be bent toward guiding the French in undertaking the reorganization and action necessary for decisive action. He also considered that political and psychological factors are of major importance in the ultimate solution of the problem. To that end he felt it vitally important to the morale of the French forces and to the satisfaction of the U.S. public that there be [a] reaffirmation at the highest government levels of the French and U.S. intention to prosecute the conflict to a satisfactory conclusion. . . .

20. CINCPAC stated that, from his own observation, a complete victory in Indochina cannot be won until sufficient native troops are available to garrison the captured villages and until native populations are won over by anti-Communist psychological warfare.

21. In a message dated 1 December 1953, Chief, MAAG Indochina submitted his monthly report on the status of actions designed to implement the "Navarre Plan," wherein he discussed the recent French airborne operation at Dien Bien Phu which General Navarre plans to develop "as a permanent defensive base astride the gateway to Luang Prabang." Chief, MAAG commented that this conservative move, followed by a base development scheme in the sparsely populated hinterland, led to [a] reasonable doubt that the French have the will to seize the initiative by operations threatening the enemy main supply lines in the northern Delta area where major enemy concentrations now exist. . . .[14]

ENCLOSURE "D"

DISCUSSION

1. By personal observation, reports, conferences, and discussions, the Mission investigated the progress being made by the French and Associated States in the military situation in Indochina.

2. Although opinions vary as to the degree of success the French have had in their attempts to wrest the initiative from the Viet Minh,[15] there is definite evidence that real progress has been made toward a more favorable military situation. A more aggressive attitude, the execution of several military operations with results varying from partially to highly successful, the growth of the indigenous armies essentially as planned, the reorganization into larger and more effective units, and the increased use of guerrilla warfare all evidence such progress. . . .[16]

10
The View from Bermuda

More than eight thousand miles away from the battlefields of Indo-China, the leaders of Great Britain, France, and the United States had been meeting in Bermuda since December 4. It was the first full-dress, international conference involving the personal participation of the Big Three heads of government in over eight years, since the gathering at Pottsdam in 1945 that ended World War II in Europe.[1]

Bermuda was at its best as the last and busiest day of the conference began on December 7. The windows of the Mid-Ocean Club, the site for the talks, looked down onto a coral pink beach and out to the glitter of a sea that seemed almost drained of color by the bright sunshine.

Inside the resort, which had been the home and the workshop of the three heads of government and their foreign ministers for the past three days, the fifth plenary tripartite meeting of the heads of government convened at 5:00 P.M.

President Eisenhower opened the session by saying that he understood that the first item to be discussed would be handled by the French and would deal with Indo-China. Foreign Minister Bidault began his presentation by announcing that he would first say a few words on the military situation. The Viet-Minh forces, he asserted, were facing a stagnation in strength. This was happily indicated, he explained, by the institution of special courts to try deserters who, by flight or other means, refused to serve in the communist army.

At the same time, however, that the Viet-Minh had reached the ceiling of strength, said Bidault, there was increasing Chinese support in transportation, signal communications, and anti-aircraft equipment. This was known to France's allies. Furthermore, reinforcements had been sent from France and had placed upon the government he represented a considerable onus of unpopularity. This last measure, he added, did not reinforce their defense in Europe.

The national forces of the Associated States—especially Viet-Nam,

(*Left to right*) British Foreign Secretary Anthony Eden, French Prime Minister Joseph Laniel, British Prime Minister Sir Winston Churchill, and French Foreign Minister Georges Bidault in Bermuda on December 3. Courtesy Dwight D. Eisenhower Library, Audiovisual Department, Abilene, Kansas.

which contained nine-tenths of the population of the Indochinese peninsula—continued to improve, claimed the foreign minister. As his colleagues knew, in Washington he had committed the French government to create, with equipment to be furnished by the United States, fifty-four additional Vietnamese battalions.[2] These were naturally a little improvised in nature, he admitted. They needed cadres and there was a limit to the transfer of cadres from old units to the new ones.[3] At the present time thirty of the fifty-four battalions had been activated and the remainder would be activated before the end of February 1954. At the same time, he added, the Viet-Nam regular army, which up to then had not

President Dwight D. Eisenhower and Secretary of State John Foster Dulles leave Washington for Bermuda on December 4. Courtesy Dwight D. Eisenhower Library, Audiovisual Department, Abilene, Kansas.

given any serious trouble, had been increased by one division of nine battalions and fourteen artillery battalions. Overall, he thought, this represented a considerable effort, financed in common by the United States and France in proportions known to his colleagues.

Turning to overall strategy, Bidault observed that by means of certain territorial sacrifices (by the French Union forces), by not trying to defend everything everywhere, and by choosing what to defend and what to attack, it had been possible to create a force of maneuver of considerable size in relation to the forces committed by both sides in the conflict. This was a great novelty, in this struggle, he declared, and the credit belonged to General Navarre who avoided dispersing his forces in an attempt to counterattack everywhere. From the military point of view, he felt, this represented a considerable improvement over the situation prevailing a year earlier.

The foreign minister wished to say that none of this would have been possible if they had not received from the United States assistance of a financial nature and equipment of all sorts, including some air assistance to be forthcoming shortly. This had made it possible to face the constantly increasing pressure from the communist adversaries. The French had sent out more men to Indo-China than had ever been contemplated, even by Marshall de Lattre.[4] He also wished to mention the aircraft carrier *Arromanches* loaned by the United States, which had furnished the financial and material means to make possible this enormous military effort. On the twelfth of December, Bidault added, the French would receive an additional group of U.S. aircraft. In his opinion, France was great lady enough to know how to say thank you with the hope that it would reach the man who had made this effort possible.

Bidault then said that he would discuss the current military situation. A first effort was being made in the delta of the Red River, he told the conference. In this part of Tonkin there were more than two thousand natives per square mile and in some areas it was most difficult to distinguish between a peasant in a rice paddy and the enemy who had just laid his submachine gun in a ditch. "The French," he explained, "had been trying to end the 'dry rot' which was caused by communist night infiltration on a broad scale in this area, which was without hills or commanding heights, where there had been one master by day and another by night."[5] The French, therefore, had worked progressively to install one master by day and night, namely the forces of the French and the Associated States.

The foreign minister said that a certain number of offensive actions had been successfully undertaken, offensive actions which had borne code names like those of World War II that General Eisenhower and Sir Winston had directed. These operations had had mysterious names like "Brochet" ("pike"). He did not feel that these names should be bandied about too much as they might offer the press the opportunity to make jokes about military operations which involved the lives of men.

These operations, Bidault claimed, had resulted in stopping the dry season offensive that the Indochinese communists had favorably prepared on the plateaus of Laos and in the two branches of the delta of the Red River for the purpose of a final accounting with the French. The communist radio had announced these operations. Consequently, large sectors of public opinion believed that since the Viet-Minh did not attack, they were seeking some political maneuver. There was, however, another reason, he stated. They had been drawn off balance by the offensives directed against them by General Navarre.

Concerning the armed forces of Viet-Nam, the foreign minister said that Vietnamese troops, who could not be supported by their own country and who had French-trained cadres, usually behaved well in combat. The supplementary Vietnamese battalions, of which he had promised fifty-four, had less cadres and there had been some surprises, but he did not doubt—and past experience had led France to believe—that, without too much delay, these units might undertake the mopping-up task that was foreseen for them.

As for the French, Bidault said, it was sometimes alleged that they were absent from this war, having sent only cadres, but there were one hundred thousand of them, and that number did not include French citizens of other territories of the French Union. Every year, he pointed out, the equivalent of one graduating class of St. Cyr was cut down.[6] This war would be lost, he argued, without the one hundred thousand French troops and white men and the support that they had received.

It was the intention of the French Command, explained the foreign minister, first to clean out the Red River Delta, then Cochin China (southern Viet-Nam), then Cambodia, and then south Annam (south-central Viet-Nam).[7] The forces of maneuver which had been concentrated enabled them to face any attack and punish the enemy severely but, at any instant, the worst kind of politics could intervene to diminish the value of the Vietnamese units.[8] Furthermore, he added, the Chinese frontier lay close at hand and the roads leading to it had been rebuilt (by the communists), and the French might find themselves at any moment facing aggression in the air or an avalanche of land forces. This would, of course, he observed, completely change the character of the war.[9]

The French were losing men and experienced cadres, said Bidault. Also, they were under the obligation of constantly rotating their troops—fighting in this harsh tropical climate—who had to face not only the enemy but mosquitos, fever, amoebic dysentary, and the weakening effect of a hot climate. They could not keep these men there indefinitely, he contended.

This then was the military situation, concluded the foreign minister. It was better than he had ever seen it before, but his colleagues must know, he added, that this front was supported by a zone of the interior (metropolitan France), which lay eight thousand kilometers (five thousand miles) away across the world.

Following further comments by Bidault on diplomatic developments concerning the Indo-China war, British Prime Minister Sir Winston Churchill addressed the conference. The prime minister said that he would like to pay his heartfelt compliments to France for her valiant effort to preserve her empire and the cause of freedom in Indo-China. He greatly admired her exertions, he declared, and was sorry, insofar as his own country was concerned, that the British had not been able to match these efforts on the vast subcontinent of India. This, he lamented, was a colossal disaster that would leave its imprint on the future.

Churchill went on to say: "History will record that Britain's desertion of her duty in India was the most serious political blunder of the past decade. I may personally not live to see all the unfortunate results that will flow from that tragedy, but there are people around this table who will come to see that this act is certain eventually to bring grief and sorrow to the entire Western world."[10]

The prime minister repeated his admiration for France and his envy of the record she had established in Indo-China under such difficult conditions. He also felt impelled, he continued, to say how much he admired the splended work of France in North Africa[11] and in Tunisia. He had often been there and had been struck by the wonderful manner in which the French cherished and nourished the civilization they had implanted. He earnestly hoped that all of the powers that were allied with France would endeavor to lend their moral support and aid in the difficult task she had undertaken in Indo-China with so much skill and resolution.

The British, Churchill pointed out, had a small but costly preoccupation in Malaya. The situation was improving there, he said, and they had not the slightest intention of wavering in their effort.

Then, returning once again to the French, the prime minister stated that he only wished to pay his tribute to France. He felt that it was a great mistake to suppose that the ancient powers of Europe had not made a contribution to the progress of these races in Asia, or that all the Europeans had done was obsolete and that it was good that it had passed away. He hoped, he added, that France would courageously persevere in her efforts.

Churchill said he would, however, suggest to Foreign Minister Bidault the great advantages to be derived from a prolongation of military service even if there was a lessening of the number of men taken. The need was for well-trained troops who would breed their own cadres and not unduly strain the main organization (professional army), and would not have to be moved too frequently. The British, he maintained, had derived great advantage from this in Malaya, Egypt, and Hong Kong—in not having to move these units to and fro so often while they bred their own cadres.

He felt that the loss of a graduating class of St. Cyr, of which Foreign Minister Bidault had spoken, was a terrible thing. A longer service term would, therefore, save lives and would give the nation a higher return. He asked that the French foreign minister not let this matter drop.

Churchill reiterated his compliments to France and only wished, he said, that he was able to pay a similar compliment to his own country on the great question of India. Dark days lay ahead in Asia, he predicted, as a result of those who thought they could do without the guidance and aid of the European nations to whom they owed so much. However, he would say no more on this subject. He knew, he admitted, that it was not a popular thing at present but he had done his utmost for it all the days of his life.

The British prime minister concluded by wishing France the best of good fortune and expressing his gratitude to the United States for giving aid to Indo-China. This aid, he was sure, would be found to have been foreseeing.

President Eisenhower, speaking next, said he would like to associate himself with the prime minister in the tribute Churchill had paid to France for the magnificent campaign waged for so long and at such cost. He added a personal tribute to General Navarre, of whom he had heard the finest reports.

The president was happy to be able to say, he announced, that he had just learned of another aircraft carrier that was to be turned over to the French in a few days, together with twenty-five transport aircraft and some helicopters. He hoped that these would soon be on the scene and doing their job.

Following further discussions on diplomatic developments concerning the Indo-China war, the conferees moved on to other subjects. The meeting was adjourned at 8:40 P.M.

Secretary of State Dulles sent the following report to the State Department on the Indo-China discussions:

Department of State
SECRET SECURITY INFORMATION

FROM: Bermuda
TO: Secretary of State
NO: SECTO 24, December 7.
SENT DEPARTMEMT SECTO 24, REPEATED INFORMATION
LONDON 19, PARIS 18, BONN 16, MOSCOW UNNUMBERED.

DEPARTMENT PASS DEFENSE
DEPARTMENT POUCH MOSCOW . . .

Bidault began with [a] detailed review [of the] military situation [in] Indochina. Pointing out [that the] Viet Minh [is] now apparently having difficulties in augmenting [its] troop strength he referred in contrast to [the] French reinforcements which have been set a difficult task in view of [the] present French public opinion and also to [the] continuing build up [of the] military forces [of the] Associated States particularly [in] Vietnam. General Navarre [is] doing well in this build up particularly re creation [of a] mobile force instead of [the] former effort [to] maintain garrisons everywhere. None of this would have been possible, stated Bidault, except for US assistance [both] financial and material.

Bidault reported [that the] first real effort [was] just made in [the] Red River delta aimed at eliminating broad Communist infiltration by night. Navarre's efforts have stopped [the] enemy's dry season offensive prepared by [the] Chinese in Laos and [in] both delta branches. Though Bidault claimed [that the] military situation [is] now better than ever before, he also stressed [the] continuing difficulties including [the] necessity for continuous rotation [of] French troops [the] long lines of communication back to France and [the] continuing casualties. . . .

Speaking with obvious feeling Churchill then complimented [the] French warmly for their effort on behalf of empire and freedom. Besides doing well in Indochina he praised their efforts in North Africa stating [that] he [was] greatly impressed by [the] French civilizing work there. In contrast Churchill expressed deep regret that [the] British [had] left India. At [the] same time he urged [the] French to consider [a] prolongation of military service which [the] British have found to be very advantageous. This permits, he stated, troops to "breed their own kind."

President [Eisenhower] associated himself completely with [the] British in complementing [sic] [the] French for their great and protracted military efforts [in] Indochina. He reported having just learned that another carrier [and] 25 transport planes (repeat planes) and some helicopters would soon be delivered by [the] US. . . .

DULLES[12]

Press accounts of that day's talks on Indo-China were considerably embellished. Arthur Veysey of the *Chicago Tribune* sent a dispatch from

Bermuda in which he reported that Foreign Minister Georges Bidault had told his colleagues that the French hoped a strong new offensive in Indo-China would crush the Viet-Minh rebels within the next few months.[13] The United Press correspondent in Bermuda, Merriman Smith, cabled this report:

> [The] United States and France were revealed at the Bermuda conference tonight to be negotiating on sending a big American military mission to Indochina to help train the Vietnam army to fight the Communists.
>
> The matter was studied by the Big 3 at a midday meeting of two hours and 20 minutes. . . .
>
> Secretary of State Dulles was reported to have convinced the French that within 18 months a large number of French troops fighting in Indochina could be withdrawn if the U.S. training mission were put into effect promptly.
>
> The projected mission would be similar to that rushed to Greece when the Truman doctrine against communism was put into effect. The United States also had a training mission in Korea when the Communists struck across the 38th Parallel in 1950.[14]

11
Evacuation

On December 8 the French launched Operation Leda in order to execute the air evacuation phase of Operation Pollux.[1] This operation, which involved 183 flights to Lai Chau by French aircraft, removed the 301st Vietnamese Infantry Battalion (301e Bataillon Vietnamien, or BVN), the 7th Company of the 2nd Thai Battalion (2e Bataillon T'ai, or BT), parts of the 2nd Moroccan Tabor (Battalion), a paratroop company, and the 327 men of the Headquarters Detachment (ZONO), which was made up entirely of Senegalese.[2] Leda was carried out successfully.[3]

In briefing the press on the new operation, the French mentioned only the evacuation of civilians from Lai Chau. The Associated Press cabled the following report from Hanoi: "The French high command announced tonight that it had started the evacuation of the 3,500 population from Lai Chau, capital of the pro-French Thai country in northwestern Indo-China in view of a possible early Viet-Minh attack there. One of the Viet-Minh's crack divisions, No. 316, has been marching in the Thai country for the last fortnight and was last reported about 50 miles southeast of the town."[4]

The Paris correspondent for the *Times* (London) filed this story:

> It was announced to-day from General Cogny's headquarters at Hanoi that the evacuation of the civilian population of Laichau, the capital of the Thai country, was being begun "as a measure of precaution."
>
> Laichau is between the Chinese border and the town of Dien Bien Phu, which French Union forces occupied at the end of last month. Some days ago the Viet-Minh 316th Division was reported to be within two days' march of either Laichau or Dien Bien Phu.
>
> Many of the Thai civil authorities have been brought out by aircraft from Laichau to Dien Bien Phu, which has now become the political as well as the economic capital of the Thai country. The Presi-

dent of the Thai Federation, M. Deo Van Long, who is 80, is in Hanoi.[5]

The United Press had an entirely different account of that day's events at Lai Chau. It sent the following wire from Hanoi:

Communist Viet Minh rebels today attacked the city of Lai Chau, in northern Tonkin Province only 20 miles south of the border of Communist China.[6]
French military headquarters here said the civilian population of the city had been evacuated.
Lai Chau is the center of a pro-French area surrounded by Communist-held territory. The city is controlled by native partisans loyal to the French.
The French command gave no details of the battle around the city, which lies between the Red and Black Rivers. No indication of the strength of the Viet Minh troops was revealed.
A spokesman for Gen. Rene Cogny, northern French commander, said the Red attack appeared aimed at overrunning a wide territory rather than the capture of any immediate local objective. Communist regular and partisan troops were used in the attack, the spokesman said.[7]

At the State Department that day PSA Director Philip Bonsal wrote a memorandum to Walter Robertson, the assistant secretary of state for Far Eastern affairs, in which he set forth his observations on the situation in Indo-China, based largely on his recent trip to that area as the State Department's representative on the second U.S. Joint Military Mission to Indo-China. The memorandum read as follows:

TOP SECRET   (WASHINGTON) December 8, 1953

Subject: General O'Daniel's visit to Indochina, November 6–15, 1953.

General O'Daniel's mission was in Indo-China from Friday afternoon, November 6, to Sunday morning, November 15. Of these nine days three were spent in the Hanoi area and one each in Laos and Cambodia.[8] A full account of the trip from the military point of view is contained in the mission's report, prepared in Honolulu from November 17 to November 20. A copy of this document is attached with the original of this memorandum. It is recommended that you read General O'Daniel's summary of his findings and recommendations.

Although I was with General O'Daniel most of the time, I had several long talks with Ambassador Heath with whom I stayed. I saw [Chief of State] Bao Dai, Prime Minister Tam and his Foreign and Defense Ministers on the Vietnamese side as well as, on the French side, in addition to the military, Commissioner General Dejean, Raymond Offry [Offroy], his deputy, and other French officials in Saigon, Hanoi, Phnom Penh [Cambodia] and Vientiane.

The purpose of this memorandum is to set down briefly my impression and thoughts regarding current conditions and prospects in Indochina.

BACKGROUND

It would be difficult to exaggerate what General Navarre has accomplished in the less than six months since he took command last May of an army whose reserves were practically exhausted and whose confidence in itself and its leaders was at a low ebb. The Viet Minh had seized and held the initiative throughout the campaign of 1952–1953. French successes had been defensive (defense of Nasan and of the major towns of Laos). And the achievement of even these results had practically exhausted all mobile reserves. The prospect for this [1953–1954] campaign season appeared to be one in which the enemy, with his increased offensive potential, would be able to attack the widespread French Union forces at a point or points of his own choosing with the confidence that the ability of the French High Command to reinforce threatened points would soon be exhausted. . . .

On the occasion of General O'Daniel's [first] visit to Indochina in late June and early July of this year, General Navarre developed his general concept of how to fight the war.[9] That concept was adopted with only minor modifications by the French Government in July and August and, in August and September, the United States Government reached agreement with the French Government for increased support by us of the French effort in Indochina to be based upon the Navarre concept. . . .

GENERAL NAVARRE'S ACHIEVEMENTS

The major achievements of General Navarre since last summer may be stated as follows:

(1) The development of a new offensive spirit which permeates the French military establishment in Indochina.

(2) The constitution of a mobile reserve or battle corps consisting at the present time of 13 Groupes Mobiles (a Group[e] Mobile is an infantry regiment plus an artillery battalion) and other elements including an airborne force of division strength.[10] There were only six such Groupes Mobiles last summer and they were, at that time, mostly tied down to specific defensive tasks. The number of Group[e]s Mobiles will be raised to twenty next summer. (This, incidentally, is the force which General Navarre's predecessor, General Salan, estimated he would need in order to come to grips effectively with the enemy regular forces.)

(3) The arrival in Indochina of the equivalent of three additional regiments from France. The decision to send such troops represents a great, and to many, an unexpected, personal triumph for General Navarre.

(4) In terms of actual operations, the French High Command took the initiative with the spectacular and successful parachute raid on Langson in July. Although the enemy has a high offensive potential and although it was generally believed at the outset of the present fighting season that he intended to use it, he has not as yet done so. To some extent this is due to various limited offensives conducted as a part of General Navarre's strategic plan for this fighting season in the North. The most important of these operations (known as Mouette and conducted between October 15 and November 3) is believed by General Navarre to have cost the enemy in killed and wounded and in material losses about one-third of the effectives of one of his regular divisions (320). Operations conducted by French Union troops and local irregulars in the Thai country northwest of the Tonkin delta have obliged the enemy to divert to that area the equivalent of perhaps one-half of another division (316). The recent capture of the relatively important town of Dien Bien Phu with its airstrip is part of this pattern. Other operations are in prospect. As a result of those already conducted, the offensive possibilities open to the enemy have been reduced and furthermore the ratio between the strength of the Franco-Vietnamese mobile forces and of the enemy's regular units has moved in favor of General Navarre who is of course also adding daily to his battle corps while that of the enemy is not being increased, quantitatively at least.

These developments should be viewed within the framework of General Navarre's over-all strategic concept. Stated very briefly, that

concept involves two offensives, one in the South and the other in
South Central Viet Nam [Operation Atlante] to begin in January
1954 and to make it possible to concentrate all available mobile
forces in North Annam [north-central Viet-Nam] and Tonkin [north-
ern Viet-Nam] for the final campaign to be initiated in October
1954. The two offensives planned for this year [the 1953–1954 fighting season] will be of unequal importance and duration. The first is
designed to clear the equivalent of perhaps half a dozen regular enemy battalions and supporting regional and people's troops from the
tip of South Viet Nam and thus to break the back of organized enemy resistance in this whole area. A single operation in considerable
force is contemplated. The second operation [Atlante] involves clearing the enemy's 15 or 16 regular battalions with supporting regional
and people's troops from the area of South Central Annam from
Cape Varella to the vicinity of Tourane, a distance of some 200
miles. A campaign lasting from January to August, 1954, is involved.
It will include a number of amphibious landings in conjunction with
the use of troops from the mountain areas in order to surround the
enemy and bring him to battle.

As a result of these two offensives, General Navarre hopes that the
entire country up to about the 19th parallel will have been cleared of
regular enemy opposition and that the final, decisive campaign can
be undertaken when the rains cease in the north in October 1954. At
that time, enemy strength will be concentrated in North Annam
(Than Hoa [sic], Vinh and Ha Tinh) and in and around the [Red
River] Delta. It is General Navarre's expectation that he will then be
in a position permanently to occupy areas which the enemy will either have to fight for under conditions unfavorable to him or abandon and retire to areas where he can no longer maintain himself as
an organized force.[11]

On December 9 Battalion 888 of Viet-Minh Division 316 set out to
repeat its ambush of December 5 by attacking the two battalions, the 1st
BPC and the 6th BPC, that had left Dien Bien Phu on December 7. This
time, however, the paratroopers were prepared and their Vietnamese
members ignored enemy appeals that they surrender and, instead, held
their ground. The communists never got close enough for hand-to-
hand fighting.

After the battle, the French Union forces systematically withdrew to
Dien Bien Phu. The area around Hill 506 was now regarded as suffi-

ciently secure to permit trucks to carry building materials to Strong-point Beatrice.

Despite this French success, the main force of Division 316 continued its advance. That day it captured Tuan Giao, the important road junction located twenty-five miles northeast of Dien Bien Phu, which had been the objective of the 8th BPC and the 3rd BT when they began their mission from Dien Bien Phu on December 1.

This new military development was the subject of news reports from both Indo-China and France. The United Press sent the following cable from Hanoi:

> Communist-led Viet-Minh rebels cut off France's two main defense bastions in Western Indo-China today in a stepped-up offensive.
>
> The Reds' 316th Division, supported by mortars and heavy artillery, seized the village of Tuan Giao, halfway between the isolated French outposts of Lai Chau and Dien Bien Phu.
>
> French Union officers said there was no way of knowing whether the Reds would turn north against the Thai capital of Lai Chau in the Black River Valley or south against Dien Bien Phu.
>
> Only three weeks ago the Loyalist French forces recaptured Dien Bien Phu, opium-rich agricultural center which guards the invasion route to neighboring Laos and is the site of one of Indo-China's best airfields. . . .
>
> . . . French spokesmen said that whichever way the Communists turn a French column will set out from the other city to attack the Reds from the rear.
>
> An airlift of American-built planes evacuated 4000 [sic] civilians of Lai Chau to Hanoi and returned with more arms and ammunition for the threatened post only 20 miles south of the Red China border.
>
> Evacuees, including women, were lodged in temporary refugee camps in Hanoi.[12]

In an update on events from four days earlier, the UP wrote: "Last Saturday [December 5] screaming Red troops attempted to recapture Dien Bien Phu in a suicidal dash through French machine-gun fire, but an armored column broke through from the south to save the garrison."[13]

The fall of Tuan Giao was also reported by the Paris correspondent for the *Times* (London):

Elements of the 316th Viet-minh Regiment [Division] were reported by a spokesman of the French high command in Hanoi this
evening to have reached the immediate neighbourhood of Laichau,
the capital of the Thai country of northern Viet Nam, the evacuation
of whose civil population was completed yesterday.

The spokesman refused to say whether it was intended to defend
the city, replying to questioners that "the French and Viet Namese
would never lose interest in Laichau either tactically or strategically,"
and that "the defence of the Thai country would not be abandoned."

The Viet-minh force is reported to have divided at the crossroads
of Tuan Giao, where it has set up its headquarters, part taking the
road to Laichau and part that to Dien Bien Phu, the new French resistance centre in the Thai country set up three weeks ago.

Everything seems thus to indicate that an important battle is in
prospect in the area.[14]

The feeling that the contest for the northwest was taking on greater
dimensions was also reflected in a telegram that Paul Sturm, the U.S.
consul in Hanoi, sent to the State Department:

SECRET   HANOI, December 9, 1953—noon.

333. Repeated information Saigon 247, Paris 147. [The] Evacuation of civilians from Laichau was completed [on December] 7th, according [to the] Chief Political Officer of [the French] Delegation
Generale. [The] Principal families were moved to Hanoi, [and the]
others to Dien Bien Phu.

[The] Status of Laichau, according to [the] informant, is now
fluid: If [the] Viet Minh attack [the] town, no effort will be made to
hold it, but whenever [the] Viet Minh are not present in force,
Franco-Thai units will continue [to] make such use of [the] town
and [its] environs as may be desirable. No fixed defensive positions
remain at Laichau.

As Dien Bien Phu passes from [an] airborne to [an] infantry
phase, General Gilles, paratroop commander, is being relieved by
Colonel De Castries, most recently in command of [the] South zone
of [the Red River] delta.

Despite rumors heard widely in official and unofficial circles here,
[the] informant says [that] he has not been able to authenticate reports that elements of Viet Minh Divisions 308 and 312 are moving

to join Division 316 in [the] Thai country. He adds that [the] objectives of Division 316 itself are far from clear at this time.

STURM[15]

Later that day Sturm had an opportunity to discuss these matters directly with General Cogny. Cogny told Sturm that the Viet-Minh might have abandoned plans for a major winter offensive against the Red River Delta and that it would probably carry its efforts to the Thai country. He confirmed that the enemy might put as many as two divisions into western Tonkin but any more than two, he thought, would be surprising. The general went on to express the hope that the reports that Divisions 308 and 312 were turning westward were well-founded since, he explained, he could ask for no development more favorable to his making serious progress in cleaning out the delta and in breaking in green Vietnamese units. He observed that the Thai country terrain and the French Union regular and guerrilla forces could be counted on to take their toll of any Viet-Minh units that were sent into the region. He emphasized, however, that none of this was yet clear: neither the Viet-Minh's objectives nor their tactics in the current campaign.

Cogny wondered, though, why the communists should bring such apparently large forces to bear in an operation that promised relatively small rewards, except possibly on the propaganda score if they were able to push the French "out of Thai country."[16] It might be, he surmised, that the aggressive French action of recent months had rendered impossible the execution of earlier Viet-Minh plans for a delta offensive and that it was obliged to attempt some other maneuver of comparable magnitude.

Concerning the evacuation of Lai Chau, Cogny said that the bulk of the town's population—two thousand men, women, and children—had been due to complete the eighty-kilometer (fifty-mile) journey on foot over jungle trail to Dien Bien Phu the night before. He had offered planes, he insisted, but the inhabitants had preferred to walk. He was particularly pleased by this trek, he added, because he considered it indicative not only of Thai courage but also of their confidence.

The general turned next to his reasons for assigning Colonel de Castries to the command of Dien Bien Phu. He stated that he had given the job to the best man for the purpose who was presently available in Tonkin. As an old cavalryman, explained Cogny, de Castries could be depended on to seize the initiative and not remain behind a defensive position.[17]

As far as Dien Bien Phu itself was concerned, Cogny said the position was now strong and was being further strengthened continually. He added that some of the paratroop battalions were being replaced by infantry units.

Cogny's optimism about the French military position in general, and about Dien Bien Phu in particular, was fully shared by General Navarre. In Saigon, Ambassador Heath cabled the State Department to relay the following information from Commissioner General Maurice Dejean concerning the latter's conversation that day with the French commander in chief:

CONFIDENTIAL   SAIGON, December 9, 1953—10 a.m.

986. Repeated information Paris 284, Hanoi unnumbered. Commanding [Commissioner] General Dejean returned [to] Saigon today. . . .

. . . Dejean had had a long briefing by Navarre and felt extremely encouraged by [the] military situation. Navarre expressed himself much as he did in my last talk with him (see my telegram 968, December 5) and felt quite certain that [the] Viet Minh would attack Dien Bien Phu where they would meet, he was quite confident, a costly repulse.[18]

12
Epilogue:
An Engagement of Forces

General Navarre's decision to launch Operation Castor was less important in itself than it was for the chain of events that it set in motion.

Within three days of the French seizure of Dien Bien Phu, General Giap had made a fundamental determination on how he would counter this action. He announced to the Viet-Nam People's Army-Central Military Committee meeting on November 23 that the French were scattering part of their mobile forces in order to defend the northwest and upper Laos against the initial movement of the 316th Division. Accordingly, he proposed to increase the Viet-Minh threat to this area and thus scatter the French forces even further. The one division, the 316th, that was already deployed toward the northwest would, therefore, be augmented by additional forces, to a total of two to three divisions or even more.

Giap's strategy in responding to Castor was revealed to the French by a Viet-Minh officer who came over to their side much later. The officer explained: "The paratroop operation at Dien Bien Phu was a pleasant surprise for our command. The first movement of the 316th Division was aimed at getting the French Command to reduce its concentration in the [Red River] delta and to scatter its forces. It was the Dien Bien Phu action which led to the decision to send fresh divisions toward the Northwest."[1]

The French reaction to the accelerated communist effort was, in turn, to reaffirm and to deepen the initial commitment of November 20 to defend the Thai country and northern Laos.

The first key date came on November 28 when General Cogny proposed to General Navarre in Hanoi that a major diversionary stab be conducted against the enemy base area north of the Red River Delta. The commander in chief objected to all three variations of the intended operation for reasons of manpower and logistics.

In his memoirs, Navarre cites another important consideration for his decision—military strategy:

> From the strategic point of view, if the change in the Vietminh plan [for the 1953–54 campaign season] eliminated the threat of an attack on the Delta, it placed a problem before us that was no less difficult.
>
> We had to confront two divergent actions. One had its origin in the region of Phu Tho, Yen Bay, Thai Nguyen [see map 5], and was oriented at first toward Laichau and Dien Bien Phu, before being inflected toward Upper Laos. The other left the region of Vinh [see map 3] in a general south to southwest direction in order to go, either by the east or by the west of the Annamite [mountain] chain, to the engagement of another opening action by the L.K.V. [the Viet-Minh's Fifth Interzone].
>
> In order to thwart the Vietminh plans, two methods could be employed—whichever strategy provided the desired means would, moreover, have to be used simultaneously [against both Viet-Minh actions].
>
> The first [strategy]—that of the direct defense—consisted of barring each of the threatened directions with sufficient forces in order to stop and throw back the enemy. It would result in a certain dispersion of our forces, almost similar to those [dispersions] of the enemy forces, but [this would be] much more apparent than real, because our possibilities of [employing] rapid strategic transports, by aerial means especially, would permit us [to execute] maneuvers that were forbidden to the enemy.
>
> The other [strategic] method—that of indirect defense—consisted of keeping our forces concentrated in the Delta, and taking action against the enemy's rear.
>
> This [latter] solution was, at first view, much more enticing than the former. It especially had the advantage of permitting a better employment of aviation, which would have been able to take action much closer to our Delta bases. But this advantage could not be overestimated because, in the Middle and Upper regions [of Indo-China] the possibilities of [employing] aviation were very limited. Above all, it had to be placed in balance with two established disadvantages of long standing in Indochina.
>
> The first was the possibility that the enemy would stop our clearing actions in the Delta if they [the clearing actions] were not very powerful, with either regional or regular forces—independent of the

offensive [divisional] part of its battle corps—forces which it had at [its] command in an amply sufficient quantity. This is what it had done, with success, the preceding year [the 1952–53 fighting season] when General Salan had attempted to take action, in leaving the Delta, against the united Vietminh [that was] operating in the Upper region [of Indo-China]: the [French] "Lorraine" operation had been stopped by [enemy] forces very inferior to ours and had not been able to attain its objective.[2]

The second disadvantage [of the indirect defense] resided in the fact, often stated in the course of the preceding campaign—and especially in 1952 in the same "Lorraine" operation—that the Vietminh, confident in the fluidity of their troops and in their capacity to rapidly change their line of communications, did not allow a threat on their rear to divert them from their objectives.[3]

All of our possibilities of action were nevertheless studied very carefully.

It was in the Vinh-Hatinh region that the [Viet-Minh] group gathered, strengthened by a division reinforced by a regiment, [that was] intended to operate in central Indochina.

In order to take action effectively against their rear, to divert their mission, one had to consider opening actions, either in the Delta on Thanh Hoa [see map 3], or in central Vietnam in the Chule region. These two ground offensives could be in conjunction with maritime landings.

They both demanded very superior means to those that it was possible to devote to them, taking into account the necessity of our opposing, at the same time, the offensive in the direction of north Laos, which appeared to be the more important one.

It was, in effect, the bulk of the Vietminh battle corps which, leaving the Phu Tho, Yen Bay, Thai Nguyen zone, was engaging itself in the direction of the Northwest.

In order to stop them in their advance, an opening action from the Delta would either have to delay them before their departure or cut their line of communications immediately thereafter, in order to compel them to make an about-turn. This solution was only valid if the enemy accepted combat. But, in this case, it would lead to provoking, in November 1953, the general battle that the inferiority of our means had specifically led us to postpone, until the development of our own battle corps would permit us to provide the required forces [for the Navarre Plan]. It involved therefore an immense risk. . . .

. . . As much in order to parry the Vietminh offensive on the Upper region [of Indo-China] as for that of the action on Central Indo-
china, we were therefore condemned, by the insufficiency of our
means, to be satisfied by directly defending the threatened regions.
The direct defense was, indeed, much more economical than the indirect defense because it permitted the territorial [French guerrilla]
forces which occupied these regions to participate in the battle. The
direct defense was not, moreover, exclusive of further actions on the
enemy communications.[4]

Navarre claims in *Agonie de l'Indochine* that there was a meeting of the
minds between himself and Cogny on rejecting the strategy of "indirectly
defending" the northwest and upper Laos by taking action against the
enemy's rear. He writes: "After a very detailed study, the project was
abandoned, by an agreement between General Cogny and myself."[5]

Cogny remembers things differently. In an interview with the Paris
newspaper L'*Express* on November 21, 1963 ("La libre confession du
Général Cogny"), Cogny gives this version of events concerning possible
French action from the delta:

> The very hour when I learned that the Viet[-Minh] battle force
> was following the traces of the 316th Division in [the] direction of
> the northwest, I initiated the idea of an attack from the Delta, includ-
> ing the necessary reconnaissance and troop movements. [Colonel]
> Vanuxem would command the shock forces which would grapple
> with the rear columns of the Viets and would force Giap to turn
> around with at least a part of his forces. We would break contact and
> would attract the Viets into the immediate approaches to the Delta
> where we would have been in the best condition to defeat them.
>
> General Navarre refused by invoking some mediocre arguments
> about the availability of the necessary forces.[6]

Gen. Georges Catroux headed the French government's 1955 commission that investigated the Dien Bien Phu operation. He later wrote
his own book on the subject, in which he makes the following observations: ". . . after having made a calculation of the means required for
these operations, General Navarre did not deem himself capable of undertaking them. He renounced them and thought he had made General
Cogny renounce them, which afterward the latter disputed."[7]

Years later, Navarre indicated that he was only too aware of his subordinate's continuing displeasure over his decision. In his autobiography,

he writes: ". . . he [Cogny] recommended actions on the Viet-Minh rear but he repeatedly clashed with my refusal, against which he vainly protested."[8]

The new garrison at Dien Bien Phu, therefore, was an active expression of the commander in chief's strategy of "directly defending" the northwest and upper Laos.

Could it be, though, that Navarre, in his memoirs, is overemphasizing his concern about an enemy attack on central Indo-China from Vinh in order to lessen his ultimate responsibility for having vetoed Cogny's plans for doing more to protect Dien Bien Phu? The answer is a categorical no. General Trapnell's December 1st report to CINCPAC clearly noted: "Navarre is uncertain whether [the] enemy threat will develop in Cent Annam [central Viet-Nam], [in] Laos or [in the] triangle [of] Lai Chau/Dien Bien Phu/Son La."

Indeed, similar concerns about the situation near Vinh were contained in earlier reports by both American military and diplomatic officials. On November 23 the U.S. Army attaché in Saigon, Col. Leo W. H. Shaughnessy, included the following comment in his cable to Washington: "[The] Southward movement [of] elements [of Viet-Minh] Div[isions] 320 and 304 and [the] Northward movement [of] Regt [Regiment] 95 with [the] resultant concentration [of] troops [in the] Vinh Area would put [the] VM [Viet-Minh] in [an] excellent position to attack to [the] West along [the] Vinh/Nape axis [thereby] threatening [the] French loc[ations] along [the] Mekong [River]."

The map that accompanied PSA Director Philip Bonsal's November 27 report to Assistant Secretary of State Walter Robertson also showed half of Viet-Minh Division 304 moving south to join Division 325, with the combined force then marching to the west into central Laos [see map 4]. In his report, Bonsal observed: "If the movement of the 325 division from its present location in central Viet Nam is continued in the direction of central Laos it would support the hypothesis that [an] invasion of Laos is the principal Viet Minh plan for the time being."

Clearly then, Navarre was justified in being concerned about the developing Viet-Minh threats in both north-central Indo-China and the Thai Highlands.

It was the degree of the latter threat, however, that lay at the heart of the disagreement between Navarre and his northern commander on November 28. Cogny's proposed offensive against the communist base area to the north of the delta stemmed from his concern that the Viet-Minh was concentrating nearly its entire battle corps against the lightly defended airhead at Dien Bien Phu.

Despite the above-quoted passage from Navarre's memoirs in which he noted that "it was, in effect, the bulk of the Vietminh battle corps which . . . was engaging itself in the direction of the Northwest,"[9] he did not, in fact, subscribe to this judgment at the time of his meeting with Cogny in Hanoi. Rather, Navarre believed that it was *elements* of the enemy divisions, not the entire divisions, that were on the move.

All impartial accounts of the November 28 meeting have since sided with Cogny on this point. The unanimous judgment can be simply put: only eight days after the seizure of Dien Bien Phu, Navarre was informed of the full dimensions of the communist threat to the new French position. General Catroux writes as follows:

> On November 28 . . . General Navarre learned from a sure source that, leaving the approaches to the Delta, the 304th division, the 308th division, the 351st heavy division, and perhaps the 312th division, would move toward the northwest between November 27 and December 5. He was moreover informed that Giap had prescribed the establishment, in the same region, of an important support base at Tuan Giao. It appeared that the major part of the [Viet-Minh] battle corps was beginning to march in order to rejoin the 316th division.[10]

Fall says: "All available sources—and General Navarre has not contradicted them since—indicate that the French commander-in-chief *knew* since at least November 28 (when he met Gen. Cogny in Hanoi) that the bulk of the enemy's battle force was in the process of getting ready for the long march into the T'ai [Thai] hill country."[11]

Writing of Navarre, Roy observes: ". . . he did not believe in the situation which the head of Military Intelligence at Hanoi had described to him on November 28. 'In front of all the charts on which the movements of the Vietminh divisions were written up,' Cogny would say later on, 'I had the impression that he did not understand.'"[12]

Did not understand? A general who had spent most of his career in French Army Intelligence? As John Keegan notes: "Navarre, though a soldier with a respectable fighting record, had more recently become identified with the activities of French military intelligence; and it was as an intelligence officer of remarkable subtlety and perception that he was best known."[13]

It is likely that this extensive intelligence background was, in fact, what prompted the commander in chief to rely on his own judgment. Nor can there be much doubt that he was genuinely skeptical about the quality of the information that he was receiving. This attitude was expressed not only to Cogny on November 28 but to General Trapnell two days later. In his December 1 report to CINCPAC on that conversation, the MAAG chief alluded to Navarre's views concerning the "inability of French intel-[ligence] to produce accurate info[rmation] on [the] size of [the] Viet-minh tp [troop] movement."

What gives added weight to the events of November 28 is what came next. For it was only five days after his fateful meeting with Cogny in Hanoi that Navarre issued his Directive No. 949, ordering that "the defense of the Northwest shall be centered on the air land base of Dien Bien Phu which must be held at all costs."

No one would later call attention to the proximity of these two events more forcefully than did Navarre's top civilian superior at the time, Prime Minister Joseph Laniel. In his 1957 memoirs, which were published a year after Navarre's (and said by some to have been a rejoinder to the latter), Laniel writes as follows:

> On November 28, General Navarre came into possession of intelligence from the Deuxieme Bureau [French Intelligence], indicating that the major part of the Vietminh battle corps had left the Delta in order to move toward the north-west, and, therefore, would directly menace Laos with an attack in force.
>
> And it was on December 3 that, in consideration of this maneuver, the commander-in-chief finalized his decision to accept battle in the north-west *by centering the defense on the base of Dien Bien Phu* which *must be held at all costs.*
>
> This decision of December 3 was signified by a "personal and secret instruction." It was in strong contradiction with the strategy pursued until that time by the commander-in-chief and which had consisted of avoiding an engagement with the Vietminh battle corps.[14]

Laniel, in short, charges that Navarre, by insisting that Dien Bien Phu be held against the growing communist threat to the northwest and upper Laos, knowingly abandoned the Navarre Plan, under which he had proposed to "try to *avoid a general battle* with the enemy battle corps" during the 1953–54 fighting season.[15]

What does Navarre himself have to say about what he learned on November 28 and its relationship to his crucial directive of December 3? He gives the following account:

The organization of the retrenched camp of Dien Bien Phu had been undertaken initially with the realization of a center of resistance of 5 to 6 battalions as an objective. It was supported by an artillery group and reinforced by partisan units. This conception corresponded to the impression that we had been given by intelligence received during the month of November, that made us think that we would, without a doubt, only deal with one division (Division 316), reinforced by one or two independent regiments or advance withholdings from other divisions. The initial layout of the retrenched camp had been established by General Gilles, on the basis of instructions that he had received from General Cogny.

From the first days of December, in proportion to the development of the enemy menace, the original conception had to be revised. Indeed, given the ascent toward the Northwest of Divisions 308, 312, of part of the 304th and of Heavy Division 351, it appeared that, even if a part of these elements were getting positioned on the route [from] Sam Neua [Laos]—[to the] Plain of Jars [Laos] [see map 3], Dien Bien Phu could be attacked by more important forces than those initially envisaged. It was, therefore, necessary to enlarge the initial retrenched camp and to stiffen the garrison.

The new layout was established by Colonel de Castries as indicated by General Cogny, and approved by me with some modifications.

From December 3, the total strength of the garrison was fixed at 9 battalions and two artillery groups.[16]

Navarre certainly paints here a more serious threat to Dien Bien Phu than he acknowledged at the time of the events. In his December 3 directive, the commander in chief spoke of *one* communist division—the 316th, which might be reinforced by the end of December—that was putting pressure on Lai Chau. It was in response to *this* menace that he raised the garrison's strength from six battalions to nine, increased its firepower, and included in his instructions a detailed scenario for both defending Lai Chau and, ultimately, driving off the enemy.

By contrast, in the above-quoted section of his memoirs, Navarre acknowledges "the ascent toward the northwest" of Divisions 308, 312, 351, and part of Division 304 *in addition* to Division 316. He implies that "a part of these elements" might be redirected to the southwest for an attack on Laos. Nevertheless, in the face of a known enemy threat that had increased from one reinforced division in November to over four divisions by early December, Navarre merely concedes that "Dien Bien Phu could be attacked by more important forces than those initially en-visaged."[17]

Were the addition of three French battalions and one artillery group intended to compensate for a quadrupling in enemy strength? At least one Viet-Nam scholar has already pondered that question. Nothing ex-plains, observes Fall, "what led Navarre to accept the fantastic proposi-tion that nine French infantry battalions (only three of which could be considered elite troops) could withstand, inside a ring of hastily built field entrenchments, the assault of three Communist divisions solidly supported by artillery firepower. . . "[18]

The answer lies in a careful examination of what Navarre says in his memoirs and, equally important, what he leaves unsaid. First, Navarre offers contradictory testimony on the vital issue of exactly when he first learned of the growing danger to Dien Bien Phu. As quoted above, in *Agonie de l'Indochine* he writes that "intelligence received during the month of November" continued to point to movement by one reinforced Viet-Minh division and that it was only "from the first days of Decem-ber" that he became aware of the increased threat.[19] In repeating this passage in his autobiography, *Le Temps des Vérités*, Navarre makes a telling alteration. The words "from the first days of December" are changed to "by mid-December."[20]

At another point in his autobiography, Navarre, in recalling a letter that he wrote to French Field Marshall Alphonse Juin on December 14, 1953, writes that "on the date when this letter was written, I still did not know that nearly all of the Viet-Minh battle corps was directed toward the Upper Region [of Indo-China]."[21]

Lastly, in referring to the December 8th evacuation of Lai Chau in *Agonie de l'Indochine*, Navarre writes: *"During the following weeks* [empha-sis added] we learned successively of the departure toward the Upper region [of Indo-China] behind Division 316, of the totality of Divisions 308 and 312, followed by elements (one, then two regiments) of Division 304, and finally by Heavy Division 351."[22]

The preponderance of Navarre's own testimony on this key point, therefore, is clear. As of early December, he remained unaware of the true extent of the peril to Dien Bien Phu. No evidence from any other source indicates that Navarre received additional information on com-munist troop movements in early December that altered his judgment of November 28 on this subject. The best proof of this lies in the fact that he based his December 3 directive on the underlying assumption that he would face, at worst, the equivalent of one reinforced communist division at Dien Bien Phu by the end of December. This was the same premise on which he had stated his belief on November 28 that it was only elements of communist divisions, not entire divisions, that were headed toward the Thai country.

The above-quoted portion of Navarre's memoirs also contains a glaring omission: he never actually mentions Directive No. 949 of December 3. Instead, a decision that was more important than Operation Castor itself—namely, that Dien Bien Phu "must be held at all costs"—is passed off as a modification of plans that had already been drawn up by Colonel de Castries on instructions from General Cogny.[23]

Navarre's only direct reference to his December 3 directive is made in *Le Temps des Vérités* in the course of pointing to Cogny's tendency to express his military reservations "in writing" so as to "cover himself with a 'paper.'"[24] But according to Navarre, Cogny never formally objected to fighting at Dien Bien Phu. "In particular," he adds, "Cogny did not protest against my instruction of December 4 [*sic*] (worked out, moreover, with his collaboration), that stipulated my intention to accept the battle of Dien Bien Phu."[25]

The actual authorship of the December 3 directive itself is not entirely clear. Roy writes: "Navarre issued [on December 3] the Personal and Secret Instructions for the Conduct of Operation No. 949, on which he had been working."[26]

Fall gives this account: "While he [Navarre] had been at Dien Bien Phu with Gen. Cogny [in late November], his own staff in Saigon had worked out the details of the future battle of Dien Bien Phu. According to officers familiar with the situation, that plan had been entirely worked out by Navarre's key planner, Col. [Louis] Berteil."[27]

Regardless of which version is true, Navarre bore final responsibility for what was a momentous decision and, inevitably, the issue posed in Laniel's memoirs returns to the fore: What happened to the Navarre Plan on December 3? Even one reinforced communist division—what Navarre expected to be at Dien Bien Phu by late December—would be a strong contingent. Might it not succeed in provoking the general engagement that the commander in chief wished to postpone until the fall of 1954?

Navarre does not directly address this question in his memoirs but, in a passage immediately following his description of Operation Castor,[28] he clearly asserts one preeminent justification for his decision to occupy Dien Bien Phu: the defense of Laos. He writes: "The battle that was going to be waged at Dien Bien Phu was on the scale of the whole Indochina theater of operations, since it had the objective of defending Laos."[29]

Does the evidence bear out this claim? A look at the contemporaneous statements of France's military leaders in Indo-China shows that the defense of Laos was, indeed, an important consideration.

On November 23 Hanoi Consul Paul Sturm reported to Washington that a spokesman for General Cogny said the French High Command had "feared that it [Viet-Minh Division 316] might be acting as [a] precursor of other major Viet Minh elements for [an] eventual attack on Laos." This cable was supplemented by the following report from Sturm twelve days later: "[French] Informants comment that [the] signature of [the] new Franco-Laotian accord on October 22 was not without its part in [the] decision to undertake 'Castor,' which offers concrete evidence of [the] military benefits [for the three Associated States] deriving from membership in [the] French Union."

Navarre, for his part, made several references to the task of defending Laos. In his final operational instructions for Operation Castor, issued on November 14, he outlined the political and strategic importance of maintaining inside the Thai tribal territory a French position that would cover Laos as well. In his November 20 message to the French government, the commander in chief reported that he had occupied Dien Bien Phu because that position would "cover the approaches to Luang-Prabang which, without this, would be in grave danger within a few weeks." He added that "an operation by Laotian forces is anticipated shortly in order to establish a land link between Luang Prabang and Dien-Bien-Phu." Three days later he told General Bull that, as a result of the Castor thrust, he had a strong base with which to provide protection to Luang Prabang. Finally, in General Trapnell's December 1 message to CINCPAC, Trapnell reported that Navarre "plans to develop Dien Bien Phu as [a] permanent defensive base astride [the] gateway to Luang Prabang."

It must be remembered, however, that Dien Bien Phu's first role was as an eventual substitute for the more vulnerable base at Lai Chau. Indeed, the November 4 decision to authorize Operation Pollux came within days of when the French learned that Division 316 was starting to move toward the northwest.[30]

As already quoted, Fall puts the situation bluntly:

> Late in 1953 it became obvious that even a modest effort on the part of the Viet-Minh forces could result in military disaster at Lai Chau, a military setback that could be complicated by the political consequences of losing the last government seat in the mountain areas. It was this political consideration which had weighed heavily

in the French decision to reoccupy another stronghold [Dien Bien Phu] in the T'ai [Thai] tribal zone."[31]

A full appreciation of these circumstances was also reflected in the various statements by the principals involved and, indeed, on five of the six previously mentioned occasions on which reference was made to the defense of Laos,[32] the subject of offering protection to Lai Chau and/or of giving assistance to the Thai partisans was also brought up.

Sturm reported on November 23 that Cogny's spokesman had said that one of the purposes of Operation Castor was "to foster [the] development of Thai guerrilla and partisan forces to supplement those already formed and based on Lai Chau." In Navarre's final operational instructions of November 14, he said that the creation of an airhead at Dien Bien Phu would provide support for Lai Chau until its eventual evacuation. He also included a special appendix that dealt with the political and administrative problems of transferring the entire Thai Tribal Federation's administration from Lai Chau to Dien Bien Phu. In Navarre's November 20 message to Paris, he expressed the concern that "the veering off toward the north-west of the 316th Division constitutes a serious menace for Lai Chau and will bring about within a short time the destruction of our guerrilla forces in the highlands." In his November 23 conversation with General Bull, the commander in chief said that the motivation for the French spoiling action at Dien Bien Phu was the fact that the 316th Division had been found moving toward Lai Chau, which he described as an important French base for the expanding maquis movement in northwest Tonkin. As a result of the Castor thrust, he added, he had a strong base with which to provide protection to Lai Chau. Finally, in Trapnell's December 1 report to CINCPAC, the MAAG Chief wrote: "Navarre states [that the] Fr[ench] intention is to regain control of [the] Thai country, [and] stimulate [a] friendly guerrilla effort in [the] region."

There were also several occasions on which the situation in the northwest was presented as the primary motive for Operation Castor, without any reference being made to the defense of Laos.

Cogny was quoted by the Associated Press on November 21 as saying that the main object of the French operation at Dien Bien Phu was to give assistance to partisans among the Thai tribesmen and to build them into a strong striking force so that they could, by stages, take back much of the Thai territory that the Viet-Minh had captured the previous winter.

Ambassador Heath reported Navarre's concern for the Thai guerrillas in the following portion of his November 21 cable to Washington:

He [Navarre] had absolute intelligence that [the] Viet Minh planned to take Lai Chau. He must resist this not because of [the] importance in itself of Lai Chau but because it was [a] necessary case for expanding [the] guerrilla operations which were harassing [the] Viet Minh rear with increasing success. He could not defend Lai Chau by increasing [the] garrison because by reason of its cup-like situation he would need 12 battalions to hold it. His battalions at Dien Bien Phu aided by [the Thai] guerrillas, should be able to thwart Viet Minh operations against Lai Chau.

It was principally to accomplish this very task that Navarre issued Directive No. 949 on December 3. He stated at the outset that the new directive emanated from the fact that a communist menace was putting pressure on Lai Chau. In the second phase of his four-phase scenario of battle, the commander in chief foresaw the enemy as being diverted from this objective by raids that would be performed by the Dien Bien Phu garrison.

On the following day, December 4, Navarre told Ambassador Heath and Senator Thye that communist troops were now moving into the Thai country both because of the French operation at Dien Bien Phu and because of the French promotion of counterguerrilla activity among the Thai mountain people. The recent development of the Thai counter-guerrilla units, he added, was a most hopeful one.

This multiplicity of statements by generals Navarre and Cogny and their respective spokesmen make two things clear. The seizure of Dien Bien Phu was intended, as one of its objectives, to defend northern Laos and to provide remote cover for its royal capital, Luang Prabang, situated 125 miles to the southwest of the new French position. This was, however, a subsidiary consideration to the more urgent task of assisting the Thai tribesmen who were a small but significant part of the French effort, and whose base at Lai Chau was under imminent military threat. The Dien Bien Phu operation, therefore, was undertaken primarily for the purpose of advancing an important but essentially local military objective in the hinterlands of the northwest. Consequently, Navarre's subsequent assertion in his memoirs that "the battle that was going to be waged at Dien Bien Phu was on the scale of the *whole* [emphasis added] Indo-China theater of operations, since it had the objective of defending

Laos" does not accurately reflect his real estimates and intentions at the time.[33]

This view is supported by two of the then highest civilian officials in France with direct responsibilities for Indo-China policy: Marc Jacquet, the secretary of state for the Associated States, and Maurice Dejean, the French commissioner general in Indo-China. Concerning the former, Roy writes: "M. Jacquet had the impression that Navarre, who did not confide his thoughts to him, seemed more preoccupied with the strategic aspect of his plan than with the special case of Laos."[34] Maurice Dejean was more blunt: "Later on [following the Dien Bien Phu operation]," writes Roy, "he [Dejean] would write, in a note to the [Laniel] government, that for the French Command the covering of Laos was simply a pretext for attempting to kill Viets [Viet-Minh soldiers]."[35]

Navarre's tardy receipt on December 4 of a formal directive from the French government advising him that he was under no obligation to defend Laos has brought criticism of the government for failing to inform him fully of its intentions in a timely manner. But no evidence has ever been presented to suggest that earlier knowledge of this directive would have prompted Navarre to call off Operation Castor or in any way to alter his military plans for the northwest.

A further and even more telling refutation of Navarre's memoirs on the central importance of Laos is provided by the order that the commander in chief issued only four days after transmitting Directive No. 949 to Hanoi.

In his December 7 instructions for Operation Atlante, Navarre wrote the following:

> The essential objective which I expect to reach [in the 1953–54 campaign season] is the disappearance of the Viet-Minh zone which spreads from south of Tourane to the north of Nha Trang and eastward to the Southern Mountain Plateau; that is, the destruction of the military forces of Lien-Khu V [Viet-Minh Fifth Interzone]. . . .
>
> In view of the considerable strategic and political results which one is entitled to expect from the complete execution of that operation, *I have decided to subordinate to it the conduct of the whole Indochina campaign during the first semester of 1954* [emphasis added].

Navarre also explains in his memoirs why he judged this operation to be necessary:

The "Atlante" operation, aiming at the liquidation of the L.K.V. was anticipated in the plan to be executed . . . from January to September [1954], the only time possible due to climactic reasons.

A narrow coastal strip, 370 kilometers [222 miles] long and an average of 70 [kilometers] [46 miles] wide, the L.K.V. had a definite economic value (rice—fisheries) and above all demographic value (about 2,500,000 inhabitants). But its political and strategic importance was even greater. It was the means of normal communication between the north (Tonkin–Annam) and the south (Cochinchina). Through it passed the emissaries, the arms and the money that fed the Vietminh rebellion in southern Vietnam and Cambodia. Its liberation and the direct passage of the region to the Vietnamese [Bao Dai] administration would have profound repercussions on morale in all of Vietnam, including the region controlled by the Vietminh. It, therefore, constituted a political test of entirely first importance.

But that was not the essential target of the operation. It would be above all a preventive parry against a very big danger. Indeed the L.K.V., with the annexes that the rebel bases [that were] installed in the Plateau of Bolevens formed for them, was a permanent threat for all of southern Indochina (Cochinchina, southern Laos and Cambodia). Considering the remoteness [from southern Indo-China] of the Chinese sources [of arms], its [the Viet-Minh Fifth Interzone's] military power had remained behind the times for a long time, quantitatively and qualitatively, in comparison to that of the northern Vietminh regions, but it was, for a year, in the course of rapid development. The L.K.V. was now becoming a base of operations where the Vietminh command counted on opening important actions in 1954 and 1955. We knew this from a sure source. Thus, for want of having taken the initiative to liquidate it in time, we found ourselves faced with an awful problem.[36]

Navarre's decision to launch Atlante just after having undertaken the commitment to Dien Bien Phu, comes under sharp criticism from both Roy and Fall. Roy observes:

Now it was the day Cogny evacuated Lai Chau by the skin of his teeth [December 7] that Navarre, far from canceling his first instructions [to defend Dien Bien Phu] issued a second series [Operation Atlante] which increased the dangers of the first. . . . He knew that he would not receive the reinforcements he had asked for and that he was under orders to adapt his operations to his means, but the principal objective which he wanted to attain was the destruction of the rebel zone on the mountain plateau of Central Annam. It was to this operation, which had nothing to do with Dienbienphu, except insofar as it endangered it further, that he wanted everything to be subordinated.[37]

Fall writes:

> It is hard to understand Navarre's decision to undertake Operation "Atlante" at a moment when the chronic French shortage of troops was strongly felt because of the battalions tied down at Dien Bien Phu. When one considers the fact that his request for massive reinforcements from France had been turned down by the French government and he had been invited, as we have seen earlier, "to adjust his operations to his means," one fails to see how he could think he could conceivably undertake "Atlante."[38]

Fall adds: ". . . the same commander-in-chief who had [on November 28] refused Gen. Cogny the use of perhaps twenty battalions for an offensive which might have at least in part alleviated the pressure on Dien Bien Phu, now was willing to use twice as many troops [for Atlante] in a sector whose conquest at that time by the French (or whose continued control by the Communists) was in no way vital to the outcome of the war."[39]

The criticisms by Roy and Fall are, undoubtedly, well taken but the most important aspect of Navarre's decision to launch Atlante is what it reveals about his plans and perceptions at the time. He was plainly confident that he was on the right course; that he, not Giap, was fundamentally in control of events; and that south-central Viet-Nam, not northern Laos, would, in fact, be the major theater of battle in the coming six months. And, most important of all, Atlante shows that Navarre, despite Laniel's charges to the contrary,[40] was, in his own mind, being faithful to the Navarre Plan. He was simply proceeding with his long-planned southern offensive, which he had outlined to the O'Daniel mission a month earlier and repeated to Senator Smith and Ambassador Heath on November 19.

It was, instead, Cogny's proposal for an offensive stab against the communist rear from the Red River Delta that Navarre judged to be the *real* violation of the Navarre Plan. As he says in his memoirs, it was the "indirect defense" of Dien Bien Phu that, he feared, "would lead to provoking, in November 1953, the general battle that the inferiority of our means had specifically led us to postpone, until the development of our own battle corps would permit us to provide the required forces [for the Navarre Plan]".[41]

If the "direct defense" of the northwest by the establishment of an air-land base, with partisan support, became the essence of the French Command's strategic approach to the coming battle at Dien Bien Phu, what can be said about its tactical considerations?

It is necessary to recall briefly the optimism with which Operation Castor was begun. It not only had the joyful hum of a successful operation, but a steady stream of visitors and a profusion of upbeat press reports as well. And yet, despite these favorable omens, the entire Dien Bien Phu enterprise was haunted from its very first days by the specter of the late and unlamented French airhead at Na-San. Would the new garrison turn into the same sort of besieged outpost?

General Gilles, for one, feared that it would and, therefore, declined the command of Dien Bien Phu. He was not alone. Many other French officers were opposed to establishing another airhead behind communist lines and, according to Fall, as noted, several senior colonels in Indo-China had already declined the position, with one stating that the defense of Dien Bien Phu would be an open invitation to disaster.[42]

Even the colonel who finally did accept the assignment had initial reservations. On November 30 at Thai Binh Colonel de Castries told General Navarre that "if you're thinking of establishing an entrenched camp, this isn't my line. I'd rather you picked somebody else." Navarre's response indicated that he knew precisely what de Castries was talking about. "Gilles would like to have another Na-San," he replied, adding: "I don't agree with him." Cogny, in his public remarks, made no secret of his joy at being rid of Na-San. During his press conference on November 22, he told a UP correspondent that "if I had been able to, I would have moved Na-San en masse to Dien Bien Phu [when he took command five months earlier]."

In view of the above sentiments, it is ironic that Na-San later came to be widely seen as the inspiration for Dien Bien Phu.

The then chairman of the U.S. Joint Chiefs of Staff, Adm. Arthur Radford, writes the following in his memoirs: "General Salan's only success in [the] fall [of] 1952 was to defend the strongly fortified position of Na San in western Tonkin. Here the Vietminh began a nine-day attack in November; they then withdrew, having suffered severe casualties.

From the French view this was a successful battle, and I was convinced that the lesson they learned there led them to try the same idea again at Dien Bien Phu a year later."[43]

Radford's thesis receives powerful support from no less an observer than Fall, who offers this analysis: ". . . what Navarre and his general staff in Saigon planned [for Dien Bien Phu] was a repetition of the siege and attack on Na-San [of] the year before, with each side operating on a somewhat larger scale but with the French eventually carrying the day because of their superiority in ground and air firepower."[44]

Both Fall and Roy point in the direction of the one man who was the most plausible link between Na-San and Dien Bien Phu: Navarre's deputy chief for operations, Col. Louis Berteil. Writes Fall:

> Navarre, sometimes at great personal risk, visited literally every sector of Indochina in the space of a few weeks [after taking up command on May 20, 1953]. He was particularly interested in the Lai Chau and Na-San airheads. His airplane was hit in several places by Communist antiaircraft fire while visiting the latter base. . . . It was during his visit to Na-San that Navarre met the commander of that base and of Mobile Group 7, Colonel Louis Berteil. . . . Berteil caught the attention of Gen. Navarre at Na-San and soon found himself on Navarre's staff as deputy chief for operations. Cogny, Berteil's immediate superior at Na-San, was to say of him ten years later that he was "pregnant" with a vast theory on the uses of fortified airheads. Cogny also asserts that it was Col. Berteil who eventually convinced Navarre not only of the usefulness of Dien Bien Phu, but also of the over-all correctness of the "air-land base" as a panacea for the dilemmas of the Indochina War.[45]

Fall, as noted, also attributes to Berteil the authorship of the December 3 directive.[46]

Roy gives a similar account:

> It was because Na San remained the sore point in the [Indochina] theater of operations that Navarre was in a hurry to visit it. . . .
> . . . [When Navarre's] plane landed at Na-San [on May 22, 1953], its wings [were] riddled with bullet holes.
> Navarre was greeted by a somewhat sad, dry, suspicious and apparently colorless man, Colonel Berteil. . . .
> He [Berteil] was extremely attentive to Navarre and showed him

round the camp with a certain respectful stiffness. Navarre instinct-
ively recognized an ally in him. Berteil was not impressive like
Cogny, who was too touchy a personality. Navarre would remember
him when the time came and would make him his operational
second-in-command to coordinate the activities of his second and
third bureaus. In fact, Berteil would rapidly become the most formidable officer in the entourage of the new Commander in Chief.[47]

Further along, in describing events on the day that Operation Castor
was launched, Roy makes the following assertion: "Berteil dreamed of
another, more powerful Na San [at Dien Bien Phu], a splendid bait
thrown to the Viets [Viet-Minh] to lure them en masse and smash
them."[48]

There is evidence that suggests that Navarre had thoughts along these
same lines himself. In General Trapnell's December 1 message to CINC-
PAC, Trapnell reported that "Navarre states [that the] Fr[ench] intention is to . . . invite [the] enemy [to] atk [attack the] Dien Bien Phu area."
Eight days later Ambassador Heath, in notifying the State Department
of Commissioner Dejean's conversation with Navarre, reported a similar
statement by the commander in chief. Cabled Heath: "Navarre . . . felt
quite certain that [the] Viet Minh would attack Dien Bien Phu where
they would meet, he was quite confident, a costly repulse."

Was Dien Bien Phu intended to be a new and improved Na-San; another hedgehog defense that would become a vast killing field for Giap's
outgunned communist troops? In his memoirs, Navarre indicates his
awareness of this view. "It has been said," he writes, "that Dien Bien Phu
had been made 'to smash the Viets [Viet-Minh].'" Denying this "overly
simplistic explanation," Navarre goes on to say: "But—if it had been the
truth—I still would not be ashamed because, regrettable as this was,
from the human point of view, 'smashing' the enemy is one of the legitimate preoccupations of all leaders of war. It was even the principal mission that General Giap assigned to his troops."[49]

Navarre's denial, though somewhat hedged, appears, on balance, to
be credible. It is likely, therefore, that his November 30 and December 9
statements were more expressions of confidence in Dien Bien Phu's defenses than scenarios for reenacting the earlier battles at Na-San.

To understand why, it is necessary first to examine the military plans
for Dien Bien Phu of the man who was most opposed to establishing a
new Na-San: Gen. René Cogny.

In Consul Sturm's cable of November 23 to the State Department, he
reported that Cogny's spokesman said one of the purposes of the new

base at Dien Bien Phu was "to send out scout in hand attack parties in all directions to seek out [the] enemy and engage him." Sturm added: "[The] Spokesman insisted that there is no intent [to] establish a new Nasan at Dien-Bien-Phu, but only a base for positive and offensive operations."

Exactly what Cogny had in mind became clearer a week later when he presented Colonel de Castries with his directive for waging a defensive-offensive battle in the geographic triangle of Dien Bien Phu-Lai Chau-Tuan Giao, a total area covering nearly five hundred square miles. The second point in the directive, issued to the Dien Bien Phu command that same day, involved orders to "gather intelligence from as far away as possible" and to use, "at least one half of its [the garrison's] strength" in operations intended to inflict heavy losses on the enemy and to delay his laying a tight siege ring around the valley.

In another telegram from Hanoi on December 5, Sturm, perhaps referring to contacts in the northern command, gave this report:

"Some sources assume (and hope) that Diem-Bien-Phu [sic], seized in operation 'Castor,' will in time become the focus of Thai partisan and guerrilla activities, in effect replacing Lai Chau militarily, and will not be transformed into another Nasan, tying down French Union battalions in static positions."

In a direct meeting with General Cogny four days later, Sturm was told that de Castries had been picked to command the new garrison because, as an old cavalryman, he could be depended on to seize the initiative and not remain behind a defensive position. Sturm, in reporting this intention to the State Department, added the following notation in parentheses: "that is, not to create another Na San."

If it is clear then that Cogny did not want Dien Bien Phu to become a retrenched camp, it is equally clear what he did want: a mooring point for long range reconnaissance and offensive operations similar to another base that the French already had operating in north-central Laos. Rather than being a reincarnation of Na-San, Dien Bien Phu was, in fact, intended to be a second Plain of Jars.

This had been Cogny's goal from the start.

In Sturm's November 23 cable to Washington, he reported that Cogny's spokesman had said that one of the purposes of the new French base was to serve as the northern counterpart to the more southerly located Plain of Jars.

Cogny definitely had Navarre's support in this objective. On November 30 the commander in chief told de Castries: "Dien Bien Phu must become an offensive base. That's why I've picked you."

Navarre made an even more revealing comment to General Trapnell that same day, which the MAAG chief, in turn, reported to CINCPAC on December 1. Cabled Trapnell: "Navarre while not admitting [the] resemblance [of] this air head [Dien Bien Phu] to Na San, has pointed to [the] similarity and strategical relationship to [the] Plain Des Jarres base with [the] probability in each instance for supporting long range recon[naissance] and clearing opns [operations]."

Finally, in his memoirs, Navarre makes the following analogies concerning Dien Bien Phu's relative capability to other French bases in northern Indo-China: "It was better than that of Nasan, of Laichau and of Luang Prabang. It was equal to that of the Plain of Jars."[50]

If it is true, therefore, that France's military leaders intended that Dien Bien Phu was to become an offensive base, then the events that had befallen the garrison by the end of the first week of December surely constituted a cruel twist of fate. Only one week had passed since Cogny had presented de Castries with his plan for waging a defensive-offensive battle in the geographic triangle of Dien Bien Phu-Lai Chau-Tuan Giao. However, with the decision to abandon Lai Chau, the concept of French Union maneuvers within this triangle had collapsed. Indeed, the minimum mission of maintaining freedom of movement within a radius of five miles around Dien Bien Phu's airfield was in danger. Serious fighting had already occurred only three miles to the northeast of the camp's central position. Gilles's departing warning to de Castries to "watch out" was well founded. For, by then, Dien Bien Phu had become—in fact, if not by design—a new Na-San.

In describing the fading hopes at Dien Bien Phu by December 7 for being able to carry out French maneuvers beyond the garrison's perimeter, Roy writes: "Nobody believed it possible any more. That didn't matter. Everybody went on pretending that they did. . . . Nobody was ready to admit that Dienbienphu had already been reduced to playing the part of a super-Na San."[51]

Did the garrison ever really attempt to become an offensive base? Not in the opinion of the official commission that the French government later appointed to investigate the Dien Bien Phu operation. The commission was headed by General of the Army Georges Catroux, one of France's most distinguished soldiers and administrators. Its report, issued on December 3, 1955, remained a state secret for over thirteen years. When it was finally published in its entirety in January 1969, the Paris correspondent for the *Los Angeles Times*, Arthur J. Dommen, summarized its salient points as follows:

The commission found fault with Navarre for his belief that Dienbienphu could interdict Vietminh infiltration into Laos. This has been used as an explanation for the choice of Dienbienphu by the French command in histories since [then]. . . .

To interdict infiltration into Laos, it would have been necessary for the French garrison to patrol and pacify a wide circle of jungle around the base, which was never even attempted.[52]

Navarre addresses this issue in the section of his memoirs immediately following his description of the evacuation of Lai Chau on December 8.[53] He concedes that Dien Bien Phu never became an offensive base but he places the responsibility for this on the tactics and priorities of the area commander, General Cogny:

> From the "unique recess" of Dien Bien Phu, General Cogny hoped now to be able to conduct "powerful offensive actions," intended to slow the putting in position of the enemy. In fact, these actions were limited to patrols and reconnaissance at a short distance. In fact, more important and more profound actions quickly appeared incompatible to him on account of the total strength [that would be] required, [and] because of the work that was necessary to perform in order to put the retrenched camp in condition to face a hostile attack, which might happen very quickly.[54] In addition, in the [hostile] encounters to which the several executed reconnaissance missions gave rise, the poor aptitude of our troops for jungle combat was clearly apparent.[55]

Navarre correctly points out above that Cogny initially "hoped . . . to be able to conduct 'powerful offensive actions,'" as, indeed, his November 30 directive made clear. It was, in fact, in pursuance of this very objective that the GAP1 offensive of December 7–9 was launched. In addition, Navarre's observation that "the poor aptitude of our troops for jungle combat was clearly apparent" is illustrated by the successful communist ambush of the GAP1 reconnaissance mission of December 5, which resulted in part from the failure of the paratroopers to take any particular precautionary measures as they were advancing into dangerous territory. However, Navarre's assertion that the garrison's actions "were limited to patrols and reconnaissance at a short distance" is more questionable. It overlooks the fact that both the GAP1 offensive of December 7–9 and the Tourret guerrilla mission that began on December 1 made deep advances into the surrounding jungle. Furthermore, both of these missions took place while the garrison was busy constructing its first important strongpoint, Beatrice, even though Navarre recalls that the strength required for both defensive preparations and important offensive actions "quickly appeared incompatible" to Cogny.

Despite the launching of these long-range missions, however, the results they gained were, at best, mixed. Although the December 7–9 stab successfully fought off a renewed Viet-Minh attack, the Tourret sortie was unable to prevent the communist seizure of Tuan Giao.

Fall analyzes the larger implications of the garrison's early efforts to act as an offensive base:

> The success of Tourret's four commando groups in infiltrating the valley twenty miles from Dien Bien Phu and of GAP1 in marching ten miles into enemy territory should not have overshadowed the stark fact that each thrust had failed to attain its objective—the disruption of Communist road traffic close to the new position and the creation of viable maquis forces inside Communist territory. . . . Dien Bien Phu indeed had ceased to fulfill its mission even before the French had a chance to build the sort of defenses that would have made it a true fortress.[56]

These shortcomings, in turn, served to undermine the very cornerstone of Navarre's decision to remain at Dien Bien Phu: the enemy's presumed logistical limitations in the northwest.

At his meeting with Cogny in Hanoi on November 28, the commander in chief had declared that the Northern Command was overestimating the logistical capabilities of the Viet-Minh battle corps. Not only did Navarre's own staff share his initial judgment on this matter but most of the staffs of the Expeditionary Corps likewise regarded the concentration of four communist divisions as a utopian project.

More importantly, this conviction was given formal expression in the all-important directive of December 3, in which Navarre made the following postulate: "In view of the remoteness of the northwestern theater of operations [from the enemy's main bases] and the logistical obligations of the Viet-Minh, it is probable that the battle will be fought according to the following scenario." Navarre elaborates on this point in his memoirs:

> . . . if the distance [between Dien Bien Phu and the Red River Delta] acted against us from the aerial point of view, it must act against the Vietminh from the logistical point of view. Dien Bien Phu was 200 kilometers [124 miles] from the Delta and more than 300 [kilometers] [186 miles] from the China frontier.[57] The roads which connected it [Dien Bien Phu] to this frontier did not exist or were

destroyed. As a result, in order to attack Dien Bien Phu, the Viet-minh battle corps was hardly able to be supplied by convoys of coolies, which only permitted it to develop limited power. In a study done in May 1953 on the operations in the Upper region [of Indo-China], General Salan expressed the opinion that the Vietminh was not able to employ heavy arms there in any important amount, due to the difficulties of transport.[58]

General Giap was only too aware of the formidable logistical obstacles that the Viet-Minh faced in attempting to engage the enemy at its new stronghold. And, like General Navarre, he was drawn to the northwest, in large part, in order to avoid a decisive showdown in the Red River Delta.[59]

Giap knew, however, that his greatest logistical challenge wasn't just the hundreds of miles between two points on a map but rather the added difficulties that were posed by the jungle, the mountains, and the poor lines of communication. It was no accident, therefore, that the Viet-Minh director of supplies was thoroughly consulted and his assent obtained before Giap formally presented his proposal for the investment of Dien Bien Phu to the D.R.V. (Viet-Minh) government on December 3. And it was in consideration of the need for a mass effort in order to carry out such an operation that the Viet-Minh commander issued his December 6 order of the day in which the population was called upon to "repair the roads, overcome all obstacles, surmount all difficulties, fight unflinchingly, defeat cold and hunger, carry heavy loads across mountains and valleys, and strike right into the enemy's camp to destroy him and free our fellow countrymen."

The immediate effect of this order was to mobilize tens of thousands of coolies from the civilian labor force in a major effort to repair existing road communications and to build a spiderweb network of new roads that would raise the logistical system to a more sophisticated level by allowing vehicles to travel along formerly impassable jungle paths. This would allow large quantities of equipment and supplies to be funneled toward the Thai country and, above all, it would enhance the distribution of Chinese aid to the Viet-Minh, increased of late, which was the one thing that Navarre openly admitted could upset his plans.[60]

Chinese assistance originated from the Kouangsi region of China and entered northeastern Viet-Nam at Cao Bang and Lang Son, whence it traveled through the Viet-Minh base areas—to the north of the Red River Delta—by way of Thai Nguyen through Tuyen Quang to Yen Bay. It then proceeded southwesterly through difficult country to the existing

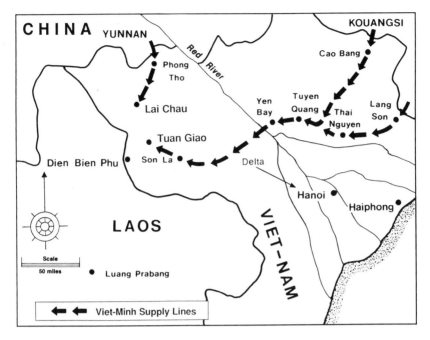

8. Viet-Minh logistical potential against Dien Bien Phu as of December 9.

road, Provincial Route 41, at Son La. With the fall of Tuan Giao on December 9, it became possible for this assistance to be forwarded to within twenty-five miles of Dien Bien Phu (see map 8).

Lancaster summarizes the importance of this supply network to the Viet-Minh as follows: "The creation of this route, covering a distance of some 220 miles, enabled supplies to be carried, wheeled on bicycles, or transported by Molotov trucks to within a short distance of the Viet Minh positions around Dien Bien Phu."[61]

In the part of Navarre's memoirs following his discussion of the garrison's lack of offensive capability,[62] he again raises the subject of enemy logistics,[63] this time indicating his awareness of the incipient Viet-Minh road network and the enhanced danger that it posed to the French position. "The information that arrived little by little," he writes,

was revealing the importance of the opposing means that were making their way toward the Upper region [of Indo-China], and the logistical effort, of an intensity without precedent, that the Vietminh was making.

Three and a half divisions (the 316th, 308th, 312th and a part of the 304th) were en route to the Northwest. Indications appeared concerning the probable intervention of the 351st Heavy Division.

Chinese aid to the Vietminh increased in very important proportions. The arrival of material and munitions was reported at the Tonkin frontier. A mass of about 75,000 coolies, who were only able to be gathered in the Upper region thanks to Chinese supplies of rice and means of transport,[64] put in order the means for about 200 kilometers [124 miles] of automobile traffic communications, and created about 100 [kilometers] [62 miles] from nothing.[65]

It appeared that the Vietminh was organizing a line of communications that automobiles could use from one end to the other. This line, about 350 kilometers [217 miles] long, originated on the Chinese frontier at Langson and at Caobang, [then] went around the Delta by [way of] Thai Nguyen, Tuyen Quang and Yen Bay (where another line of possible supplies converged which, by [way of] the Red River, reached Lao-Kay), then, by a route for the most part constructed from nothing, [it] rejoined the R.P. 41 [Provincial Route 41] (Hoa Binh–Laichau) near Nasan and ended at Tuan Giao, where a very important logistical base was put into working order, which was intended to supply the siege corps at Dien Bien Phu.[66]

Navarre then goes on to describe a second line of enemy communications that reached Tuan Giao:

"[It] came from China as well, [and traveled] by [way of] Ban Nam Coum and Laichau, but it utilized poor trails or mediocre waterways and was not used very much. It served only to direct a contribution of rice."[67]

Navarre's assertion that the region of China closest to Dien Bien Phu was of little significance in terms of offering logistical support to the Viet-Minh is challenged by virtually all authoritative accounts. For what greatly increased the importance of China's Yunnan region—along Viet-Nam's northwestern border—was an event that occurred almost simultaneously with the fall of Tuan Giao: the evacuation of Lai Chau. Writes Fall: "Tuan Giao was [to become] the major Communist supply staging area near Dien Bien Phu and, as soon as Lai Chau had fallen into Communist hands, [it] had also become the terminal for the shortest supply road between the battlefield and Communist China."[68]

Keegan agrees that the communists were in a strong position to exploit the French loss of Lai Chau: "[Viet-Minh] strength was growing in the northwestern highlands, where they now had a forward base [Tuan Giao] and the spur of a supply road running down from China. . . . [Giap's] engineers, with Chinese help, had recently constructed an all-weather road almost as far as Lai Chau (the Thai highlanders' capital) and on it he had assembled a sizable fleet of trucks."[69]

H. G. Martin also mentions this alternative route in *Brassey's Annual:* ". . . to cut out the long lift from the North-East frontier [of Viet-Nam] and to ensure adequate ammunition supplies, . . . [Giap] organized a main supply route by Molotova [truck] lorry northward through Laichau directly to the northern frontier with China."[70]

O'Ballance provides the most detailed account of this road:

> In late 1953, the Viet Minh opened up a good, all-weather road from Kokiu, south of Kunming [China], to the border town of Phong Tho [Viet-Nam], and then through towards Lai Chau [see map 8], which enabled supplies to be brought right up to the Viet Minh divisions north of Laos. The [Viet-Minh] Supply Service was working well and the road transport system was efficient, and was rapidly replacing human porters in the rear areas. There were already 9 transport companies, each of between 35 and 40 trucks. . . . The majority of the drivers were Chinese. The trucks were mainly either American, taken in Korea, or Russian Molotovas. . . .
>
> . . . The sudden evacuation of Lai Chau . . . had the strategic disadvantage of allowing the Viet Minh to extend their motor road from Kunming, which had already passed the frontier at Phong Tho, down through Lai Chau towards Tuam Giao [*sic*].[71]

It is evident that, for the Viet-Minh, the one-two punch of gaining Lai Chau and Tuan Giao gave them a tremendous logistical advantage and a major victory in their battle to take Dien Bien Phu; for the French, the early loss of both positions represented a serious military setback.

Why didn't Navarre order the immediate evacuation of Dien Bien Phu? This question was raised by the 1955 French government commission.

Paris correspondent Arthur Dommen of the *Los Angeles Times* summarized that portion of the commission's report as follows: "In view of . . . [the] 'illusion' [that Dien Bien Phu could interdict Viet-Minh infiltration into Laos][72] and other drawbacks of the fortified camp at Dienbienphu, the commission declared, Navarre's decision to stick with his original strategic plan and accept a siege battle against the Vietminh was faulty.

He should, instead, have paid greater attention to planning the evacuation of the camp while it was still feasible."[73]

Navarre addresses this issue in his memoirs and offers a familiar explanation for his decision not to order an evacuation: the defense of Laos. He writes:

> . . . to evacuate Dien Bien Phu would signify a renunciation of the defense of North Laos, such that we would abandon it without combat, such that [after] we had carried forward the defense of Luang Prabang and Vientiane, [we would be accepting] a solution whose certain inefficacy I mentioned earlier.[74] It was, therefore, abandoning the mission. It would be a shameful escape, which French prestige could not endure, and which would involve incalculable consequences. Finally, in any case, two to three battalions and almost all the material would have been lost.[75]

It is difficult to avoid the feeling that, once again, Navarre is placing greater emphasis on the defense of Laos in his memoirs than figured in his actual calculations at the time. Furthermore, the military reasons that he advances in his memoirs for refusing to evacuate Dien Bien Phu seem to be almost an afterthought to the questions of "abandoning the mission," "a shameful escape," and "French prestige." But weren't such essentially political considerations more properly the concern of Paris than of the commander in chief in Saigon? And was the loss of two or three battalions and attendant material, as significant as these might be, of greater importance than the execution of the Navarre Plan to which, as already noted, Navarre remained firmly committed?

In order to find a more credible answer to this question, it necessary to take a careful look at the chronology of events.

The operative words in the French commission's criticism of Navarre were that he did not plan the evacuation of Dien Bien Phu "while it was still feasible."[76] By this criterion, however, the rapidly deteriorating military situation in early December would have made it necessary for the evacuation of Dien Bien Phu to be carried out, at the latest, in conjunction with the evacuation of Lai Chau—in other words, within days of when the commander in chief had ordered that the new airhead "must be held at all costs." In short, the necessity for an evacuation *simply was not recognized* while there was still time for it to be carried out successfully.

Navarre cites the commission's views on this point in his autobiography:

It is not possible to blame me, the [French] commission said first of all, for having occupied Dien Bien Phu, the strategic importance of which is inconstestable. But it was grievous of me [said the commission] to have accepted battle there: I should have conducted the evacuation in the first days of December when the volume of forces that the Viet-Minh was bringing to the Upper Region [of Indo-China] was revealed to me. To this criticism it is possible to make [this reply]. . . .

. . . at the beginning of December I had not yet determined the importance of the enemy forces that were directed on Dien Bien Phu.[77]

Writes Fall:

In retrospect, the first week of December, 1953, was the decisive moment when the fate of Dien Bien Phu was sealed. . . .

Militarily, Navarre, during the first week of December, still had the choice of completely withdrawing the garrisons of Lai Chau and Dien Bien Phu by airlift and—having shielded the major part of northern Laos by means of the air-land base of the Plain of Jars with its three easily-defended airstrips—concentrating the bulk of his battle force for a major offensive against the enemy's main logistical centers [Cogny's plan] while carrying out, if he wanted to, his original plan of eliminating the large Communist pocket in the south [Operation Atlante].[78]

Laniel strongly supports this position:

[General Navarre's] decision of December 3 . . . was the strategic origin of the military defeat of Dien Bien Phu. . . .

. . . There is no doubt that from December 4, 1953 there developed a strategic error that was going to be fatal for us. Whereas all the intelligence indicated to the commander in chief that Dien Bien Phu was on the point of being invested, the latter chose deliberately to remain there in order to wage battle. The evacuation of the place, or all other measures of protection, were still able to be considered at this point.[79]

Norman E. Martin makes the following observation in *Military Review:*

. . . for the first time in airborne warfare there existed [at Dien Bien Phu] a set of circumstances permitting the planned withdrawal by air of an airborne force of tactical significance. The complete destruction and dispersal of Vietminh forces in the immediate objective area [on November 20, 1953] and the relative isolation of the objective area from enemy reinforcements made withdrawal simple to execute, and on a leisurely basis, during the latter part of November and early December 1953.[80]

Finally, Navarre himself concedes in *Agonie de l'Indochine* that the option of evacuating Dien Bien Phu was lost beyond early December:

The retrenched camp of Dien Bien Phu had been initially conceived, as has been said earlier, to bar the route to Upper Laos to the reinforced Division 316, that is to say to resist the efforts of a large division, but without important heavy means.

Perhaps it would have been possible to evacuate when, at the beginning of December, we received information indicating the probable ascent of all or part of Divisions 308, 312 and Heavy Division 351. The evacuation should have been executed before December 10 because, after that date, Division 316 had arrived in the proximity of Dien Bien Phu and it had, therefore, become impossible without enormous losses.[81]

Navarre, in fact, goes further and makes the following admission: "Even before the arrival of Division 316, there were enough Vietminh forces (regular Regiment 148 and regional battalions) around Dien Bien Phu so that the [French] elements charged with covering the last airplane embarcations would not have been able, without enormous losses, to retreat through the jungle of northern Laos."[82]

It is clear, then, from General Navarre's own words and from the testimony and evidence from all other sources, that the Navarre Plan died at Dien Bien Phu on December 9, 1953. For as of that date, only nineteen days after the launching of Operation Castor, all of the basic calculations—strategic, tactical, logistical, and intelligence—had been made that would soon bring about the general engagement of forces in the northwest that the commander in chief had firmly proposed to delay for at least one year, until the French were in a stronger position to meet such a test. In the process, the military plans had been set in motion on both sides that were destined to make Dien Bien Phu the decisive battle in the seven-year-old French Indo-China war.

The Dien Bien Phu operation has been roundly criticized in retrospect by many American officials who were directly involved in formulating U.S. policy toward Indo-China at the time.

In an interview on June 28, 1965, Donald Heath, the former U.S. ambassador to Saigon, recalled having been "rather flabbergasted" by the French military undertaking.[83]

Walter Robertson, the former assistant secretary of state for Far Eastern affairs, made similarly disapproving remarks in an interview on April 18, 1967: "General Navarre evolved a rather complicated plan which . . . in the end produced a tremendous debacle at Dien Bien Phu. . . .

The French gambled on the assumption that the Viet-Minh could not surround . . . [the] high terrain around Dien Bien Phu with artillery. There they underestimated the resourcefulness and the ability of the communists."[84]

What neither Heath nor Robertson bothered to recall, however, were their own contemporaneous reactions to the seizure of Dien Bien Phu. In his November 21 telegram to the State Department, Heath matter-of-factly reported that "General Navarre told me last night he was much encouraged over [the] success of [the] three-battalion parachute drop at Dien Bien Phu." He made no other comments or criticisms. Robertson, in his address of December 2, confined his remarks on Indo-China to saying that "we believe the tide is now turning." There is no evidence to indicate that the observations expressed by either man gave a false or misleading impression of their attitudes at the time.

In their reminiscences, Heath and Robertson offered differing versions of how U.S. military officials reacted to Operation Castor.

Heath told of "a rather surprising belief among our military personnel in the chances for [the operation's] success."[85] Robertson, on the other hand, gave this account: "[The French] decided upon this plan of concentrating their crack troops at Dien Bien Phu, which was not a strategic position in the judgment of our military experts, from the standpoint of the overall war. It was a very unstrategic position, in our opinion, militarily—and I say our opinion, the opinion of our military experts—because it was a low area surrounded by high terrain."[86]

Opinions are especially divided concerning how the French action was assessed by one military man in particular: Gen. Thomas Trapnell, the chief of the U.S. Military Assistance Advisory Group in Indo-China.

Melvin Gurtov writes: "What is not generally realized is that Major General Thomas J. H. Trapnell . . . concurred in the Dienbienphu operation."[87] Bernard Fall agrees and goes further, observing that Trapnell, on his November 29 trip to Dien Bien Phu (and on subsequent visits) "expressed nothing but admiration for the job being done there" and "beamingly hovered over this French military enterprise like a mother hen."[88]

An opposing view is given by James M. Gavin, a member of the U.S. Army in 1953, who, in writing about Operation Castor, says: "Our military adviser in Saigon, Major General Thomas Trapnell, had never thought well of the scheme."[89] It appears, on balance, that Gavin's version is closer to the truth, although for reasons that are instructive.

Trapnell's analysis of Castor, as contained in his December 1 report to CINCPAC, was, indeed, critical but not because he believed the operation to be a dangerous action that might put the French in a vulnerable, overextended position. Rather, he disapproved of the operation because it was, in his view, "[a] conservative move [that] has been followed by [a] base development scheme in [the] sparsely populated hinterland [and which] leads to [a] reasonable doubt [that the] Fr[ench] have [the] will to seize [the] initiative by opns [operations] threatening enemy supply lines from China in [the] northern Delta area where maj[or] enemy concentrations now exist." Trapnell, in short, saw the new French airhead as a case of poor priorities and a lack of resolve, rather than the result of a potentially serious military misjudgment.[90]

There is testimony as to how the Joint Chiefs of Staff (JCS) privately felt about the merits of the Dien Bien Phu operation from both Gavin and William B. Rosson, who, like Gavin, was a member of the U.S. Army at the time. Gavin asserts that "the Joint Chiefs of Staff had been doubtful about the Dien Bien Phu strategy from the beginning."[91]

Rosson agrees, observing: "From the standpoint of the JCS, . . . the diversion of a [French] force approaching divisional size from the critical Tonkin [Red River] Delta was unsound. Nor could the JCS justify commitment of a significant portion of an already over-burdened air transport fleet and of substantial numbers of fighters and light bombers operating at maximum radii [in order] to succor the airhead."[92]

These accounts are contradicted, however, by a man who was in an even better position to know the truth: Matthew B. Ridgway, then a member of the JCS. In an interview on April 15, 1976, the former army chief of staff was asked the following question: "At what point do you believe [that] you personally, and the other members of the JCS, first became aware of the importance and dangerous nature of the Dien Bien Phu operation?"[93]

Replied Ridgway: "Initially, in spite of the isolation of Dien Bien Phu, we were not too worried about it. We had a high estimate of the combat effectiveness of the French."[94]

Lending support to Ridgway's side of the story is the December 2 address of JCS Chairman Adm. Arthur Radford, in which he said the following: "Indo-China . . . is a very real part of the overall conflict between the free world and communism. Today, I am happy to say that there is reason to be optimistic about its eventual outcome. Militarily, the forces of freedom can win."

Admiral Radford would later be among those who would lay the blame for the Dien Bien Phu operation on French thinking that supposedly grew out of their earlier stand at Na-San. In his memoirs, Radford criticizes the seizure of Dien Bien Phu as "a move reminiscent of the defensive concepts of previous years"[95] and, as already noted, he expands on this criticism in another part of his memoirs: "From the French view this [Na-San] was a successful battle, and I was convinced that the lesson they learned there led them to try the same idea again at Dien Bien Phu a year later."[96]

There is testimony, however, that Admiral Radford may have had a very different view of the Na-San precedent at the time. In an interview on February 4–5, 1975, John O'Daniel, the former head of the two U.S. joint military missions that visited Indo-China in 1953, was asked the following question concerning his first mission in July of that year: "Do you recall any particular aspect of your conversations with CINCPAC [Admiral Radford] enroute to Indo-China?"[97] O'Daniel answered: "Admiral Radford told me that he was impressed with [the] casualties [that the] French had inflicted on the enemy at Na-San. He wanted to see more of the same."[98]

No one would later be a greater critic of the French seizure of Dien Bien Phu than the man who was America's commander in chief in 1953, Dwight D. Eisenhower. In an interview on July 28, 1964, he said: "[The French] came along with this Dien Bien Phu plan. As a soldier I was horror-stricken. I just said, 'My goodness, you don't pen troops in a fortress, and all history shows that they are just going to be cut to pieces.' . . . And I told the [U.S.] Defense [Department] people and the State Department. I said, 'I just think this is terrible.'"[99]

Eisenhower repeated these sentiments three years later. In an interview on July 20, 1967, he said:

> [The French] came along and told us about their plan of Dien Bien Phu: establishing a Dien Bien Phu fortress.
>
> I said, "I can't think of anything crazier. No experienced soldier would ever establish a force, an immobile force, in a place, in a

fortress, and then ask the enemy to come to invest it. That's just silly. Almost every investment in history, with one or two exceptions, has ended with the surrender of the garrison. What are you really asking to do? I won't go along with this scheme."[100]

In less animated language, Eisenhower also describes his concerns about Dien Bien Phu in his memoirs:

> It was difficult then—as it is now with the advantage of hindsight—to understand exactly why (a year in advance of the buildup contemplated in the Navarre Plan) the French decided to send ten thousand crack troops into this position, strong as it was, whose only means of resupply was by air. . . .
> . . . Whatever the reasons, the occupation of Dien Bien Phu caused little notice at the time, except to soldiers who were well acquainted with the almost invariable fate of troops invested in an isolated fortress. I instructed both the State and Defense Departments to communicate to their French counterparts my concern as to the move.[101]

Both Walter Robertson and former presidential Press Secretary James Hagerty support Eisenhower's contention that he made his views about Dien Bien Phu known to the French.

In his interview in April 1967, Robertson observed: "We [the U.S.] felt so strongly that it [the French occupation of Dien Bien Phu] was bad tactics that General Eisenhower, not as President of the United States but as a military expert himself, a military commander himself, sent a private message opposing this tactic. He thought it was an unstrategic position, an indefensible position."[102]

In an interview in January 1968, Hagerty recalled: "President Eisenhower told his French friends—and by that I mean government friends—[that] it [Dien Bien Phu] was a completely untenable military position, and that this was no place to make a stand."[103] In a subsequent interview, Hagerty added: "President Eisenhower's serious advice to the French government was that this [Dien Bien Phu] was no place to defend."[104]

Given the strong feelings about Dien Bien Phu that both Eisenhower and his associates later remembered him as having, it is surprising, indeed, that the president raised no objections whatever to the new French base on the occasion when he had the best opportunity for doing so: at the Bermuda Conference.

When discussions among the Big Three turned to the subject of Indo-China on the afternoon of December 7, Foreign Minister Bidault did not specfically mention the Dien Bien Phu operation, but he referred to it indirectly by saying that France had succeeded in stopping the dry season offensive that the communists had prepared on the plateaus of Laos. He also had ample praise for General Navarre, crediting him with having drawn the Viet-Minh off balance by the offensives that he had directed against it while, at the same time, avoiding the dispersement of his own forces by refusing to counterattack everywhere. Bidault wound up his remarks by saying that the military situation in Indo-China was better than he had ever seen it before.

In Eisenhower's own brief comments on Indo-China, he did not challenge Bidault's optimistic assessment of the situation and even said that he would like to pay personal tribute to General Navarre, of whom he had heard the finest reports. He made no mention of Dien Bien Phu. Neither did the president mention the French garrison nor express any concern about the conduct of the war in his December 10 memorandum on the Bermuda Conference. He wrote as follows:

> Indo-China was . . . a subject on which Bidault expounded at great length. There was nothing particularly new that was developed out of his discussion, but it is clear that the French (possibly correctly) consider that the situation there is in better shape than it has been for a long time. While this does not mean that they are too hopeful about securing an early and real military victory, it does mean that for the first time they are talking positively in terms of a possible military victory.
>
> The United States has been supplying equipment for that operation at a very generous rate. In fact, I believe that in some regards they have more equipment than they can use. In addition, we are right now turning over a second aircraft carrier, some C-47 transports (25) and some helicopters. All of this is designed to give them better air support and greater flexibility in the use of their paratroop battalions.
>
> The American and the British delegations had little comment to make on Bidault's presentation.[105]

The U.S. reaction to Bidault's comments on Indo-China receives the following treatment from Marquis Childs in his book, *Eisenhower: Captive Hero:*

In December 1953, the President met in Bermuda with Prime Minister Winston Churchill and French Premier Joseph Laniel. . . . the [Bermuda] conference in . . . [one] respect proved to have been a sad deception. The heads of government and their foreign ministers in reviewing the world situation had accepted from Georges Bidault a rosy picture of the war in Indochina that was almost entirely false. The United States was paying up to nearly a billion dollars annually of the cost of that conflict, and Bidault encouraged the hope that with only a little more time and a little more money the war against the Communist Viet-minh would be brought to a successful conclusion. Whether American diplomatic reporting from that area was hopelessly deficient or whether the President and Dulles preferred to accept the optimistic view, they seem to have put full credence in Bidault's wishful dream, which concealed such a fearful reality.[106]

The questions raised by Childs deserve further exploration. To what extent was U.S. policy toward Indo-China being guided by diplomatic reporting that was "hopelessly deficient?" Attention must focus first on the U.S. man on the scene at the northern Indo-China battlefront: Hanoi Consul Paul Sturm.

Sturm's telegrams of November 23, December 5, and December 9, and his December 9 meeting with General Cogny were very revealing of the attitudes and intentions of the French Northern Command. It is also clear that as late as December 5, Sturm did not yet foresee the growing importance of Dien Bien Phu and, indeed, thought that the main communist target was still the Red River Delta.

This was indicated by the portion of his December 5 report, which read as follows: "It is too early to affirm [a] basic change in Viet Minh fall campaign plans, which have been generally assumed to hinge on [a] major effort against [the] Delta by regular forces now outside [the Delta]." Four days later Sturm was beginning to pick up enough static to warn of "rumors heard widely in official and unofficial circles here . . . that elements of Viet-Minh Divisions 308 and 312 are moving to join Division 316 in [the] Thai country."

The importance of this revelation, however, was largely offset later that day by General Cogny's boastful remarks to Sturm, which the consul also relayed to the State Department. Cogny said he hoped the reports that Divisions 308 and 312 were turning toward the northwest were well founded as he could ask for no development more favorable to his making serious progress in cleaning out the Red River Delta and in breaking in green Vietnamese units. The general added that the Thai country terrain and the French Union regular and guerrilla forces could be counted on to take their toll of any Viet Minh units that were sent into the region.

Cogny's concerns of November 28 had clearly been replaced by a more conservative reading of the Viet-Minh threat to Dien Bien Phu as well as by a renewed confidence stemming both from his appointment of Colonel de Castries and from the implementation of his November 30 directive.

As Cogny went on to say that day, in assigning Colonel de Castries to command Dien Bien Phu, he believed that he had given the job to the best man for the purpose who was then available in Tonkin. As an old cavalryman, observed Cogny, de Castries could be depended on to seize the initiative and not remain behind a defensive position. The general added that the Dien Bien Phu position was now strong and was being further strengthened continually. Such an optimistic assessment by the Northern commander himself was no less likely to be persuasive to a U.S. consular official in Hanoi than was Bidault's presentation to Eisenhower in Bermuda.

Hints of a more sinister explanation for American hopefulness come from Joseph and Stewart Alsop in their book, *The Reporter's Trade*. Writing of Joseph's visit to Paris in late 1953, during what is described as "the sad winter of Dienbienphu," the Alsop brothers go on to make the following charge: "The State Department had virtually commanded our embassy in Saigon to emphasize the positive in all of its reports. Hence the normally capable staff of the Paris embassy had been grossly misled about the gravity of the situation by reports from Saigon that were much too optimistic; and the [Paris] embassy staff had in turn misled the resident American correspondents."[107]

If Ambassador Heath's reports from Saigon were "much too optimistic," then it was only because he was uncritically passing on General Navarre's prognostications just as Sturm, for his part, was doing with Cogny's forecasts from Hanoi. There is no evidence to indicate that the State Department actively sought to influence the contents of the cable traffic from its Vietnamese missions.

That does not mean, however, that the hand of responsibility rests lightly on the State Department and on one man in particular: the director of the Office of Philippine and Southeast Asian Affairs, Philip Bonsal.

Midlevel State Department officials like Bonsal, who were the recipients of diplomatic reports from large geographic areas of the world and who had the responsibility of sifting and summarizing this information for policymakers, were, to some degree, the hinge on which U.S. foreign policy turned. And yet, curiously, Bonsal's secret intradepartmental memorandums on the military situation in Indo-China contained less insight on the approaching battle at Dien Bien Phu than did some contemporaneous reports in the print media.

The PSA director's memorandum of November 27 to Assistant Secretary Robertson revealed that within one week of the French seizure of Dien Bien Phu, U.S. intelligence was aware that a Viet-Minh force of over two divisions was headed in that direction. Bonsal speculated that the French action had been carried out "in anticipation of this [enemy] movement" and went on to conclude his memo with the following observations:

> Viet Minh attacks against Franco-Vietnamese installations in that area [Dien Bien Phu] may be an indication of renewed Viet Minh incursions against Laos, or else an effort to clear away forces [the Thai guerrillas] having a harassing capacity against the Viet Minh.
>
> If the movement of the 325 division from its present location in central Viet Nam is continued in the direction of central Laos it would support the hypothesis that [an] invasion of Laos is the principal Viet Minh plan for the time being.
>
> We have insufficient information of the enemy movements or of the French plans to arrive at any firm conclusion as to the importance of this development. The enemy movement may not take its final form for several weeks. Nevertheless, the Viet Minh are moving some forty to fifty thousand troops away from the [Hanoi-Haiphong] perimeter for a still undisclosed purpose.

Bonsal, therefore, did not evince any particular concern about the Dien Bien Phu position itself in his report nor, indeed, did he think it certain that the new French base was the ultimate target of the latest Viet-Minh maneuvers. He preferred, instead, to take a wait-and-see attitude.

By contrast, as early as November 23, *Time* foresaw the likelihood that French and Viet-Minh troop movements were pointing toward an important battle at Dien Bien Phu: "The Viet-Minh," wrote *Time*, "were reported to be moving up their 316th Division, and it seemed possible that the Communists might break their own tactical rules by fighting a pitched battle for Dienbienphu, rather than let Navarre's men stay in possession."

On the very day that Bonsal wrote his November 27 memo, the Associated Press sent the following dispatch from the new garrison:

A Vietminh division—perhaps 10,000 men—was reported moving from the east today upon the Thai tribal town which French Union forces captured a week ago. . . .

The westbound rebel division was identified as No. 316. Presumably pulled out of the line menacing the French-held Red River Delta, it was reported less than 50 miles from this town . . . . French Gen. Rene Cogny said the division would require several days to complete the march.

Eleven days later the growing communist pressure in the area finally forced the evacuation of Lai Chau, the beginnings of which were widely reported by the press on December 8. The AP cabled from Hanoi that the evacuation was being carried out "in view of a possible early Viet-Minh attack there." The Paris correspondent for the *Times* (London), in reporting the same story, wrote that "some days ago the Viet-minh 316th Division was reported to be within two days' march of *either* [emphasis added] Laichau or Dien Bien Phu."

Yet, despite this evident deterioration in the military situation in the northwest and although General Navarre had already told American authorities that one motivation for the French seizure of Dien Bien Phu was to provide protection for Lai Chau, whose capture by the enemy must be resisted,[108] Bonsal displayed no concern about military developments in the lengthy report of his "impression and thoughts regarding current conditions and prospects in Indochina" which he sent to Assistant Secretary Robertson on the very day that Lai Chau was being evacuated.

Specifically, the PSA director described the military situation as follows:

It would be difficult to exaggerate what General Navarre has accomplished in the less than six months since he took command last May of an army whose reserves were practically exhausted and whose confidence in itself and its leaders was at a low ebb. . . .

The major achievements of General Navarre since last summer may be stated as follows:

. . . In terms of actual operations, the French High Command took the initiative with the spectacular and successful parachute raid on Langson in July. Although the enemy has a high offensive potential and although it was generally believed at the outset of the present fighting season that he intended to use it, *he has not as yet done so* [emphasis added]. To some extent this is due to various limited offensives conducted as a part of General Navarre's strategic plan for this fighting season in the North. The most important of these operations (known as Mouette and conducted between October 15 and November 3) is believed by General Navarre to have cost the enemy in killed and wounded and in material losses about one-third of the effectives of one of his regular divisions (320). Operations conducted by French Union troops and local irregulars in the Thai country northwest of the Tonkin delta have obliged the enemy to divert to that area the equivalent of perhaps one- half of another division (316). The recent capture of the relatively important town of Dien Bien Phu with its airstrip is a part of this pattern. Other operations are in prospect. As a result of those already conducted, the offensive possibilities open to the enemy have been reduced. . . .

Two observations deserve to be made here. The first is that Bonsal's description of the results of Operation Mouette made no mention of the considerably less favorable report on that operation that he had received on December 1 from F. S. Tomlinson, the counselor of the British embassy in Washington. The second point concerns Bonsal's estimate that the communists were only diverting toward the Thai country "the equivalent of perhaps one-half of . . . division (316)" when he himself had sent the following report to Assistant Secretary Robertson on November 27: "Two [Viet-Minh] divisions [308 and 316], plus elements of a third [304] are moving from their recent positions North and West of the Hanoi-Haiphong perimeter in the direction of Son-La/Lai-Chau."

How could Bonsal on December 8 have failed to include such highly relevant and potentially serious information, of which he was fully aware and which he had already made known to his superiors eleven days earlier? And how could they, in turn, have failed to detect the flaws and omissions in Bonsal's analyses, as was indicated by the favorable note that Everett F. Drumright, Robertson's deputy, wrote on the top of the December 8 memorandum: "Seen by WSR [Walter S. Robertson] on 12–12–53. A very well put memo."[109]

A clue to the explanation lies in the opening sentences of Bonsal's report in which he described General O'Daniel's mission to Indo-China, and then added the following lines: "A full account of the trip from the military point of view is contained in the mission's report, prepared in Honolulu from November 17 to November 20. A copy of this document is attached with the original of this memorandum. It is recommended that you read General O'Daniel's summary of his findings and recommendations."

A close examination of the O'Daniel mission's report reveals that Bonsal's characterization of Operation Mouette as having cost the Viet-Minh "about one-third of the effectives of one of his regular divisions (320)" and his description of the communist force that was heading toward the northwest as consisting of "the equivalent of perhaps one-half of . . . division (316)" were taken almost verbatim from the O'Daniel report.[110]

That report, in fact, holds the key to understanding the widespread optimism that permeated official Washington's attitude toward the Indo-China war at this critical juncture. For the State Department was not alone in its decision to place primary reliance on the O'Daniel report and to accord a lower priority to less sanguine reports from other sources.

On December 7, the day prior to when Bonsal wrote his memorandum to Robertson, the Pentagon's Joint Strategic Plans Group (JSPG) circulated its draft memo to the Joint Chiefs on the O'Daniel report, which was approved by the Joint Strategic Plans Committee two days later. The JSPG summarized the central conclusion of the O'Daniel report as follows: "Real military progress in implementation of the 'Navarre Plan' is evident. To a limited extent, the French and Associated States have succeeded in regaining the initiative in the conflict. As a result, prospects for victory appear increasingly encouraging." Then, as its first recommendation, the JSPG went on to say: "It is recommended that: a. The report of the [O'Daniel] Mission be accepted as a basis for further planning in connection with operations in Indochina."

In Enclosure "C" (Facts Bearing on the Problem) of its report, the JSPG included General Trapnell's critical comments of December 1 on the Dien Bien Phu operation and CINCPAC's reservations of December 2 concerning the optimistic tone of the O'Daniel report, but it essentially dismissed these dissenting opinions in Enclosure "D" (Discussion) with the following observation: "Although opinions vary as to the degree of success the French have had in their attempts to wrest the initiative from the Viet-Minh, there is definite evidence that real progress has been made toward a more favorable military situation."

Therefore, the three-week-old report of the O'Daniel mission, though widely believed by U.S. military personnel in Indo-China to be overoptimistic at the time that it was written[111] and quickly superseded by subsequent events, became, as of December 9, the centerpiece of American military and diplomatic planning in connection with the future course of the Indo-China war.

The one event that did more than anything to render the O'Daniel report out of date was the French occupation of Dien Bien Phu. The report was completed on November 19, the day before Operation Castor

was launched, and there is no evidence to indicate that either General
O'Daniel or any other U.S. official was told in advance of the operation.[112] Nevertheless, the report did contain one reference to the northwest that set forth the prevailing, "pre-Castor" wisdom toward that theater of the war.

In Enclosure "C" (Facts Bearing on the Problem) of its draft report,
the JSPG summed up this portion of the O'Daniel report as follows:

> Positive action taken since July 1953 to organize and expand the
> action of [the] Associated States guerrilla forces has met with consid-
> erable success. Presently, French Union guerrilla forces operating in
> the northwest section of Indochina have forced the Viet Minh to de-
> ploy one regiment plus one battalion to counteract this guerrilla ac-
> tion. Approximately 6,000 guerrillas are now being directed by the
> para-military organization and the prospects for the future appear
> good.

The O'Daniel report thus adopted the view that the movement of part
of the 316th Division toward the Thai country was essentially defensive,
not offensive, in character and therefore represented a military setback
for the communists. This judgment, in turn, increased the credibility of
subsequent French declarations concerning the Dien Bien Phu operation's prospects for success and helps to explain why the initial compla-
cency of U.S. policymakers toward the new French airhead stands in
such sharp contrast to the deep concerns that they were later to portray
in their memoirs and reminiscences.

As "The Pentagon Papers" observes: "The temptation to 'go along'
with the French until the Viet Minh was defeated was all the more attractive because of the expectation of victory which pervaded official Washington. Before Dien Bien Phu, General O'Daniel consistently reported
that victory was within reach if the United States continued its
support."[113]

When former Army Chief of Staff Matthew Ridgway was asked in his
April 1976 interview about the perennially optimistic outlook of General
O'Daniel's reports on Indo-China, he made this observation: "I never
served closely with General O'Daniel. Personally, and this is not for attri-
bution, I was not impressed with him. I thought he was inclined to be
over-optimistic. He was a good commander himself but not a particularly
good judge of other commanders."[114]

This subject was raised directly with O'Daniel himself when the following question was put to him during his February 1975 interview: "On

your second visit [to Indo-China] in November 1953 you reported that 'real military progress in implementing the "Navarre Plan" is evident' and that the French had definitely established a far better military situation than existed during the previous year. In retrospect, do you feel this assessment was too optimistic?"[115]

O'Daniel replied: "In retrospect, yes."[116]

And so by early December 1953 the U.S. had officially accepted France's mistaken interpretation of recent events in Indo-China, especially the movement of Viet-Minh troops toward the northwest. An important new enemy initiative was under way against Dien Bien Phu but the true dimensions and significance of this development remained undetected by both the French and the Americans.

The Indo-China War had taken a dramatic turn.

Appendixes

A. U.S. Estimate of Heavy Support by the Viet-Minh

NATIONAL INTELLIGENCE ESTIMATE

NIE 91   WASHINGTON, 4 June 1953.
PROBABLE DEVELOPMENTS IN INDOCHINA THROUGH MID-1954

THE PROBLEM

To estimate French Union and Communist capabilities and probable courses of action with respect to Indochina and the internal situation throughout Indochina through mid-1954. . . .

The Viet Minh probably will continue to receive a steady flow of material assistance from the Chinese Communists, and the amount may increase at any time. The Viet Minh do not have, and probably cannot develop within the period of this estimate, the capability to make such effective use of heavy equipment—artillery, armor, and aircraft—from the Chinese Communists as to permit successful attacks against strong concentrations of regular French forces.*

B. General Navarre's Description of the "Navarre Plan"

CONFIDENTIAL   SAIGON, November 19, 1953–2 p.m.

879. . . . I accompanied Senator Smith and Dr. Francis Wilcox on [a] call on General Navarre who explained [the] "Navarre plan" while dep-

---

*From U.S. Department of State, *Foreign Relations of the United States, 1952–1954,* vol. 13 [Indochina], pt. 1, pp. 592, 600.

recating having his name attached to it. Navarre stated that circumstances would require him to wage an essentially defensive war in north-[ern Viet-Nam] until [the] summer [of] 1954, but this would not preclude French tactical offensives in that region or [the] cleaning up of [the] Tonkin [Red River] delta. Meanwhile, as [the] Vietnamese army [was] built up, he planned offensive operations to destroy Viet Minh Forces in south and central Vietnam. This should be accomplished by next June [1954] by which time, as a result of [the] expansion of his own forces, of [the] military and economic losses and difficulties which would be inflicted on [the] Viet Minh, by using some of [the] new Vietnamese National Army units and freeing certain French Union units from their present state of warfare duties, he would have a sufficient striking force to force [the] main Viet Minh Armies in [the] north to decisive battles. He hoped that by April 1, 1955 or certainly by May, or June, to have inflicted [a] military defeat on [the] Viet Minh. This did not mean that hostilities would then be entirely over since there were vast regions of forests, jungle, and mountains from which [the] Viet Minh could still indulge in guerrilla harassment. It might take another two years or so to wipe out such last-stand guerrilla operations but that campaign would be essentially a police rather than [a] military operation and Vietnam would have forces to cope with it alone. . . .

HEATH*

C. Text of the Joint U.S.–French Communiqué of September 30, 1953

The forces of France and the Associated States in Indochina have for 8 years been engaged in a bitter struggle to prevent the engulfment of Southeast Asia by the forces of international communism. The heroic efforts and sacrifices of these French Union allies in assuring the liberty of the new and independent states of Cambodia, Laos and Vietnam has earned the admiration and support of the free world. In recognition of the French union effort the United States Government has in the past furnished aid of various kinds to the Governments of France and the Associated States to assist in bringing the long struggle to an early and victorious conclusion.

---

*From U.S. Department of State, *Foreign Relations of the United States, 1952–1954,* vol. 13 [Indochina], pt. 1, p. 876 and n.1.

The French Government is firmly resolved to carry out in full its declaration of July 3, 1953 by which it announced its intention of perfecting the independence of the three Associated States in Indochina, through negotiations with the Associated States.

The Governments of France and the United States have now agreed that, in support of plans of the French Government for the intensified prosecution of the war against the Viet Minh, the United States will make available to the French Government prior to December 31, 1954 additional financial resources not to exceed $385 million. This aid is in addition to funds already earmarked by the United States for aid to France and the Associated States.

The French Government is determined to make every effort to break up and destroy the regular enemy forces in Indochina. Toward this end the government intends to carry through, in close co-operation with the Cambodian, Laotian, and Vietnamese Governments, the plans for increasing the Associated States forces while increasing temporarily French forces to levels considered necessary to assure the success of existing military plans. The additional United States aid is designed to help make it possible to achieve these objectives with maximum speed and effectiveness.

The increased French effort in Indochina will not entail any basic or permanent alteration of the French Government's plans and programs for its NATO forces.*

D. Prime Minister Joseph Laniel's Statement of July 3, 1953 Concerning the Associated States

The Government of the French Republic, meeting in Council of Ministers, has conducted an examination of French relations with the Associated States of Indo-China.

It considers that the time has come to adapt the agreements they have concluded with France to the position which, with her full support, they have been able to secure in the community of free peoples.

Respectful of national traditions and human freedoms, France, during nearly a century of cooperation, has led Cambodia, Laos and Viet-Nam

---

*From U.S. Department of State, *Foreign Relations of the United States, 1952–1954,* vol. 13 [Indochina], pt. 1, p. 812; U.S. Department of State, *Department of State Bulletin,* Oct. 12, 1953, vol. 29, no. 746, pp. 486–87.

to the full flowering of their individuality and has maintained their national unity.

By the agreements of 1949, she recognized their independence and they agreed to associate themselves with her in the French Union.

The Government of the [French] Republic wishes today to make a solemn declaration.

During the four year period which has passed since the signing of the agreements, the brotherhood of arms between the armies of the French Union and the national armies of the Associated States has been further strengthened, thanks to the development of these national armies which each day are taking a more important part in the struggle against the common enemy.

During the same period, the civil institutions of the three nations have put themselves in a position to assume the totality of the powers belonging to modern States, while the international audience accorded to their Governments has expanded to include the majority of the countries which make up the United Nations.

In these circumstances, France considers that there are grounds to perfect the independence and sovereignty of the Associated States of Indo-China by ensuring, in agreement with each of the three interested Governments, the transfer of the powers that she has continued to hold in the interests of the States themselves because of the perilous circumstances resulting from the state of war.

The French Government has decided to invite each of the three Governments to reach agreement with it on the settlement of the questions which each of them may deem it necessary to raise in the economic, financial, judicial, military, and political fields, respecting and safeguarding the legitimate interests of each of the contracting parties.

The Government of the Republic expresses the hope that agreement on these various points will strenthen the friendship which unites France and the Associated States within the French Union.*

---

*From Allan W. Cameron, ed., *Viet-Nam Crisis: A Documentary History,*, vol. 1 (1940–56) (Ithaca, N.Y.: Cornell University Press, 1971), pp. 199–200; Gareth Porter, ed., *Vietnam: The Definitive Documentation of Human Decisions*, vol. 1 (Stanfordville, N.Y.: Earl M. Coleman, 1979), pp. 451–52; and Peter V. Curl, ed., *Documents on American Foreign Relations, 1953*, published for the Council on Foreign Relations (New York: Harper & Brothers, 1954), pp. 347–48.

E. Units of the French Union Forces Stationed at Dien Bien Phu as of December 6

AIRBORNE
HQ, Airborne Divisional Element (EDAP),
6th Colonial Parachute (6 BPC)
2nd Battalion, 1st Parachute Regiment (II/I RCP)
1st Colonial Parachute (1 BPC)
1st Foreign Legion Parachute (1 BEP)
5th Vietnamese Parachute (5 BPVN)
8th Parachute Assault (8 BPC)
17th Airborne Engineers Company
35th Airborne Artillery Regiment (2 batteries) (35 RALP)
1st Foreign Legion Heavy Airborne Mortar Co. (1 CEMLP)
342nd Parachute Signal Company (elements)

INFANTRY
3rd Thai Battalion (BT 3)

ARTILLERY
Laotian Autonomous Artillery Battery (BAAL)

ENGINEERS
3rd Company, 31st Engineers (31/3 BG)*

F. James Hagerty's Announcement of the Bermuda Conference

IMMEDIATE RELEASE   NOVEMBER 10, 1953
JAMES C. HAGERTY, PRESS SECRETARY TO THE PRESIDENT

THE WHITE HOUSE

The President has directed me to issue the following statement:

It has been decided to hold the Three Power Conference at Bermuda which was planned for the beginning of July but had to be put off. President [Dwight D.] Eisenhower and Secretary of State [John

---

*From Bernard B. Fall, *Hell in a Very Small Place: The Siege of Dien Bien Phu* (New York: J. B. Lippincott, 1967), p. 479.

Foster] Dulles will represent the United States; M. [Joseph] Laniel, President of the Council of Ministers, and M. [Georges] Bidault, Foreign Minister, will represent France; and [Prime Minister] Sir Winston Churchill and Mr. [Anthony] Eden, Foreign Minister, will represent Britain. It is hoped to meet from December 4th to December 8th and various matters of common concern to the three Powers will be discussed.*

G. Total Casualties for French Union Forces in Indo-China between 1945 and October, 1953**

Type of Forces	Dead/Missing	Wounded	Sick/Evacuated
French	15,681	18,608	27,732
Foreign Legion	6,907	4,573	5,019
Africans	10,118	9,143	8,848
Native			
Expeditionary Forces	21,599	17,243	—
Indochinese			
National Armies	10,069	5,804	—
Total	64,374	55,371	41,599

*From Dwight D. Eisenhower Library, Abilene, Kansas, White House Central Files, Official File 116 [Foreign Affairs—Foreign Policy Series], box 588, folder: 116–0 Bermuda Conference.

**From John J. McCuen, *The Art of Counter-Revolutionary War: The Strategy of Counter-Insurgency* (Harrisburg, Penn.: Stackpole Books, 1966), p. 260.

Notes

1. Operation Castor

1. The word "Dakota" was the nickname for the Douglas C-47 transport aircraft. It could carry a payload of 5,500 pounds for a distance of 900 miles, at a top speed of 175 miles per hour.

   Bernard Fall says that the C-47 left on a "lone" mission at 5:00 A.M. in order to appraise the weather conditions (Bernard B. Fall, *Hell in a Very Small Place: The Siege of Dien Bien Phu*, p. 1). Jules Roy says that the plane began its flight at 4:30 A.M. in the company of a four-engine "Privateer" naval aircraft that was to evaluate the weather conditions *for* the C-47 (Jules Roy, *The Battle of Dienbienphu*, p. 38).

2. The abbreviation "Gatac" stood for Groupement Aérien Tactique (Air Force Tactical Group). The French had five air commands in Indo-China that were responsible for the northern, central, and southern sections of Viet-Nam, as well as for both Laos and Cambodia. Gatac Nord was the staff unit responsible for northern Viet-Nam.

3. Roy says that the C-47 radioed to Hanoi as early as 6:30 A.M. that the *crachin* was clearing (Roy, *The Battle of Dienbienphu*, p. 39). But, according to Fall, the fate of the airdrop was initially in some doubt, with visibility over Dien Bien Phu "almost completely blocked" by the fog at 6:30 A.M. Not until 7:00 A.M., he says, did the upper layers of the clouds begin to "thin out noticeably" (Fall, *Hell in a Very Small Place*, pp. 1–2).

4. These battalions were made up of both French and Vietnamese troops. Fall writes: "Bigeard's 6th BPC contained more than 200 Vietnamese troops out of 651 men. . . . These proportions differed slightly from unit to unit but there was no strictly 'French' unit in Indochina that did not have a large number of locally raised Vietnamese troops . . . [and] such mixed French-Vietnamese units on the whole fought far better than purely Vietnamese units and also purely European units (who did not have the benefit of the knowledge of local terrain and language of their Vietnamese comrades)." (Fall, *Hell in a Very Small Place*, p. 8).

5. The name "Viet-Minh" was an abbreviation for Viet Nam Doc Lap Dong Minh Hoi (League for the Independence of Viet-Nam). This communist

"united front" organization, founded in 1941, was disbanded in 1951 when it was merged with the Lien Viet (League for the National Union of Viet-Nam), thus forming the Viet-Nam Front of National Union. The name Viet-Minh, however, had persisted in use.

6. In 1950 the commander of the Viet-Nam People's Army, Gen. Vo Nguyen Giap, had assembled his infantry regiments into five divisions. Each division consisted of four regiments and each regiment was composed of three battalions. The divisions were designated as the 304th, 308th, 312th, 316th, and 320th. In 1951 the Viet-Minh heavy artillery battalions were grouped together to form the 351st Heavy Division. It consisted of three regiments, two of artillery and one of engineers. In early 1953 a sixth infantry division, the 325th, was added.

7. Philippe Devillers and Jean Lacouture summarize General Navarre's military background as follows: "On May 8, 1953, the French government appointed as Commander in Chief General Henri Navarre, aged 55, until then Chief of Staff to [French Field] Marshall [Alphonse] Juin, Commander in Chief of Allied Forces in Central Europe, and regarded as one of the most brilliant strategists in the French Army. The General took up his command in Saigon on May 20" (Philippe Devillers and Jean Lacouture, *End of a War: Indochina, 1954*, p. 34).

8. See map 2. William Simcock gives the following explanation for the geopolitical importance of the Red River Delta in the French Indo-China War:

> In Viet-Nam [military] operations were centered chiefly on and around the great Red River Delta, a triangular expanse of flat riceland bounded on its landward sides by mountains which were controlled for the most part by the Viet-Minh. The delta is some 80 miles across its seaward base and slightly better than 100 miles from base to apex. This is the heartland of North Viet-Nam and the setting for its . . . chief seaports and nine-tenths of its population. (Of areas of similar size, the Red River Delta has the highest density of population per square mile in the world). (William Simcock, "Dien Bien Phu: Yesterday's Battlefield," *Canadian Army Journal* 12 [July 1958], p. 36)

9. Roy, *The Battle of Dienbienphu*, p. 42.

10. Ibid. The climactic conditions for military movement in Indo-China were much better during the dry, winter season months of November through April than during the rainy, summer season months of May through October. The winter months were thus referred to as the "campaign season" or "fighting season."

11. Devillers and Lacouture, *End of a War*, p. 43; Roy, *The Battle of Dienbienphu*, pp. 41–42.

12. See fig. 2. Different sources offer an amazing variety of information on the length and width of the valley, ranging from the Associated Press's 5 miles by 2 miles (*New York Herald Tribune*, Nov. 22, 1953, p. 2) to Wilfred G. Burchett's 15 miles by 5 miles (*The Furtive War: The United States in Vietnam and Laos*, p. 136).

13. See fig. 3. Roy writes the following impressionistic description of these

heights: "Hills surround the basin, as round and gentle as breasts, or as sharp limestone masses rising in irregular tiers to pointed peaks which formed a jagged amphitheater around the basin" (Roy, *The Battle of Dienbienphu,* p. 37).

14. Roy observes that the Xas looked "more like wild beasts than men" (Roy, *The Battle of Dienbienphu,* p. 37).

15. See map 2. Dien Bien Phu's location accounted for how it had acquired its name, since "Dien Bien Phu" was not really a place name. It was the designation for a Thai village, the true name of which was Muong Thanh and which was still known only by that name in the mountainous Thai country. Muong in the Thai language, like phu in Vietnamese, meant "administrative center." Dien and bien were the Vietnamese words, respectively, for "big" and "frontier." "Dien Bien Phu" could, therefore, be translated as "big administrative center on the frontier." It was known to the Vietnamese by the more formal title of "Seat of the Border County Prefecture" (ibid, p. 36; Fall, *Hell in a Very Small Place,* p. 22).

16. Major Bigeard would later give the following description of his battalion's drop: "When we came down on November 20 we were told there would be no Vietnamese [Viet-Minh at Dien Bien Phu]. But there were two companies exactly where we jumped. Some of my men were killed before they even touched the ground, others were stabbed where they landed" (Michael Maclear, *The Ten Thousand Day War: Vietnam, 1945–1975,* p. 30).

17. *Newsweek* says that the similarity in uniforms extended to "identically camouflaged helmets" (*Newsweek,* Dec. 14, 1953, p. 40), whereas Fall writes that the respective uniforms were the same "except for the flat woven palm-leaf helmet worn by the Viet-Minh soldiers" (Fall, *Hell in a Very Small Place,* p. 11).

18. Fall points to one blessing in disguise for the paratroopers. In Operation Castor, he writes, "as in almost all major airborne operations, the very chaos and dispersion of the drop pattern confused the enemy and prevented the immediate destruction of the dropped units. There was at first no clearly distinguishable center of effort upon which the enemy could concentrate its fire and troops" (ibid).

19. The fighters struck with what was later described as "surgical precision" (ibid., p. 12).

20. The circumstances of the 1st BPC's arrival at Dien Bien Phu are painted very differently by Fall and Roy. Fall says that, after embarking at 1330 (1:30 P.M.), the battalion's "jump at 1500 [3:00 P.M.] on DZ Natasha, now fully held by the men of the 6th BPC, was largely uneventful" (ibid., p. 14). Roy gives this account: "At 1400 hours [2:00 P.M.], the 1st Battalion, Colonial Paratroops, was dropped on Natacha [sic] where Bigeard was barely beginning to sort things out. Half of his battalion was cut off, and as yet he did not have a zone where helicopters could land to pick up the wounded. Violent fighting was spreading confusion everywhere" (Roy, *The Battle of Dienbienphu,* p. 44).

21. The Associated States were the three Indochinese states of Viet-Nam, Laos,

and Cambodia which, under the French Constitution, were "associated" with France by their membership in the French Union.

22. Fall gives the following description of Viet-Minh Division 316: "The 316th Division was not the best of all Communist outfits, but it was excellently suited for operations in the highlands because two of its three infantry regiments, the 176th and the 174th, were recruited from among tribesmen who spoke the same language as the inhabitants of the T'ai [Thai] highlands" (Fall, *Hell in a Very Small Place*, p. 39). Note: the word "Thai," according to Fall, was often spelled "T'ai" in French documents in order to avoid confusion with neighboring Thailand (Siam) (Fall, *The Two Viet-Nams*, p. 472).

23. Roy, *The Battle of Dienbienphu*, pp. 44–45; Bernard B. Fall, *Street Without Joy*, 4th ed., rev., pp. 315–16; and Joseph Laniel, *Le Drame Indochinois: De Dien-Bien-Phu au Pari de Genève*, pp. 35–37. Luang Prabang was the royal residence town of Laos while the more secure Vientiane was the administrative capital. See map 2.

24. Roy gives the lowest casualty figures of any source, "ten men had been killed, . . . ten seriously wounded, and twenty-one slightly wounded, eleven of them in landings" (Roy, *The Battle of Dienbienphu*, p. 43). However, he gives this information while the fighting was still in progress. Fall lists "11 dead and 52 wounded" at the conclusion of the battle (Fall, *Hell in a Very Small Place*, p. 14). *Newsweek* reports the highest total casualties at "26 dead and 47 wounded for the victorious French and Vietnamese" (*Newsweek*, Dec. 14, 1953, p. 40). For deaths alone the largest figure is given by Major Bigeard, who writes: "The combat lasted all day, with forty men killed on our side" (Maclear, *The Ten Thousand Day War*, p. 30).

25. Fall says that "ninety dead in full uniform were found on the battlefield" but adds that "subsequent discovery of graves hurriedly dug at the edge of the valley indicated that Communist losses might have been greater" (Fall, *Hell in a Very Small Place*, p. 15). According to Roy, "the Vietminh had left ninety-six dead" (Roy, *The Battle of Dienbienphu*, p. 44). *Newsweek* lists "97 known dead and an estimated 350 wounded for the Vietminh" (*Newsweek*, Dec. 14, 1953, p. 40). Finally, *Time* reports that "the French said they killed more than a hundred of the enemy" (*Time*, Nov. 30, 1953, p. 42).

2. Digging In .

1. Fall, *Hell in a Very Small Place*, p. 20. Fall contends that the "uniformly overstated figures" in the headlines "indicated that French official sources had deliberately provided the press with exaggerated statistics" (ibid.).

2. *New York Times*, Nov. 21, 1953, p. 3. The actual distance between Hanoi and Dien Bien Phu was 187 miles rather than the 125 miles reported by the United Press.

3. Ibid.

4. Ibid.

5. The abbreviation "1st BEP" stood for 1er Bataillon Étranger de Parachutistes (1st Foreign Legion Parachute Battalion). It had a total of 653 paratroopers, including 336 Vietnamese.

6. The command organ was known as "EDAP," an abbreviation for Elément Divisionnaire Aéroporte (Airborne Division Command Element).

7. U.S., Department of State, *Foreign Relations of the United States, 1952–1954,* vol. 13 (Indochina), pt. 1, p. 881. The number at the beginning of the cable referred to the total number of messages that the Saigon embassy had sent to the State Department during 1953.

8. *New York Herald Tribune,* Nov. 22, 1953, p. 2.

9. A *maquis* is a hiding place for guerrilla fighters.

10. Roy, *The Battle of Dienbienphu,* p. 48; Navarre, *Agonie de l'Indochine, 1953–1954* p. 198, n. 2. According to Navarre, Cogny amplified on this statement the next day by saying: "If the retrenched camp of Na-San had been put on rollers, I would have transported it to Dien Bien Phu as soon as I took command five months ago" (Navarre, ibid.).

Na-San, located seventy miles to the east of Dien Bien Phu and about midway between Dien Bien Phu and the Red River Delta (see map 2), was occupied by the French in October 1952 in response to a Viet-Minh invasion of the Thai Highlands. Navarre's predecessor as commander in chief, Gen. Raoul Salan, hastily transformed Na-San into a fortified camp that became the center of French resistance. In late November 1952 the Viet-Minh assailed the camp twice but the garrison beat back both attacks and the communists suffered an estimated seven thousand casualties, including one thousand dead. Na-San was successfully evacuated by the French on August 12, 1953. The type of entrenched camp that was established at Na-San was what the French called a *base aero-terrestre*—an "air-land base"—or, in American military parlance, an "airhead." It involved a strongly defended position that was resupplied by transport aircraft and supported, in case of direct enemy attack, by combat aircraft.

11. *New York Herald Tribune,* Nov. 22, 1953, p. 2.

12. Ibid.

13. Ibid.

14. Ibid. Roy describes the parachutes as looking like "a huge wash spread out" (Roy, *The Battle of Dienbienphu,* p. 47).

15. *New York Herald Tribune,* Nov. 22, 1953, p. 2.

16. Fall compares these early days of the operation to "a vast Boy Scout jamboree" (Fall, *Hell in a Very Small Place,* p. 53).

17. Roy, *The Battle of Dienbienphu,* pp. 50–51.

18. *Washington Post,* Nov. 23, 1953, p. 4. The "sweeping" action south of Lai Chau by the Thai partisans and other loyal troops, which the AP reported, may, in fact, have been part of a reassignment of forces from this French airhead. The French commander at Lai Chau, Lieutenant Colonel Trancart, ordered the withdrawal to Dien Bien Phu of the 1st Thai Partisan Mobile Group (Groupement Mobile de Partisans T'ai, or GMPT 1) on November

13, 1953. Fall gives the following account of that maneuver: "The withdrawal of the 700 men through terrain which they knew well did not at first present any special problems. However, roving units of [Viet-Minh] Regiment No. 148 finally caught up with them when they were two days' march away from Dien Bien Phu [about November 21], and the last leg of their march became a continuous battle against well-laid Communist ambushes. These had to be broken up with mortar fire and continuous counterattacks" (Fall, *Hell in a Very Small Place*, pp. 19–20).

19. *Washington Post*, Nov. 23, 1953 p.4.
20. *Times* (London), Nov. 23, 1953, p. 6.

3. Main Front: The Northwest

1. Navarre makes the following brief reference to this operation: "On November 22 the connection was made with Laichau" (Henri Navarre, *Agonie de l'Indochine* 1935–1954, [Paris: Librairie Plon, 1956] p. 201).

2. Various scholars on Viet-Nam have written about the racial divisions that have historically existed between the Vietnamese and the different ethnic minority groups of that country. Joseph Buttinger writes: "The contrast between the low and mountainous parts of Vietnam is underlined . . . by the racial and cultural differences of the people in the higher regions from those in the plains. The thinly spread mountain population consists almost exclusively of the various ethnic minorities, while the Vietnamese themselves, ever since their existence was first recorded by Chinese historians over two thousand years ago, have always crowded the valleys and deltas and refused to settle in higher altitudes" (Joseph Buttinger, *The Smaller Dragon: A Political History of Vietnam*, p. 26). Such ethnic territoriality had political ramifications since, as Bernard Fall points out, "in the highlands, the fierce Thai, Muong, and Tho tribes tolerated Vietnamese overlordship with about as much good grace as the latter tolerated their own submission to the Chinese . . . and Vietnamese annals are full of mountaineer uprisings." (Fall, *The Two Viet-Nams*, p. 16). Bringing the story more up to date, William Simcock writes:

Lai Chau was then [1953] the capital of the Thais, a large minority group of distant Chinese origin who were no longer Chinese nor yet Viet-Namese. They are remotely akin to the Siamese or Thailanders. They have their own speech, script and culture. Their domain, known as the Thai Bac country, was geographically included within the boundaries of Tonkin, [in northern] Viet-Nam but as a people they had remained apart. This was as much due to the nature of the terrain, the lack of communications and the primitive self-sustaining village level of economy as to their different culture and language, and the tradional concept of close-knit family and village associations.

The Thai Bac country was, in fact, a primitive backwater which had little to offer to the Viet-Minh at the time and which had therefore been left uncontested to the small number of French troops who were stationed within it. Now, however, [in late November 1953] . . . the Viet Minh were moving into it. (Simcock, "Dien Bien Phu: Yesterday's Battlefield," p. 40)

3. The Fairchild C-119 "Flying Boxcar" could carry an 11,500 pound payload for 1,000 miles, at a maximum speed of 296 miles per hour. The use of a U.S. C-119 transport aircraft in this bulldozer drop involved an ongoing support program for the French effort in Indo-China by the U.S. Far Eastern Air Forces. This latest phase of the program was started on November 14, 1953 when five C-119s were sent to Cat-Bi Air Base in northern Viet-Nam, near Haiphong, in order to train French air crews for air drops. Most of the French personnel had an adequate knowledge of English and linguistic problems were negligible. However, this was the first known attempt to drop a bulldozer from a Flying Boxcar and the failure may have been due to an error by the French crews in the conversion of American measures of weight.

4. National Archives, Washington, D. C., Civil Reference Branch, Record Group 59, General Records of the Department of State, Indochina, 1950–1954, Decimal File 751G.00/8–151–751G.00/12–3153, Box 3675, Hanoi Consulate telegram 310 from Paul J. Sturm to the Secretary of State, Nov. 23, 1953.

5. See map 3 for the geographic references in Shaughnessey's report.

6. The abbreviation FTVN stood for Forces Terrestres du Nord Viet-Nam, which was the Ground Forces Command of North Viet-Nam, headed by General Cogny.

7. The abbreviation EMIFT was the designation for Navarre's staff. It stood for État-Major Interarmées et Forces Terrestres (Joint and Ground Forces General Staff). The abbreviation G-2 was part of the U.S. Army's nomenclature. It stood for Intelligence Division.

8. The abbreviation RP 41 stood for Provincial Route 41. It was a paved road that connected Dien Bien Phu with the Red River Delta and was accessible to sturdy automobiles during the dry season.

9. Two other sources put the origin of this Viet-Minh action at more than two weeks earlier. Navarre writes: "In the last days of October, we learned successively that our Thai country underground resistance forces were being attacked by two regular [Viet-Minh] regiments, and that Division 316, leaving the surroundings of the Delta, was marching on Laichau" (Navarre, *Agonie de l'Indochine*, p. 188). Navarre's account is supported by Devillers and Lacouture. The 316th Division, they write, "left its bases in Thanh Hoa province on October 27 and moved northwest toward the highlands along Provincial Route 41" (Devillers and Lacouture, *End of a War*, p. 44).

10. National Archives, Washington, D. C., Military Reference Branch, Record Group 218, U.S. Joint Chiefs of Staff, Geographic File, 1951–1953, Box 7, Folder: "CCS 092 Asia (6–25-48) Sec. 50," message from USARMA, Saigon, Vietnam to CSUSA, Washington, D. C., Nov. 23, 1953.

11. Navarre's account appears to support Fall's version of the 1st BPC's arrival at Dien Bien Phu on November 20 (see chapter 1, n. 20). In his memoirs, Navarre sums up Operation Castor as follows: "On November 20, as anticipated, an airborne group of three battalions jumped on Dien Bien Phu and seized it, surmounting a lively resistance, opposed by a Vietminh regional battalion that was completely surprised. It was joined, on the 21st and the 22nd, by three other battalions and the artillery group. . . . The operation was remarkably manned and executed by General Gilles" (Navarre, *Agonie de l'Indochine*, p. 201).

12. According to Fall, "the valley [of Dien Bien Phu] grew almost 2,000 tons of rice a year" (Fall, *Hell in a Very Small Place*, p. 9). Navarre writes of the valley: "Its production of rice was very excessive and able to assure, over several months, the maintenance of 20,000 to 25,000 men" (Navarre, *Agonie de l'Indochine*, p. 194).

13. Operation Mouette was called off on November 8, 1953, after having lasted for twenty-four days.

14. Nha Trang was located on the coast of southern Viet-Nam, northeast of Saigon. Tourane (later called Da Nang) was located on the coast of central Viet-Nam, south of Hue. See map 7.

15. Roy, *The Battle of Dienbienphu*, pp. 55–56. On July 17, 1953 three French paratroop battalions attacked Lang Son, located in the communist-held territory of northeastern Viet-Nam, near the Chinese border (see map 5). "Operation Hirondelle," as this action was called, resulted in the destruction of large Viet-Minh stocks of equipment, weapons, ammunition, and fuel, after which the paratroopers returned safely to the Red River Delta.

16. Navarre had not forgotten Cogny's remarks when he wrote his memoirs. Citing numerous "declarations that he [Cogny] made to the press . . . without being obligated to do so," Navarre says that he had "many times" asked Cogny "to refrain from doing this" (Navarre, *Agonie de l'Indochine*, pp. 198–99, n. 2). He adds: "In assuming this attitude General Cogny infringed very uselessly on the traditions of honor in the Army because, since it was a question of decisions at my echelon, his responsibility had been covered up because of the fact that I had made them [the decisions], even if he had been to a great extent the inspiration for them" (ibid., pp. 198–99).

17. The word "hedgehog" is frequently used in discussing the type of entrenched camps that the French had constructed at Lai Chau and Na-San. Fall refers to such air-land bases as "strongly defended hedgehog positions" (Fall, *Hell in a Very Small Place*, p. 31). The hedgehog is a small insect-eating mammal of Europe, with a shaggy coat and sharp spines on the back which bristle and form a hedgelike defense when the animal curls up. A "hedgehog defense," in military terms, refers to a method of defensive warfare characterized by the setting up of fortified strongpoints offering resistance on all sides, thus causing trouble to the enemy even after they have been bypassed. This was used especially by the Soviet Army during the German invasion of World War II.

18. *Time*, Nov. 30, 1953, p. 42.

19. *Times* (London), Nov. 23, 1953, p. 6.

20. Fall, *Hell in a Very Small Place*, pp. 20–21. Fall confirms the importance of the opium connection to the Viet-Minh. He writes: "The valley [of Dien Bien Phu] had long been known as one of the most important opium collection and processing centers in all Indochina. Raw opium of a value of more than 10 million piasters (then about $1 million) was collected there every year, and the Viet-Minh considered opium an important medium for illegal purchase of American weapons and European medical drugs on the black markets of Bangkok and Hong Kong" (ibid., p. 9).

21. Ibid., p. 20.

22. *Time*, Nov. 30, 1953, p. 42.

23. Devillers and Lacouture write: "At the end of September [1953] the Politburo of the Lao Dong party met under Ho's [Ho Chi Minh's] chairmanship, and examined [General] Giap's operational plans for the winter of 1953–54. From November 19 to 23, the central military committee worked out its plan of operations with the senior commanders in the light of the political bureau's instructions" (Devillers and Lacouture, *End of a War*, p. 46).

24. By "our initiative" and "our offensive," Giap was referring to the movement of the 316th Division toward the Thai Highlands.

25. Gareth Porter, ed., *Vietnam: The Definitive Documentation of Human Decisions*, vol. 1, p. 483.

26. Ibid. Yves Gras offers the following insight on how Viet-Minh military strategy evolved during the fall of 1953:

> The necessity to renounce its offensive against the [Red River] delta [because of Operation Mouette] did not take the Viet-Minh by surprise. Its logistical constraints obliged it to prepare its operations far in advance. When the Central Committee of [the] Lao Dong [party] had met at the end of September in order to fix the objectives for the 1953–1954 campaign, Giap had proposed to it two different plans, one aimed against the delta and the other [against] Laos. The logistical preparations had been made from these two hypotheses. The choice of the plan that would finally be engaged could therefore be reserved until the last moment. The Viet-Minh thus held two irons in the fire.
>
> During "Operation Mouette," Giap had kept himself from engaging several divisions of the [Viet-Minh] battle corps. . . . He let the 320th Division, whose intervention was not foreseen in the upper region [of Indo-China], confront alone the French penetration, forbidding even the 304th [Division], which was in the vicinity, to assist it. His battle corps remained intact and available to enter the campaign when, at the end of October, he modified his plans [see n. 9 above]. Learning no doubt of the risk of the "military adventure" that would be a decisive battle in the interior of the delta, where important [French] reinforcements had arrived, he brought the principal effort of the winter campaign to the northwest. (Yves Gras, *Histoire de la Guerre d'Indochine*, pp. 519–20)

4. Portents

1. The Viet-Minh used a political code, an operational code, and a supplies code. The French Command possessed the supplies code and was, therefore, capable of deciphering orders concerning enemy personnel and material. Numerous French listening posts constantly intercepted such orders and transmitted them to Saigon and Hanoi for decoding.

2. The successful drop of the second bulldozer was carried out in two sorties; the blade, which weighed 5,000 pounds, was dropped separately. According to Roy, the bulldozer "rested on a metal platform widened by a guard of planks which struck [sic] out like arms and prevented it from tipping over. Lead weights had lowered its center of gravity" (Roy, *The Battle of Dienbienphu*, p. 54). Col. Maurice F. Casey, commander of the U.S. 483rd Troop Carrier Wing (Medium) of the 315th Air Division (CC), noted that this was the heaviest single item ever dropped in the Far East.

   Subsequently, on November 27, seven French crews, four of which had been replaced at Haiphong because of the language barrier, were transported to Clark Air Base in the Philippines with their American instructors. Each crew was given approximately fourteen hours of transition training in heavy drops and four drops were made at Dien Bien Phu on December 3.

3. In reporting this story, the United Press put the enemy position at "fifty miles east of Dienbienphu and seventy-five miles west of Hanoi," a total distance of only 125 miles (*New York Herald Tribune*, Nov. 27, 1953, p. 5). As in its initial dispatch on Operation Castor (see chapter 2, n. 2), the UP was more than sixty miles short of the actual distance of 187 miles between the two points.

4. *Atlanta Constitution*, Nov. 28, 1953, p. 2.

5. Ibid.

6. Ibid.

7. This referred to Divisions 308 and 316 in northern Viet-Nam and to Divisions 304 and 325 in central Viet-Nam. Along with his memorandum, Bonsal sent a map of northern and north-central Indo-China that showed the dispositions of the various Viet-Minh divisions. See map 4.

8. Division 308 was moving from north of the perimeter and Division 316 and elements of Division 304 were moving, respectively, from west and southwest of the perimeter.

9. National Archives, Washington, D. C., Civil Reference Branch, Record Group 59, General Records of the Department of State, Indochina, 1950–1954, Decimal File 751G.00/8-151—751G.00/12-3153, Box 3675, memorandum from Philip W. Bonsal to Walter S. Robertson, Nov. 27, 1953. Bonsal's memorandum to Robertson was drafted by Robert E. Hoey, the State Department's officer in charge of Vietnam-Laos-Cambodia affairs in the Office of Philippine and Southeast Asian Affairs (U.S., Department of State, *Foreign Relations of the United States, 1952–1954*, vol. 13 [Indochina], pt. 1, p. 886, n. 1).

5. Command Decision

1. See map 5. The relevant information in the map's key reads: "Actions envisaged by us [generals Navarre and Cogny] for cutting Vietminh communications" (Navarre, *Agonie de l'Indochine*, p. 207).

2. Ibid., p. 167, n. 1; Fall, *Hell in a Very Small Place*, p. 43. Fall contends that Cogny "never contradicted" Navarre's memoirs concerning the accuracy of this information.

3. Both Navarre and Fall confirm that a third operation was considered but they present totally different descriptions of it. In Navarre's recollection, it was merely a variant form of the second operation:

    We then considered doing it [the attack against Thai Nguyen] under the form of a "go and return" of two or three weeks, during which we would almost entirely dismantle the Delta. The efficacy of this would be very limited, both in space (because facilities of avoidance existed for the Vietminh) and in time (because it was not possible to prolong "the impasse" in the Delta). Furthermore, during the only period when it would be feasible, important forces of the Vietminh battle corps would still be stationed in the surroundings of the Delta and would be able to intervene in the Thai Nguyen region, making success very problematical. (Navarre, *Agonie de l'Indochine*, pp. 167–68.)

    In any event, argues Navarre, the first plan that was considered—against Yen Bay—was "the only really effective one" (ibid., p. 167). In Fall's description, the operation was of a much lower magnitude and not necessarily aimed against Thai Nguyen. He writes: "The third alternative consisted of a smaller-scale paratroop operation along the lines of Dien Bien Phu itself, but close enough to the French battle line in the Red River Delta for the paratroops to be rescued within a few days by an armored battle group. This operation would be pretty much a copy of Operation 'Swallow' (Hirondelle) undertaken by the French against Lang Son in July, 1953" (Fall, *Hell in a Very Small Place*, pp. 41–42).

4. French thinking about the limitations on the effective use of heavy support by the Viet-Minh was shared by the United States. See appendix A for excerpts from a U.S. National Intelligence Estimate (NIE) of June 4, 1953 on "Probable Developments in Indochina Through Mid-1954" (U.S., Department of State, *Foreign Relations of the United States, 1952–1954*, vol. 13 [Indochina], pt. 1, pp. 592, 600). Participating with the Central Intelligence Agency (CIA) in the preparation of this NIE were the following member organizations of the Intelligence Advisory Committee: the intelligence organizations of the Department of State, the army, the navy, the air force, and the joint staff, which was the planning group that served the Joint Chiefs of Staff.

5. According to Roy, "wagered" was the exact word that Navarre used (Roy, *The Battle of Dienbienphu*, pp. 60–61).

6. *U.S. News & World Report*, Dec. 4, 1953, pp. 22–23.

7. Roy, *The Battle of Dienbienphu,* p. 62. Navarre gives this account of why de Castries was chosen to replace Gilles:

It is good, I believe, to indicate here the actual reasons for this change of command, about which many erroneous and suggestive commentaries have been made.

General Gilles usually commanded all of the parachute troops [paratroopers] of Indochina. Responsible for their training and for the formation of new units that were anticipated in the [military] plan, he was not able, without great inconvenience, to be kept from his command.

On the suggestion of General Cogny, I designated Colonel de Castries for the replacement. The choice was made the object of criticism, as an afterthought.

Why choose a horseman, it was said, when the command of a retrenched camp would normally go to an infantryman? Because neither General Cogny nor I had the "button spirit" [placing importance on military decorations] and Colonel de Castries seemed to the two of us to be the best man to do the job that we expected from the defender of Dien Bien Phu. We had designated him, therefore, neither "because he was horseman" nor "although he was a horseman."

Why, it was also asked, give a command to a colonel that, normally, would have fallen on a general? Because, in Indochina, to make up for a very important shortage, it was normal for a colonel to exercise the command of a general—and also because General Cogny and I did not have the fetishism of decorations [placing importance on military insignia] any more than the spirit of the button.

Be that as it may, I remain convinced that none of those whom I could have designated—had he been a general and an infantryman—would have done better than Colonel de Castries. (Navarre, *Agonie de l'Indochine,* pp. 204–5).

According to Roy, Cogny's selection of de Castries involved more than purely military considerations. He writes:

Cogny had another reason to be pleased at seeing Castries shipped off to Dienbienphu. He did not get along well with the colonel, who had just arrived from Amiens [France] to take command of the southern zone of the delta and who had insisted on being received with ten white-gloved motorcyclists and a solemn Mass. Castries never missed a chance of hinting to his new chief that he was in the way. His [de Castries's] posting to Dienbienphu would solve everything. In point of fact, it would be Vanuxem who would take Castries's place. . . . (Roy, *The Battle of Dienbienphu,* pp. 62–63).

Furthermore, Fall casts doubt on Navarre's assertion (above) that he and Cogny considered de Castries to be "the best man to do the job." Writes Fall: "Several senior colonels in Indochina had been offered the Dien Bien Phu command but chose to turn down the offer. At least one of them stated frankly that he felt that the defense of Dien Bien Phu would be an open invitation to disaster" (Fall, *Hell in a Very Small Place*, p. 54). In turn, when Navarre wrote his autobiography, *Le Temps des Vérités* (in which the chapters on Indo-China were largely condensed from *Agonie de l'Indochine*), he refuted this account of de Castries's selection: "It has been written that several generals and colonels had been sounded out before Colonel de Castries and had refused. This is false" (Henri Navarre, *Le Temps des Vérités*, p. 325, n. 1).

8. Navarre makes the following observations in his memoirs:

> . . . the basin of Dien Bien Phu was the largest of the whole Upper region [of Indo-China]. The bottom was a genuine plain, 16 kilometers [9.9 miles] by 9 kilometers [5.6 miles], level, open and allowing the employment of armor in excellent conditions.
>
> The large crests that dominated it were at a distance of of 10 to 12 kilometers [6.2 miles to 7.4 miles] from the airfield which would establish the retrenched camp. This distance was superior to the useful range of possible opposing artillery. The latter was only able, therefore, to take a position on the descending slopes toward the interior of the basin. It would be likewise concerning . . . [an enemy effort] that intended to interdict the air space over the site of the airport. In the opinion of all the artillerymen, it was impossible [to do this], because the [enemy] batteries would be seen by [French] observatories in the basin, either during their emplacement, or when they were fired. They would therefore be "silenced" by our anti-battery artillery and by our aviation bombardment. (Navarre, *Agonie de l'Indochine*, pp. 195–96).

9. Fall, *Hell in a Very Small Place*, p. 40. The decision to evacuate Lai Chau had been made well before the occupation of Dien Bien Phu and was, in fact, linked with Operation Castor. Fall explains:

> Late in 1953 it became obvious that even a modest effort on the part of the Viet-Minh forces could result in military disaster at Lai Chau, a military setback that could be complicated by the political consequences of losing the last government seat in the mountain areas. It was this political consideration which had weighed heavily in the French decision to reoccupy another stronghold in the T'ai [Thai] tribal zone. On November 4, 1953, it was decided to evacuate Lai Chau and to transfer the government of the T'ai Federation to the new airhead at Dien Bien Phu. The French commander at Lai Chau, Lieutenant Colonel Trancart, was informed of the planned evacuation of Lai Chau (dubbed Operation "Pollux") on November 13. . . .
>
> On the following day, November 14, Gen. Navarre issued final operational instructions (known in French military parlance as IPS, or "personal and secret instructions") to the regional commanders who would have to cooperate with one another in the matter of the Dien Bien Phu operation. . . .
>
> In the IPS of November 14, Navarre . . . outlined the political and strategic importance of maintaining inside the T'ai tribal territory a

French position which would cover Laos as well. The operation, set for November 20, provided for the creation of an airhead at Dien Bien Phu that would establish a land link with French forces in northern Laos and would provide support for Lai Chau until its eventual evacuation. The three directives of November 14 contained a special appendix dealing with political and administrative problems, since the evacuation of Lai Chau implied the transfer of the whole T'ai Tribal Federation's administration to Dien Bien Phu. (Ibid., pp. 19, 38).

The connection between the occupation of Dien Bien Phu and the evacuation of Lai Chau was embodied in the very names that were given to these two operations. Writes Fall: "Some sources have erroneously translated the code name 'Castor' into the English equivalent 'Beaver' [see chapter 3 for Sturm's cable to the State Department of November 23]. This is an error. As the second code name 'Pollux' clearly indicates, the planners meant to refer to the twin brothers of Greek mythology, Castor and Pollux, to emphasize the twin aspect of the landing at Dien Bien Phu and the evacuation of Lai Chau" (ibid., p. 467, n. 14).

Lieutenant Colonel Trancart's order to withdraw the 1st Thai Partisan Mobile Group (GMPT 1) from Lai Chau to Dien Bien Phu was a preliminary phase of "Operation Pollux" (see chapter 2, n. 18). When Trancart was first informed of Pollux on November 13, according to Fall, "he was ordered at the same time to 'repress' any rumors about the fact that this was going to take place" (Fall, *Hell in a Very Small Place*, p. 37). This attempt to squelch leaks, along with the "personal and secret" nature of General Navarre's directives of November 14, indicates a firm determination to maintain tight security on Operation Pollux. That may account for why the commander in chief initially withheld mention of Pollux from everyone, including his own government. In his telegram to Marc Jacquet on November 20 (see chapter 1), in his remarks to Ambassador Heath on the same day (see chapter 2), and during his visit with General Bull on November 23 (see chapter 3), Navarre spoke only of Operation Castor.

10. Fall, *Hell in a Very Small Place*, p. 40.

11. Ibid. Muong Khoua was located in northern Laos, approximately thirty-seven miles southwest of Dien Bien Phu. Navarre referred to this link-up operation in his telegram to the French government of November 20.

12. Numerous authors have discussed both de Castries's pedigree and his predilections. Fall writes:

> Colonel Christian Marie Ferdinand de la Croix de Castries, born in Paris in 1902, looked every inch the blue-blooded aristocrat he was. As his official biography showed (the French Army's public information office had soon realized how much this impressed American journalists) the de Castries' ancestors had served France with the sword since the Crusades. . . .
>
> . . . A daredevil pilot since 1921, holder of two world championships for horseback riding (the high jump in 1933 and the broad jump in

1935), the young nobleman with the profile of a Roman emperor was irresistable to women. His close brushes with the outraged husbands of his female conquests were countless. A reckless gambler, he was also debt-ridden. (Fall, *Hell in a Very Small Place*, pp. 54–55).

Roy says the following about de Castries:

... [he] typified the aristocratic officer whose character, name, war record and legend could lead, despite all obstacles, to the highest posts in the army.... A remarkable horseman, he had been world champion for the high jump in 1933 with Vol-au-Vent, and for the long jump, two years later, with Tenace. His file was stuffed with youthful indiscretions and gambling debts. A horse to ride, an enemy to kill, a woman in his bed—that could have been his motto. An attractive motto—if you didn't look at it too closely. He was a man of another age whom wars, women and horses linked to our own (Roy, *The Battle of Dienbienphu*, pp. 64–65).

Dean Brelis offers the following anecdote about de Castries: "Colonel de Castries was a romantic. He was a proud cavalry officer, and he still talked of how a French cavalry officer won his spurs by going through a decathlon of a final examination in the field that tested his horsemanship, [and] his swordsmanship. One of the more delightful aspects of the obstacle course was that he had to drink a magnum of champagne and service a well-experienced prostitute to her satisfaction, all in a half hour's time" (Dean Brelis, *The Face of South Vietnam*, p. 13).

13. Roy, *The Battle of Dienbienphu*, p. 64.
14. National Archives, Washington, D. C., Military Reference Branch, Record Group 218, U.S. Joint Chiefs of Staff, Geographic File, 1951–1953, 092 Asia (6-25-48), Sections 45–51, Box 7, message from USARMLO, Singapore to DEPTAR, Washington, D.C. for ACofSG2, and CNO, Department of the Navy, Washington, D.C., Nov. 30, 1953.

6. First Sortie

1. Both Fall and Burchett say that the distance between Dien Bien Phu and Tuan Giao was fifty miles (Fall, *Hell in a Very Small Place*, p. 59; Burchett, *The Furtive War*, p. 133). The incredibly steep mountains that separated these two points may have made the actual journey fifty miles but a glance at a map (see map 3) shows the straight-line distance to be about half that. Donald Lancaster confirms this, saying that Tuan Giao was "situated twenty-five miles from Dien Bien Phu" (Donald Lancaster, *The Emancipation of French Indochina*, p. 287, n. 48).
2. The guerrilla units were known officially as Groupements de Commandos Mixtes Aéroportés (Composite Airborne Commando Groups) or GCMA. (The French word *mixte*, in military parlance, may stand for "joint," "miscellaneous," "provisional," "composite," etc.) Joseph Buttinger notes that these units had been in operation since late 1951 (Joseph Buttinger, *Vietnam: A*

Dragon Embattled, vol. 2, p. 1069, n. 109). According to Edgar O'Ballance, however, they "had languished for lack of official, high-level enthusiasm" (Edgar O'Ballance, *The Indo-China War, 1945–1954: A Study in Guerrilla Warfare,* p. 201). George K. Tanham agrees and sees this French oversight as a misplaced opportunity. He explains:

> . . . [A] serious obstacle to Viet[-Minh] progress was created by minority groups, most of whom lived in the mountainous areas. . . . these groups regarded the Vietminh as a Vietnamese government, and thus as one to be feared and distrusted [see chapter 3, n. 2]. . . . However, the French were slow to exploit their advantage in this respect. It was not until 1953 that they organized guerrilla groups in the mountains to strike at Vietminh lines of communication. By that time, their dilatory tactics over the granting of independence [to the Associated States] and their inability to protect the minorities had lost them much of the latter's support. (Tanham, *Communist Revolutionary Warfare: From the Vietminh to the Vietcong,* pp. 53–54).

The various GCMA maquis groups had a total force of about 15,000 in operation behind communist lines. The commandos were considered too weak to influence the outcome of any particular operation but they were useful for long-range reconnaissance and it was said that some of the groups had even penetrated into Communist China. The most significant action by such a unit involved the parachuting of forty Meo tribesmen near Lao Kay in northern Viet-Nam on October 4, 1953 in an unsuccessful attempt to destroy Viet-Minh communications lines at a vital point of entry on the Sino-Vietnamese border (see map 5).

The relationship between the guerrilla units and the French Central Intelligence services was analogous to that between the American Special Forces and the U.S. Central Intelligence Agency (CIA) in South Viet-Nam in the mid-1960s. In the introduction to Maj. Roger Trinquier's book, *Modern Warfare: A French View of Counterinsurgency,* Fall writes of the guerrilla commander:

> By mid-1951, Major Trinquier received command of all behind-the-lines operations in Indochina. . . .
>
> By late 1953, almost 20,000 men were under his command—probably the largest unit ever commanded by an army major—and engaged in operations covering several thousand square miles of enemy territory. Native tribesmen were flocking to his maquis in greater numbers than could be armed and trained. (Trinquier, *Modern Warfare,* p. xiii).

Writing of the French commando units in *Hell in a Very Small Place,* Fall observes: "Their commander, Major Roger Trinquier, had a great deal more authority than his lowly military rank would indicate, since he and his free-wheeling subordinates could operate largely on their own. . . . The French members of the GCMA's were hand-picked [for these missions] . . . and usually spoke one or more of the mountain dialects perfectly. They were also capable of getting along with a minimum of western conveniences for several months, if not years, on end" (Fall, *Hell in a Very Small Place*, p. 58). In December 1953 the name of the commando units was changed from GCMA to Groupements Mixtes d'Intervention (Composite Intervention Groups), or GMI, when their mission was extended beyond airborne commando operations.

3. Can Tho was located in the Mekong Delta, southwest of Saigon. See map 7.
4. This strategic plan, known widely in the summer and fall of 1953 as the "Navarre Plan," is described in great detail by Navarre in his memoirs:

I come now to the operational part of the plan. . . . The prospects [at the time of Navarre's arrival in Indo-China as commander in chief in May 1953] . . . can be summed up as follows.

In the near-term, that is to say before October–November [1953], it was not very probable that the Viet-Minh would begin very important operations. They would be impeded by the rainy season that had already begun, and by the fatigue of their troops who, although not having undergone very severe defeats in the course of the spring [1953] campaign, had led, during long months, hard operations in a very difficult terrain (the Upper Tonkin region and Upper Laos). Therefore, we would probably be allowed a certain delay.

For a three or four month term, that is to say in the autumn [of 1953] or in the beginning of [the] winter [of 1953–54], it was, on the other hand, anticipated that the enemy would launch an offensive of very great breadth, which would extend more or less unceasingly until the end of May 1954, that is to say until the next rainy season. By this offensive, he would endeavor to obtain, if not a definitive decision, at least the conquest of essential military and political bases, permitting him, [by] the next year or two years later, to obtain this [definitive] decision. We would suffer this shock with [military] means [that were] very inferior to those of the enemy.

In a distant future, that is to say a term of about two years, on the condition that the productiveness of mobile forces would be able to be reversed to our favor by the constitution of our battle Corps, it would be possible for us, in turn, to take the offensive.

The chief idea of the whole operational plan must therefore be the following:

During the 1953–1954 campaign, considered the dangerous point, try to *avoid a general battle* with the enemy battle corps and *constitute our battle corps.*

During the 1954–1955 campaign, on the other hand, *seek a general battle,* once our battle corps had a sufficient mass and training.

This idea was the basis of the plan that General Salan [Navarre's predecessor] had left to me as a heritage. It became my own.

Another essential notion was the separation of the Indochinese theater of operations into two distinct spaces, respectively situated to the north and south of the 18th parallel. (At the altitude of the 18th parallel, there exists a barrier, constituted by the Door of Annam [central Viet-Nam], extending to the west by a limestone chain ending at the Mekong [River] near Thakek [in west-central Laos near the border with Thailand]. It is the only natural frontier between northern and southern Indo-China. . . .) In the northern region, the Viet-Minh were able to concentrate much larger mobile forces than ours, because nearly the whole of his battle corps was located there. In the southern region, on the other hand, with the exception of the Lien-Khu V [L.K.V. or Viet-Minh Fifth Interzone] where the equivalent of a very large regular division was able to emerge at any moment [in the area between Nha Trang and Tourane], the Viet-Minh had scarcely any regional forces.

Consequently, if the strategic offensive was not possible for us in the north, for the moment, because of the inferiority of our forces, it was possible in the south, where we were able to achieve a certain superiority of means. . . .

. . . These considerations made me draw up the following plan of operations, very close to the one proposed by General Salan in his study of May 1953.

(1) During the 1953–1954 campaign, retain a strategically defensive attitude to the north of the 18th parallel, and seek to avoid a general battle there. On the other hand, take the offensive, as soon as possible, to the south of the 18th parallel, in order to cleanse central and southern Indo-China and recover some resources there. In particular, try to liquidate the L.K.V.

(2) Once obtaining superiority in mobile divisions, that is to say starting with the autumn of 1954, take the offensive to the north of the Door of Annam [the 18th parallel], with the aim of creating a military situation that would permit a political solution to the conflict.

This plan was established in terms of the potential enemy functions, such as they were known to us, and such as this [enemy] increase had been forecast.

Two formal reservations had been made, to which the [French] Government's attention had been called (by a memorandum in July 1953 and by a presentation before the Committee of National Defense on July 24, 1953).

On the one hand, we could, as a result of the progress made by the enemy in the organization of his battle corps, undergo very serious reverses in the course of the 1953–1954 campaign.

Besides, the plan was only worthwhile to the extent that Chinese aid to the Viet-Minh remained at the present size. In the case of a massive increase of this aid, no plan had in fact been considered as possible. (Navarre, *Agonie de l'Indochine*, p. 43 and n. 2; p. 80; p. 81 and n. 1; p. 82 and n. 1).

This description of the Navarre Plan, as presented in Navarre's memoirs, is an essentially accurate portrayal of the commander in chief's military strategy as he, in fact, perceived it in the fall of 1953. This is shown from the record of a conversation that Navarre had with three American visitors on the day before he launched Operation Castor. At this meeting, Navarre outlined his battle plans for the coming year to Sen. H. Alexander Smith (Rep., N.J.), a member of the Senate Foreign Relations Committee; Dr. Francis Wilcox, the chief of staff for the committee; and Ambassador Donald Heath. Heath sent a report on this discussion to the State Department in Saigon embassy telegram 879 of November 19, 1953. The text of the telegram appears in appendix B (U.S. Department of State, *Foreign Relations of the United States, 1952–1954,* vol. 13 [Indochina], pt. 1, p. 876 and n. 1).

Senator Smith subsequently made the following observations about the Navarre Plan in his study mission report: "While we were in Indochina we studied at some length the Navarre plan. I am convinced that it is based on sound principles and holds considerable promise for the termination of hostilities in Indochina. French and Vietnamese leaders have agreed to go on the offensive and to prosecute the war more vigorously than they have in the past. If they carry out their present plans I believe the Communists can be defeated" (U.S. Congress, Senate Subcommittee on the Far East of the Committee on Foreign Relations, 83rd Congress, 2nd Session, *The Far East and South Asia: Report of Senator H. Alexander Smith, Chairman, Subcommittee on the Far East, Senate, Committee on Foreign Relations, on a Study Mission to the Far East,* p. 15).

5. See chapter 3 for Navarre's comments on this subject to General Bull on November 23.

6. This refers to the task force under the command of Colonel de Crèvecoeur.

7. Savannakhet was located in west-central Laos along the Mekong River border with Thailand. See Colonel Shaugnessy's report (chapter 3) and Philip Bonsal's memorandum (chapter 4) for previous discussions of this enemy threat by U.S. officials.

8. National Archives, Washington, D. C., Military Reference Branch, Record Group 218, U.S. Joint Chiefs of Staff, Geographic File, 1951–1953, 092 Asia (6–25–48), Sections 45–51, Box 7, report from Chief, MAAG to CINCPAC, Dec. 1, 1953.

9. The O'Daniel report made the following assessment of the operation: ". . . a limited offensive of approximately [three French divisions] . . . (Operation "Mouette") [was directed] south from the Delta against a concentration of two (2) Viet Minh divisions. . . . the French report that this operation, completed [on] 8 November, inflicted large casualties on the enemy and put the 320th Viet Minh division out of action for a prolonged period (about one-third of this Division was reported destroyed)" (U.S. Army Center of Military History, Washington, D. C., Historical Services Division, Historical Records Branch, U.S. Joint Military Mission to Indochina, "Progress Report on Military Situation in Indochina as of 19 November 1953," p. 2).

10. Participating with the Central Intelligence Agency (CIA) in the preparation of this National Intelligence Estimate were the following member organizations of the Intelligence Advisory Committee: the intelligence organizations of the Department of State, the army, the navy, and the joint staff.

11. The Eisenhower administration had originally planned to allocate $460 million in military assistance to the French Union forces in Indo-China during the 1953–1954 fiscal year. Of this sum, Congress appropriated $400 million. Following the presentation by the French of the Navarre Plan, the U.S. National Security Council decided on September 9, 1953, to grant an additional $385 million toward the implementation of this French military strategy. The "U.S.-French Supplementary Aid Agreement on Indochina" was signed in Paris on September 29, 1953, and a joint communiqué announcing this agreement was released the following day. See appendix C, for the text of that communiqué (U.S. Department of State, *Foreign Relations of the United States, 1952–1954,* vol. 13 [Indochina], pt. 1, p. 812; U.S., Department of State, *Department of State Bulletin,* Oct. 12, 1953, vol. 29, no. 746, pp. 486–87).

12. In a major address on Indo-China on July 3, 1953, one week after becoming prime minister of France, Joseph Laniel took note of the four-year-old agreements by which Viet-Nam, Laos, and Cambodia had associated themselves with France in the French Union (see chapter 1, n. 21) and went on to state that "France considers that there are grounds to perfect the independence and sovereignty of the Associated States of Indo-China." See appendix D, for the full text of this address (Cameron, ed., *Viet-Nam Crisis,* pp. 199–200; Porter, ed., *Vietnam,* pp. 451–52; and Peter V. Curl, ed., *Documents on American Foreign Relations, 1953,* pp. 347–48). As of November 1953 Laos was the only one of the three Associated States to have reached agreement with France. On October 22, 1953, the governments of Laos and France signed a treaty of association and several conventions that simultaneously reaffirmed the independence of Laos and its membership in the French Union. By contrast, neither Viet-Nam nor Cambodia had yet opened negotiations with France, owing in part to the internal political situations in both countries.

13. U.S., Department of State, *Foreign Relations of the United States, 1953–1954,* vol. 13 (Indochina), pt. 1, pp. 894–95.

14. U.S., Department of State, *Department of State Bulletin,* vol. 29, no. 755, Dec. 14, 1953, pp. 814, 816. The countries where Robertson claimed that communist attacks had been "decisively repelled" included the Philippines, Malaya, Burma, Indonesia, and Korea (ibid., p. 816).

15. National Archives, Washington, D. C., Military Reference Branch, Record Group 218, U.S. Joint Chiefs of Staff, Chairman's File, Admiral Radford, 1953–1957, 091 Indo China, Box 59, address by Admiral Radford to the USMA student conference, Dec. 2, 1953.

7. Commitment to Battle

1. Fall, *Hell in a Very Small Place,* p. 44; Georges Catroux, *Deux Actes du Drame Indochinois-Hanoi: Juin 1940; Dien Bien Phu: Mars-Mai 1954,* p. 155; Laniel, *Le Drame Indochinois,* p. 38; and Roy, *The Battle of Dienbienphu,* p. 66. See

chapter 1, n. 2 concerning the five air commands that the French used in Indo-China.

2. A sampan is a small, flat-bottomed boat that has traditionally been used in the harbors and rivers of China and Japan.

3. "Democratic Republic of Viet-Nam" (D.R.V.) was the official name used by the Viet-Minh opposition government to the Associated State of Viet-Nam.

4. U.S., Department of State, *Foreign Relations of the United States, 1952–1954*, vol. 13 (Indochina), pt. 1, p. 899.

5. In Heath's report of this conversation to the State Department, the message was garbled at the very point where he quoted Navarre's estimate of how many Viet-Minh troops were headed toward the northwest. It read: "[According to Navarre] . . . the equivalent of (garble) [parentheses in original] division was now moving into Thai country" (ibid., pp. 899–900). The use of the singular word "division," however, would indicate that the cable was meant to read "one division" or possibly "one reinforced division." This would square with both the formal appraisal of enemy strength that was contained in Navarre's directive of December 3 and with accounts of Navarre's thinking from all other sources (see previous text, this chapter).

6. The insertion of the word "minus" was an apparent reference to the fact that part of Viet-Minh Division 304 was known to be heading southward from the vicinity of Thanh Hoa toward Vinh. Cho Bo was located on the western rim of the Red River Delta, about midway between Hanoi and Moc Chau. See map 3.

7. The acronym "Cas" stands for Controlled American Source and refers to the United States Central Intelligence Agency (CIA) (letter from U.S., Dept. of the Army, Intelligence and Security Command, Ft. George G. Meade, Maryland, to the author, Oct. 20, 1994).

8. The words "now closed in" meant that lead elements of Division 316 were close to Tuan Giao. See map 3.

9. National Archives, Washington, D. C., Military Reference Branch, Record Group 319, Army Chief of Staff, ACSI Message File, Vietnam, 1953, Box 52, message from USARMA, Saigon, Vietnam to CSUSA, DeptAr, Washington, D.C. for G-2, Dec. 4, 1953.

8. Strongpoint Beatrice

1. "Strongpoint Beatrice" was the first of ten fortified positions that the French would eventually establish at Dien Bien Phu, each of which was given a woman's name. In addition to Beatrice, there were Gabrielle, Anne-Marie, Françoise, Isabelle, Dominique, Claudine, Huguette, Éliane, and Junon. There are differing accounts as to how the particular names of the strongpoints came to be chosen. Lancaster writes that the positions "had been named after ladies of whose company the garrison were deprived" (Lancaster, *The Emancipation of French Indochina*, p. 294). One of the strongpoints, however,

may have been named after a song. "Anne-Marie," according to Roy, "was the heroine of a German song that the [French Foreign] Legion used to sing as it marched along ('Anne-Marie, tell me where you are going? I'm going to town where the soldiers are . . . ')" (Roy, *The Battle of Dienbienphu*, p. 84). Fall offers the most original explanation. "It has been rumored," he writes, "that all the fortified positions of Dien Bien Phu had been given the names of Col. de Castries' mistresses. That rumor has remained unverified" (Fall, *Hell in a Very Small Place*, p. 62).

2. See map 6. According to Fall, "the average elevation of the French-held areas in the center of the plain of Dien Bien Phu was around 350 to 380 meters [1,150 to 1,248 feet]" (Fall, *Street Without Joy*, p. 317).

3. Fall, *Hell in a Very Small Place*, p. 61.

4. *Washington Post*, Dec. 6, 1953, p. 10.

5. National Archives, Washington, D. C., Civil Reference Branch, Record Group 59, General Records of the Department of State, Indochina, 1950–1954, Decimal File 751 G.00/8–151—751 G.00/12–3153, Box 3675, Hanoi Consulate telegram 327 from Paul J. Sturm to the Secretary of State, Dec. 5, 1953.

6. *Los Angeles Times*, Dec. 6, 1953, sec. 2A, p. 2.

7. See appendix E for a listing of the airborne, infantry, artillery, and engineer units that were stationed at Dien Bien Phu as of December 6. Unless otherwise indicated, all of the units listed are battalions. French designations are in parentheses (Fall, *Hell in a Very Small Place*, p. 479).

8. *Los Angeles Times*, Dec. 7, 1953, p. 24.

9. See AP story quoted earlier in this chapter.

10. *Times* (London), Dec. 7, 1953, p. 6. The *Times* story incorrectly attributed the communist ambush to units of the Viet-Minh 148th Independent Regiment, which had formerly occupied Dien Bien Phu, instead of to lead elements of the 316th Division.

11. Fall, *Hell in a Very Small Place*, p. 45.

12. Roy, *The Battle of Dienbienphu*, p. 74. Fall contends that Giap's order "should have put Navarre on notice that the Viet-Minh indeed was determined to stand for battle in the jungle valley [of Dien Bien Phu]" (Fall, *Hell in a Very Small Place*, p. 45). Roy, however, doubts that the French commander was aware of the order's existence. He writes: "This [order] was a major document, which the [French] listening posts did not intercept because it was probably not broadcast by radio [see chapter 4, n. 1]. . . . In it [the order] Giap clearly stated the object to be attained and defined the mission of every man in the [Viet-Nam] People's Army. . . . It may be assumed that extraordinary precautions were taken to prevent the enemy from laying hands on a document which left no doubt whatever about the intentions of the Vietminh command" (Roy, *The Battle of Dienbienphu*, pp. 74–75).

13. Of the other two regiments that made up the 304th Division, one was to remain on guard near the delta and the other was being directed toward central Viet-Nam for an upcoming operation against central Laos.

9. Pollux and Atlante

1. *Life*, Dec. 14, 1953, p. 35.
2. *Newsweek*, Dec. 14, 1953, p. 40.
3. The Piste Pavie ("Pavie Track" or "Pavie Trail"), which connected Lai Chau with Dien Bien Phu (see map 6), was, according to Fall, "a narrow jungle path which could not even accommodate jeeps in most places and in some places was even difficult for mules" (Fall, *Hell in a Very Small Place*, p. 63). It had been named in honor of August Pavie, a French explorer and diplomat, who, while serving as a vice consul in Laos in the 1880s, signed a protectorate treaty with the Thai tribes. He also signed a series of treaties with the Siames and the British that stabilized the western borders of Laos, thus earning for him the title of "Father of Modern Laos" (Bernard B. Fall, *Anatomy of a Crisis: The Laotian Crisis of 1960–1961*, p. 28).
4. The following extracts from Cogny's telegram appear in Navarre's autobiography: "Lai Chau is without military value and [is] a veritable mousetrap . . . Dien Bien Phu is, on the contrary, defensible. . . . Reinforcing Dien Bien Phu will enhance the effectiveness of the offensive actions that are anticipated from this unique recess" (Navarre, *Le Temps des Vérités*, p. 324, n. 1). In writing about Cogny's decision to evacuate Lai Chau on December 7, Fall makes the following personal observation: "I had been to Lai Chau a few weeks earlier, and the impossibility of its prolonged defense seemed obvious" (Fall, *Hell in a Very Small Place*, p. 63, n. 1). By contrast, Navarre offers a somewhat divided judgment on the timing of Operation Pollux. In the course of describing the plans for Operation Castor, Navarre notes that "the garrison at Laichau was later recalled to Dien Bien Phu, when a dangerous threat of attack was defined" (Navarre, *Agonie de l'Indochine*, p. 201).
   Further on, however, when directly discussing Pollux, Navarre implies that Cogny's decision to launch the operation was not dictated by imminent military necessity: "In the first days of December, the advance guards of the 316th Division were reported to be some distance from Laichau. General Cogny, whose first intention, approved by me, had been to hold Laichau and to 'act on a Laichau/Dien Bien Phu pairing' for as long as possible, decided to evacuate Laichau. Indeed, now, he thought that it was preferable to concentrate the defense on the 'unique recess' of Dien Bien Phu" (ibid., p. 203). In repeating the latter passage in his autobiography, *Le Temps des Vérités*, Navarre makes clear that he fully supported Cogny's decision to evacuate Lai Chau. First, he drops the above words "approved by me" and "for as long as possible" concerning Cogny's original intention to "act on a Laichau/Dien Bien Phu pairing." Second, he adds the following sentence: "I approved this decision [to evacuate] in consideration of Laichau's role, which was of little strategic importance, and of the indefensible character of the position" (Navarre, *Le Temps des Vérités*, p. 324).
5. Concerning this reserve, Navarre writes: "On the suggestion of General Gilles, [the] commander of the airborne troops [that were] charged with the

operation [Castor], I decided to allow 3 parachute battalions to remain at Dien Bien Phu which were destined to constitute the counter-attack reserve. Indeed, this role could only be taken by an infantry of high offensive quality, and the parachute battalions offered the best guarantee in this regard" (Navarre, *Agonie de l'Indochine*, p. 201, n. 1).

6. Roy, *The Battle of Dienbienphu*, p. 78. The official name for de Castries's new command was "Groupement Operational du Nord-Ouest" (Northwestern Operational Group). Observes Roy: "It was known for short as 'GONO,' a medical slang term which I would have regarded as a bad omen" (ibid., p. 77).

7. Fall puts the date for Instruction No. 964 on December 12 but Devillers and Lacouture, Catroux, and Roy all say that the instruction was issued on December 7 (Fall, *Hell in a Very Small Place*, p. 45; Devillers and Lacouture, *End of a War*, p. 45; Catroux, *Deux Actes du Drame Indochinois*, p. 157; and Roy, *The Battle of Dienbienphu*, p. 76).

8. Fall, *Hell in a Very Small Place*, pp. 45–46; Catroux, *Deux Actes du Drame Indochinois*, p. 157.

9. The Joint Chiefs of Staff had referred the O'Daniel mission's report of November 19 (designated "J.C.S. 1992/256") to the Joint Strategic Plans Committee for comment and recommendation. The Joint Strategic Plans Committee, in turn, directed (J.S.P.C. 958/135/D) the Joint Strategic Plans Group on December 3 to prepare a draft report. Prior to the completion of this report, the Joint Logistics Plans Committee requested collaboration because of the logistical implications.

10. The abbreviation CG USARPAC stood for Commanding General, U.S. Army, Pacific, and referred to General O'Daniel. The title "CHIEF, MAAG, INDOCHINA" stood for Chief, [U.S.] Military Assistance Advisory Group, Indo-China, and referred to General Trapnell.

11. The words "forced a redeployment of a portion of the enemy forces" referred to the movement of Viet-Minh Division 316 toward the northwest.

12. The words "one regiment plus one battalion" were a further reference to Viet-Minh Division 316. In a preliminary message that General O'Daniel sent to the Joint Chiefs of Staff on November 19 in order to summarize the major findings of his mission, he reported that a "large part [of the] effectives . . . [of] div[ision 316] has been diverted to meet French Union operations including guerrilla, commandos and Maquis in [the] Thai country" (U.S., Department of State, *Foreign Relations of the United States, 1952–1954*, vol. 13 [Indochina], pt. 1, p. 879).

13. The commander in chief, Pacific (CINCPAC) was Vice Adm. Felix Stump, who had succeeded JSC chairman, Adm. Arthur Radford, in that position.

14. See chapter 6 for the complete text of the report by MAAG Chief General Trapnell.

15. In addition to the reservations that had been expressed by CINCPAC and the MAAG chief (and duly noted in the draft report) concerning the French position, the U.S. Army attaché in Saigon, Colonel Shaughnessey,

responded on November 24 to the assertions in the O'Daniel report by stating flatly that there was no concrete evidence that the French Union forces
would be able to take decisive action to win the Indo-China war in the fore-
seeable future. In summarizing the six month period since the arrival of General Navarre, the attaché made the following observations: (1) Despite a series of French raids and limited objective offensive actions in northern Viet-
Nam, the Viet-Minh retained the initiative and the French were in a basically
defensive posture; (2) although the French now had larger and better organized mobile reserves than had been available six months before, these had
been formed as the result of the arrival of reinforcements, and there had been
no appreciable decrease in the number of French units committed to static
defensive missions; and (3) there had been no significant improvement in the
training of the Vietnamese Army, nor in the French psychological warfare
program, but the organization and conduct of French Union guerrilla warfare had improved (National Archives, Washington, D.C., Military Reference Branch, Record Group 319, Army-Operations, General Decimal Files
1953, 091.I, Box 37, Folder: "G-3 091 Indo China [Sec. III] [Cases 41–],"
summary of comments by the U.S. Army attaché in Saigon regarding the
report of the U.S. Joint Military Mission to Indochina, prepared by the U.S.
Army's Office of the Assistant Chief of Staff [G-2] for Intelligence, Dec. 17,
1953.) In subsequently forwarding a summary of the attaché's statements on
the O'Daniel report to the chief of staff of the army, the army's Office of the
Assistant Chief of Staff (G-2) for Intelligence observed that "the Attache's
views are in general accordance with comments from high U.S. military
officials who have expressed the opinion or who have implied that the 19
November 1953 report of Lieutenant General O'Daniel on French progress
under the Navarre plan is somewhat over-optimistic" (Ibid., comments by
the U.S. Army's Office of the Assistant Chief of Staff [G-2] for Intelligence
on the Army Attache's views regarding the report of the U.S. Joint Military
Mission to Indochina, Dec. 17, 1953). Among the other "high U.S. military
officials" who shared the attaché's opinion of the O'Daniel report was Gen.
Paul W. Caraway. Caraway, who had accompanied Vice President Richard
M. Nixon during the latter's visit to the Far East in the fall of 1953, wrote
the following in a report on Indo-China: "Conversations confirmed as cor-
rect the bulk of the information available in the Department of the Army.
General O'Daniel's report was definitely optimistic" (National Archives,
Washington, D.C., Military Reference Branch, Record Group 319, Army
Chief of Staff, General Decimal Files 1953, Decimal File 680.2, Box 835,
ACofS, G-3, to CofS, Nov. 23, 1953). Even before the O'Daniel report had
been written, Caraway made the following personal observation on Nover-
mber 13 concerning O'Daniel's general attitude toward the trip: "[General
O'Daniel] feels that Navarre will do all he promised [during the first O'Da-
niel mission]. He has developed a certain amount of resistance to any criticism of Navarre or of the French efforts" (National Archives, Washington,
D.C., Military Reference Branch, Record Group 319, Army Chief of Staff,

General Decimal Files 1953, Decimal File 680.2, Box 835, ACofS, G-3, to CofS, Nov. 13, 1953).

16. National Archives, Washington, D.C., Military Reference Branch, Record Group 218, U.S. Joint Chiefs of Staff, Geographic File, 1951–1953, 092 Asia (6–25–48), Sections 45–51, Box 7, Folder: "CCS 092 Asia (6–25–48), Sec. 50," draft report J.S.P.C. 958/136 by the Joint Strategic Plans Committee (in collaboration with the Joint Logistics Plans Committee) to the Joint Chiefs of Staff on "Report of U.S. Joint Military Mission to Indochina," Dec. 7, 1953. On December 9 the Joint Strategic Plans Committee approved the December 7 draft report prepared by the Joint Strategic Plans Group, subject to minor changes, none of which affected the extended excerpts from the draft report, as presented in this chapter.

10. The View from Bermuda

1. The Bermuda meeting of the western Big Three was originally planned, at Prime Minister Churchill's request, for June 1953. The talks were rescheduled for July when the French government of René Mayer fell on May 21 and they were postponed indefinitely after Churchill suffered a stroke on June 24. See appendix F for the text of presidential Press Secretary James Hagerty's announcement of the Bermuda Conference on November 10, 1953 (Dwight D. Eisenhower Library, Abilene, Kansas, White House Central Files, Official File 116 [Foreign Affairs-Foreign Policy Series], Box 588, folder: "116–0 Bermuda Conference," Hagerty statement to the press, Nov. 10, 1953).

2. Bidault was referring to a tripartite meeting of the Big Three foreign ministers that was held in Washington from July 10 to 14, 1953.

3. The word "cadre," in military parlance, can, strictly speaking, mean staff officers, or it can refer, in a more general sense, to a group that forms a nucleus of trained personnel around which an expanded military unit can be built.

4. Gen. Jean de Lattre de Tassigny was both the commander in chief of the French Expeditionary Corps in Indo-China and the high commissioner of Indo-China from December 1950 to January 1952.

5. U.S., Department of State, *Foreign Relations of the United States, 1952–1954*, vol. 5 [Western European Security], pt. 2, p. 1825.

6. The French Military Academy at St. Cyr was the counterpart of Britain's Sandhurst or America's West Point. Casualties among the French officer corps in Indo-China were the subject of a "top secret" report that the State Department had sent to the U.S. National Security Council on August 5, 1953. The report read: "Since World War II, the war in Indochina has been a heavy drain on French military and financial resources. . . . and in the seven years [since the war began] the French Union has had 148,000 casual-

ties" (U.S., Department of State, *Foreign Relations of the United States, 1952–1954*, vol. 13 [Indochina], pt. 1, p. 714). By October 1953, according to John McCuen, total casualties had grown to 161,344, a figure which included 64,374 dead and missing, 55,371 wounded, and 41,599 sick or evacuated. See appendix G, for McCuen's breakdown on these casualties according to the various types of French Union forces (McCuen, *The Art of Counter-Revolutionary War*, p. 260).

By 1953 draftees into the French Army were no longer being sent to Indo-China since, as Bernard Fall explains, "the French Parliament, by an amendment to the Budget Law of 1950, restricted the use of draftees to French 'homeland' territory (i.e., France and Algeria, and French-occupied areas of Germany), thus severely limiting the number of troops that could be made available to the Indochina theater of operations" (Fall, *Hell in a Very Small Place*, p. viii). As a result, says Fall, "the war bit deeper into the vitals of the French professional army" (ibid., p. vii) and the State Department report to the NSC observed that the 148,000 casualties "had' absorbed a large percentage of the officers and non-commissioned officers of the regular French army" (U.S., Department of State, *Foreign Relations of the United States, 1952–1954*, vol. 13 [Indochina], pt. 1, p. 714). Robert Randle says specifically that by the fall of 1953, the Indo-China war "had consumed 25 per cent [sic] of the officers and 40 per cent of the non-commissioned officers of the French army" (Robert F. Randle, *Geneva 1954: The Settlement of the Indochinese War*, p. 6).

In an address entitled "The Communist Campaign in the Far East," that was made before the Chamber of Commerce of Louisville, Kentucky on October 14, 1953, the U.S. assistant secretary of state for Far Eastern affairs, Walter Robertson, said: "The war has been horribly costly to France. Last year [1952] the casualties among French officers in Indochina was 568—18 more than the entire number, 550, that graduated from the French Military Academy of St. Cyr" (U.S., Department of State, *Department of State Bulletin*, Nov. 2, 1953, vol. 29, no. 749, p. 593). Roy gives this breakdown on casualties among French Union forces as of May 1953: "Since it had begun, the Indochinese War had killed 3 generals, 8 colonels, 18 lieutenant colonels, 69 majors, 341 captains, 1,140 lieutenants, 3,683 NCO's and 6,008 soldiers of French nationality; 12,019 Legionnaires and Africans; and 14,093 natives. These figures did not include the missing—over twenty thousand—or the wounded or those repatriated on health grounds—over 100,000" (Roy, *The Battle of Dienbienphu*, p. 12).

7. Bidault's outline of French strategy was not an entirely accurate representation of the Navarre Plan. See General Trapnell's report (chapter 6), Navarre's memoirs (chapter 6, n. 4), and appendix B.

8. Bidault was referring to internal politics within the Associated State of Viet-Nam.

9. American officials had foreseen the likelihood that the French would raise

the issue at Bermuda of possible enemy air action against their forces in Indo-China. The Joint Chiefs of Staff history of the war in Viet-Nam describes the measures that were taken as follows:

> In preparation for the [Bermuda] conference, the Joint Chiefs of Staff directed the Joint Intelligence Committee [on November 13, 1953] to evaluate repetitive French reports indicating that the Chinese Communists might support the Viet Minh with jet aircraft. The committee could not find corroboration for French fears. It reported to the [Joint] Chiefs [on November 25] that although the Chinese were capable of furnishing jet or conventional aircraft support for the Viet Minh, U.S. intelligence did not indicate either an increase in this capability or an intent by the Chinese to intervene with jets in Indochina. The Joint Chiefs agreed, and so informed the Secretary of Defense [on December 1]. They took no other action in preparing material for use in the Indochinese phase of the Bermuda discussions (Joint Chiefs of Staff, *The History of the Joint Chiefs of Staff. The Joint Chiefs of Staff and the War in Vietnam: History of the Indochina Incident, 1940–1954,* vol. 1, p. 325)

10. Dwight D. Eisenhower Library, Abilene, Kansas, Dwight D. Eisenhower: Papers as President of the United States, 1953–1961 (Ann Whitman File), International Meetings Series, Box 1, Folder: "Bermuda-Miscellaneous," memorandum by President Eisenhower on the Bermuda Conference, Dec. 10, 1953.

11. Churchill's mention of "North Africa" was an apparent reference to Morocco and Algeria.

12. National Archives, Washington, D.C., Civil Reference Branch, Record Group 59, General Records of the Department of State, Council of Ministers (Bermuda Conference), 1953–54, Decimal File 396.1/10–1953—396.1/8–1954, Box 1452, Bermuda telegram 24 from the Secretary of State to the State Department, Dec. 7, 1953.

13. *Chicago Tribune,* Dec. 8, 1953, p. 7.

14. *Atlanta Constitution,* Dec. 8, 1953, p. 1. No official account of the Bermuda Conference confirms Dulles's purported offer of additional U.S. military personnel for Indo-China beyond those already stationed there as part of the U.S. Military Assistance Advisory Group (MAAG). However, newspapers in both France and Britain echoed the UP report. In a telegram to the State Department the next day giving a "roundup" of French press reaction to the Bermuda Conference, Attaché Theodore Achilles included the following item: "[The] *Aurore* leads [its] front-page with [a] heavy head[line], 'American instructors for [the] Vietnam army? Such is [the] offer of Eisenhower at Bermuda.' [The] Report that [the] US has offered [a] military mission, similar to [the] one to Greece, for Indochina appears in [a] number of papers" (National Archives, Washington, D. C., Civil Reference Branch, Record Group 59, General Records of the Department of State, Council of Ministers [Bermuda Conference], 1953–1954, Decimal File 396.1/10–1953—396.1/8–1954, Box 1452, Paris Embassy telegram 2215 from Theodore C.

Achilles to the Secretary of State, Dec. 8, 1953). In a similar report on "Tuesday press comment on Bermuda" from British newspapers, Ambassador Winthrop Aldrich included the following information: "[The] *Mail's* correspondent Broadbent believes '[that the] US agreed to expand immediately its military omissions [missions] in Indochina' and 'American experts will be sent without delay to train Vietnam forces and release some French troops'" (Ibid., London Embassy telegram 2500 from Winthrop W. Aldrich to the Secretary of State, Dec. 8, 1953).

11. Evacuation

1. Leda was the mythological mother of Castor and Pollux.
2. The initials ZONO stood for Zone Opérationnelle Nord-Ouest (Northwestern Operational Zone). This area centered around Lai Chau and was commanded by Lieutenant Colonel Trancart.
3. Navarre writes the following concerning the implementation of Leda and Pollux: "The regular garrison of Laichau rejoined Dien Bien Phu by air on December 8. Part of the support units rejoined it by land. The others went underground" (Navarre, *Agonie de l'Indochine*, p. 204).
4. *Chicago Tribune*, Dec. 9, 1953, sec. 4, p. 1.
5. *Times* (London), Dec. 9, 1953, p. 6. Fall writes the following concerning Deo Van Long: "On [December 8] . . . the old leader and his entourage of graceful princesses and ballet dancers embarked on a C-47 transport plane for Hanoi" (Fall, *Hell in a Very Small Place*, p. 63).
6. The actual distance between Lai Chau and the Chinese frontier was thirty miles.
7. *Washington Post*, Dec. 9, 1953, p. 3. No other source corroborated the UP's story of a Viet-Minh attack against Lai Chau on December 8.
8. The remaining four days of the mission's visit were presumably spent in Saigon where the French High Command was headquartered.
9. This "general concept" was a reference to the Navarre Plan.
10. A French *groupe mobile* (mobile group) consisted of two or three thousand troops (the size of a U.S. regimental combat team) and included some tank and artillery elements. In 1953 it remained the largest tactical unit with which the French operated in Indo-China. By contrast, the Viet-Minh's six infantry divisions and one heavy division were modeled on Chinese-type, ten-thousand-man divisions. See chapter 1, n. 6, concerning the organization of the Viet-Minh divisions. In comparing the head-to-head fighting potential of a French *groupe mobile* and a Viet-Minh division, John Prados observes: "The [Viet-Nam] People's Army had no tanks and until 1953 did not have many artillery guns either, but its divisions were still too large for an average *groupe mobile* to engage" (Prados, *The Sky Would Fall*, p. 17).
11. U.S., Department of State, *Foreign Relations of the United States, 1952–1954*, vol. 13 [Indochina], pt. 1, pp. 903–906. Bonsal's memorandum was favorably

received by his superiors at the State Department. Everett F. Drumright, the deputy assistant secretary of state for Far Eastern affairs, later wrote the following note on the top of the memorandum: "Seen by WSR [Walter S. Robertson] on 12–12–53. A very well put memo" (ibid, p. 903, n. 1).

12. *Los Angeles Times*, Dec. 10, 1953, p. 16.

13. Ibid. This attack is not corroborated by any other source and the description given by the UP bears little resemblance to the Viet-Minh ambush that did occur that day. See chapter 8.

14. *Times* (London), Dec. 10, 1953, p. 8.

15. U.S., Department of State, *Foreign Relations of the United States, 1952–1954*, vol. 13 (Indochina), pt. 1, pp. 915–16.

16. National Archives, Washington, D.C., Civil Reference Branch, Record Group 59, General Records of the Department of State, Indochina, 1950–1954, Decimal File 751G.00/8–151–751G.00/12–3153, Box 3675, Hanoi Consulate telegram 334 from Paul J. Sturm to the Secretary of State, Dec. 10, 1953.

17. In reporting this portion of Cogny's remarks to the State Department, Sturm added in parentheses: "that is, not to create another Na San" (ibid.).

18. U.S., Department of State, *Foreign Relations of the United States, 1952–1954*, vol. 13 (Indochina), pt. 1, p. 914. Telegram 968 reported on Heath's visit with Navarre on December 4, in the company of Senator Thye.

12. Epilogue: An Engagement of Forces

Note: Any quoted text in this chapter for which detail regarding source is not given has already appeared in chapters one through 11.

1. Roy, *The Battle of Dienbienphu*, p. 59.

2. Fall confirms Navarre's view of "Operation Lorraine." Referring to Cogny's proposal for a diversionary attack from the Red River Delta in order to relieve the pressure on Dien Bien Phu, he writes as follows:

A similar operation, code-named "Lorraine," had been tried in November, 1952. . . .

. . . Operation "Lorraine" was . . . disastrous. Although involving close to 30,000 men, including several airborne and armored battalions, it not only ran out of steam before it was able to reach Yen Bay [see map 5] but on the return to the delta, a part of the French troops fell into a large-scale ambush at the gorges of Chan-Muong and sustained heavy losses. "Lorraine," too, had been mounted in good part for the purpose of compelling the Communist divisions that had begun to invade the T'ai [Thai] highlands [see chapter 2 n. 10] to fall back in order to rush to the defense of their own rear areas. (Fall, *Hell in a Very Small Place*, pp. 41–42)

3. Fall confirms Navarre on this point as well, writing: "The [Lorraine] strategy

had failed because Giap had never departed from his strategy of leaving smaller units to fend for themselves even at great costs because he was absolutely certain, thanks to his excellent intelligence network, that such French offensive operations would always sooner or later run out of steam" (ibid., pp. 42–43).

4. Navarre, *Agonie de l'Indochine*, pp. 164, 166–68.
5. Ibid., p. 168.
6. Fall, *Hell in a Very Small Place*, p. 42.
7. Catroux, *Deux Actes du Drame Indochinois*, p. 154.
8. Navarre, *Le Temps des Vérités*, p. 430.
9. Quoted earlier in this chapter. See quotation preceding reference in text for note 4.
10. Catroux, *Deux Actes du Drame Indochinois*, p. 154.
11. Fall, *Hell in a Very Small Place*, p. 45.
12. Roy, *The Battle of Dienbienphu*, p. 76.
13. John Keegan, *Dien Bien Phu*, p. 61.
14. Laniel, Le Drame Indochinois, *pp. 38–39*.
15. See chapter 6, n. 4.
16. Navarre, *Agonie de l'Indochine*, pp. 212–13.
17. Ibid., p. 213.
18. Fall, *Hell in a Very Small Place*, p. 49.
19. Navarre, *Agonie de l'Indochine*, pp. 212–13.
20. Navarre, *Le Temps des Vérités*, p. 330.
21. Ibid., p. 303, n. 1.
22. Navarre, *Agonie de l'Indochine*, p. 170.
23. This portion of Navarre's memoirs appears earlier in this chapter. See passage preceding reference in text for note 16.
24. Navarre, *Le Temps des Vérités*, p. 430.
25. Ibid.
26. Roy, *The Battle of Dienbienphu*, p. 66.
27. Fall, *Hell in a Very Small Place*, p. 44.
28. See chapter 3, n. 11.
29. Navarre, *Agonie de l'Indochine*, p. 202.
30. See chapter 3, n. 9.
31. See chapter 5, n. 9.
32. That is, mentions by Consul Sturm twice, General Navarre three times, and General Trapnell once.
33. Quoted earlier in this chapter. See quotation preceding reference in text for note 29.
34. Roy, *The Battle of Dienbienphu*, p. 29.
35. Ibid., p. 24.
36. Navarre, *Agonie de l'Indochine*, pp. 174–75.
37. Roy, *The Battle of Dienbienphu*, p. 76.
38. Fall, *Hell in a Very Small Place*, p. 46.

39. Ibid.
40. The relevant passage from Laniel's memoirs appears earlier in this chapter. See quotation preceding reference in text for note 14.
41. Quoted earlier in this chapter. See quotation preceding reference in text for note 4.
42. See chapter 5, n. 7.
43. Stephen Jurika, ed., *From Pearl Harbor to Vietnam: The Memoirs of Admiral Arthur W. Radford*, p. 350.
44. Fall, *Hell in a Very Small Place*, p. 50.
45. Ibid., p. 30.
46. The relevant passage from Fall's book appears earlier in this chapter. See quotation preceding reference in text for note 27.
47. Roy, *The Battle of Dienbienphu*, pp. 10–11.
48. Ibid., p. 44.
49. Navarre, *Agonie de l'Indochine*, p. 199.
50. Ibid., p. 196.
51. Roy, *The Battle of Dienbienphu*, pp. 77–78.
52. *Washington Post*, Jan. 26, 1969, sec. B, p. 5.
53. See chapter 11, n. 3.
54. In a footnote at this point, Navarre observes: "It had been allowable for General Cogny to obtain the required strength by accelerating the consignment to Dien Bien Phu of battalions [that were] anticipated for supporting the garrison, at a figure fixed by me. Chiefly preoccupied by the [Red River] Delta, General Cogny did not do it. It had been equally possible for him to send the supplementary manpower under the form of detachments of prisoners" (Navarre, *Agonie de l'Indochine*, p. 204, n. 1). Note: the words "at a figure fixed by me" refer to Dien Bien Phu's assigned strength of nine battalions.
55. Ibid., p. 204.
56. Fall, *Hell in a Very Small Place*, p. 62.
57. By the words "China frontier," Navarre explains, he is referring to "points of the Chinese frontier where supplies [for the Viet-Minh] entered [Viet-Nam]" (Navarre, *Agonie de l'Indochine*, p. 195, n. 1).
58. Ibid., p. 195.
59. See chapter 3, n. 26 concerning Giap's strategic thinking on this point. For Navarre's strategy, see the quotation from his memoirs that appears earlier in this chapter, preceding reference in text for note 41.
60. See chapter 6, n. 4.
61. Lancaster, *The Emancipation of French Indochina*, p. 287, n. 48.
62. Quoted earlier in this chapter. See quotation preceding references in text for notes 54 and 55.
63. Quoted earlier in this chapter. See quotation preceding references in text for notes 57 and 58 for Navarre's initial comments on enemy logistics.
64. In a footnote at this point, Navarre writes: "It was estimated until then that 20,000 coolies was the maximum strength that was able to be assembled and maintained by the Vietminh in the Upper region [of Indo-China], as a result

of lack of rice and the difficulties of transport" (Navarre, *Agonie de l'Indochine*, p. 206, n. 1).

65. The words "from nothing" (*de toutes pièces*) are apparently intended to mean that about one hundred kilometers of roads were built where no previous paths existed upon which to build them.

66. Navarre, *Agonie de l'Indochine*, pp. 205–206. See map 5 for Navarre's map of "Vietminh Lines of Communication" toward Dien Bien Phu (ibid., p. 207). The information in the map's key reads as follows: "Principal lines of supply of the [Viet-Minh] siege corps of Dien Bien Phu; Secondary lines of supply; Actions envisaged by us [generals Navarre and Cogny on November 28] for cutting Vietminh communications" (ibid.).

67. Ibid., p. 206. See map 5. In a footnote at this point, Navarre observes: "It is therefore entirely inaccurate that, as was claimed, the location of Dien Bien Phu in proximity (80 kilometers) [50 miles] to the Chinese frontier favored the Vietminh. This was not the Chinese region—near which the retrenched camp was located—that issued the decisive aid." (ibid., p. 206, n. 3). Note: Dien Bien Phu was actually located about 85 miles from the Chinese frontier, not 50 miles as Navarre claims.

68. Fall, *Hell in a Very Small Place*, p. 59.

69. Keegan, *Dien Bien Phu*, pp. 67, 75.

70. H. G. Martin, "The War in Indo-China," *Brassey's Annual: The Armed Forces Year-Book, 1954*, p. 249.

71. O'Ballance, *The Indo-China War, 1945–1954*, pp. 204, 207–208.

72. See portion of Dommen's summary, quoted earlier in this chapter, preceding reference in text for note 52.

73. *Washington Post*, Jan. 26, 1969, sec. B, p. 5.

74. See Navarre's earlier quotation in this chapter, preceding reference in text for note 29.

75. Navarre, *Agonie de l'Indochine*, p. 239.

76. This quotation is taken from the portion of Dommen's summary, preceding reference in text for note 73.

77. Navarre, *Le Temps des Vérités*, p. 439. For Navarre's other remarks on his awareness of the growing Viet-Minh threat, see the series of quotations from earlier in this chapter, preceding references in text for notes 19 through 22.

78. Fall, *Hell in a Very Small Place*, pp. 47–48.

79. Laniel, *Le Drame Indochinois*, pp. 38–39, 51.

80. Norman E. Martin, "Dien Bien Phu and the Future of Airborne Operations," *Military Review*, vol. 36, no. 3 (June 1956), p. 25.

81. Navarre, *Agonie de l'Indochine*, pp. 238–39. For Navarre's comments on the initial conception of the camp and the developing enemy threat, see his quotation from earlier in this chapter, preceding reference in text for note 16.

82. Ibid., p. 239, n. 1.

83. Melvin Gurtov, *The First Vietnam Crisis: Chinese Communist Strategy and United States Involvement, 1953–1954*, pp. 180–81, n. 63.

84. Dwight D. Eisenhower Library, Abilene, Kansas, Oral History Transcripts,

Oral History Transcript 121, interview with Walter S. Robertson, April 18, 1967, pp. 72–73. The collection is hereafter cited as Oral History Transcripts.

85. Gurtov, *The First Vietnam Crisis,* pp. 180–81, n. 63.

86. Oral History Transcripts, Robertson interview, pp. 72–73.

87. Gurtov, *The First Vietnam Crisis,* pp. 50–51.

88. Fall, *Hell in a Very Small Place,* pp. 106, 108.

89. James M. Gavin, *Crisis Now,* p. 41.

90. Navarre, for his part, had a less than tender opinion of Trapnell's professional abilities. He writes: "General Trapnell [was] a second-class military personality, but very efficacious and a very correct man, anxious to remain scrupulously within the limits of his duties" (Navarre, *Agonie de l'Indochine,* p. 136).

91. Gavin, *Crisis Now,* p. 41.

92. William B. Rosson, "Four Periods of American Involvement in Vietnam: Development and Implementation of Policy, Strategy and Programs, Described and Analyzed on the Basis of Service Experience at Progressively Senior Levels," p. 17.

93. U.S. Army Center of Military History, Washington, D.C., Historical Services Division, Historical Records Branch, File EY SEA-RS-489, synopsis of interview with Matthew B. Ridgway, April 15, 1976, p. 1. The collection is hereafter cited as Historical Records Branch.

94. Ibid.

95. Jurika, ed., *From Pearl Harbor to Vietnam,* p. 377.

96. Quoted earlier in this chapter. See quotation preceding reference in text for note 43.

97. Historical Records Branch, File EY SEA-RS-494, summary of interview with John W. O'Daniel, Feb. 4–5, 1975, p. 1.

98. Ibid.

99. Oral History Transcripts, Transcript 14, interview with Dwight D. Eisenhower, July 28, 1964, pp. 25–26.

100. Oral History Transcripts, Transcript 11, interview with Dwight D. Eisenhower, July 20, 1967, pp. 64–65.

101. Dwight D. Eisenhower, *Mandate for Change: The White House Years, 1953–1956,* p. 339.

102. Oral History Transcripts, Robertson interview, p. 73.

103. Oral History Transcripts, Transcript 91, interview with James C. Hagerty, Jan. 31, 1968, p. 112.

104. Oral History Transcripts, Transcript 91, interview with James C. Hagerty, April 17, 1968, p. 544.

105. Dwight D. Eisenhower Library, Abilene, Kansas, Dwight D. Eisenhower: Papers as President of the United States, 1953–1961 (Ann Whitman File), International Meetings Series, Box 1, Folder: "Bermuda-Miscellaneous," memorandum by President Eisenhower on the Bermuda Conference, Dec. 10, 1953.

106. Marquis Childs, *Eisenhower: Captive Hero. A Critical Study of the General and the President,* pp. 200–201.

107. Joseph and Stewart Alsop, *The Reporter's Trade,* pp. 48–49.

108. See Ambassador Heath's cable on his talk with General Navarre (chapter 2) and Navarre's subsequent conversation with General Bull (chapter 3).

109. Bonsal declined to answer a series of written questions concerning this period of his tenure as PSA director (letter from the author to Philip W. Bonsal, Oct. 28, 1987; letter from Philip W. Bonsal to the author, Nov. 19, 1987).

110. See chapter 6, n. 9 concerning the O'Daniel report's comments on Operation Mouette. See chapter 9, nn. 11, 12 concerning the report's references to the military situation in the northwest.

111. See chapter 9, n. 15.

112. French plans for Operation Castor, according to Admiral Radford, "had not even been mentioned to General O'Daniel during his [November 1953] visit" (Jurika, ed., *From Pearl Harbor to Vietnam,* p. 377). O'Daniel confirmed this in his February 1975 interview, saying: "Neither I nor any other American I know of was consulted about the Dien Bien Phu operation until it was actually underway" (Historical Records Branch, O'Daniel interview, p. 3).

113. U.S., Department of Defense, *United States–Vietnam Relations, 1945–1967* (The Pentagon Papers), vol. 1, sec. II.A.1, p. A-39.

114. Historical Records Branch, Ridgway interview, p. 1.

115. Historical Records Branch, O'Daniel interview, p. 3.

116. Ibid.

Bibliography

Archives and Libraries

Dwight D. Eisenhower Library, Abilene, Kans.:
Audiovisual Department: Picture nos. 72-590-2, 72-591-3.
Dwight D. Eisenhower, Papers as President of the United States, 1953–1961, (Ann Whitman File).
International Meetings Series.
International Series.
Oral History transcripts 11, 14, 91, 121.
White House Central Files; Official File 116, Foreign Affairs–Foreign Policy Series

National Archives, Washington, D.C.:
Civil Reference Branch: Record Group 59, General Records of the Department of State, Indochina, 1950–54; Record Group 59, Council of Ministers (Bermuda Conference), 1953–54.
Military Reference Branch: Record Group 218, U.S. Joint Chiefs of Staff, Chairman's File, Admiral Radford, 1953–57; Record Group 218, and Geographic File, 1951–53; Record Group 319, Army Chief of Staff; Record Group 319, Army-Operations; Record Group 330, Secretary of Defense, Assistant Secretary of Defense (International Security Affairs), Office of Military Assistance.
Still Picture Branch: Picture nos. 306-PS-53-9838, 306-PS-55-4100.

U.S. Air Force, Office of Air Force History, Bolling Air Force Base, Washington, D.C.:
"History, 483rd Troop Carrier Wing (Medium), 315th Air Division (Combat Cargo), July 1, 1953–December 31, 1953.
315th Air Division (Combat Cargo), "History, 1953–1954, Special Report–Far Eastern Air Forces, Participation in French Indo-China."

U.S. Army Center of Military History, Washington, D.C., Historical Services Division, Historical Records Branch:
Files EY SEA-RS-489, SEA-RS-494.
U.S. Joint Military Mission to Indochina, "Progress Report on Military Situation in Indochina as of 19 November 1953."

U.S. Army Military History Institute, Archives, Carlisle Barracks, Penn., Joseph A. McChristian Papers.

Articles, Books, and Documents

Alsop, Joseph, and Stewart Alsop. *The Reporter's Trade.* New York: Reynal, 1958.

"Armed Truce Only: No Peace in Korea." *U.S. News & World Report,* December 4, 1953, pp. 22–23.

Backlund, Donald R. "Stalingrad and Dien Bien Phu: Two Cases of Failure in Strategic Resupply." *Aerospace Historian* 17 (Summer–Fall, 1970).

"Bold French Get the Jump on Vietminh." *Life,* December 14, 1953, p. 35.

Boudarel, Georges. *Giap.* Paris: Éditions Atlas, 1977.

Bowers, Ray L. *The United States Air Force in Southeast Asia: Tactical Airlift.* Washington, D.C.: Office of Air Force History, 1983.

Brelis, Dean, and Jill Krementz. *The Face of South Vietnam.* Boston: Houghton Mifflin, 1968.

Burchett, Wilfred G. *The Furtive War: The United States in Vietnam and Laos.* New York: International Publishers, 1963.

Buttinger, Joseph. *The Smaller Dragon: A Political History of Vietnam.* New York: Frederick A. Praeger, 1958.

———. *Vietnam: A Dragon Embattled,* vol. 2. New York: Frederick A. Praeger, 1967.

Cameron, Allan W., ed. *Viet-Nam Crisis: A Documentary History,* vol. 1 (1940–56). Ithaca, N.Y.: Cornell University Press, 1971.

Catroux, Georges. *Deux Actes du Drame Indochinois-Hanoi: Juin 1940; Dien Bien Phu: Mars–Mai 1954.* Paris: Librairie Plon, 1959.

Childs, Marquis. *Eisenhower: Captive Hero. A Critical Study of the General and the President.* New York: Harcourt, Brace, 1958.

"Churchill: In the Last Stage." *Newsweek,* October 26, 1953, p. 49.

Curl, Peter V., ed. *Documents on American Foreign Relations, 1953.* Published for the Council on Foreign Relations. New York: Harper & Brothers, 1954.

Devillers, Philippe and Jean Lacouture. *End of a War: Indochina, 1954.* New York: Frederick A. Praeger, 1969.

Doyle, Edward et al. *Passing the Torch: The Vietnam Experience.* Boston: Boston Publishing Co., 1981.

Eisenhower, Dwight D. *Mandate for Change: The White House Years, 1953–1956.* Garden City, N.Y.: Doubleday, 1963.

Fall, Bernard B. *Anatomy of a Crisis: The Laotian Crisis of 1960–1961.* Garden City, N.Y.: Doubleday, 1969.

———. "Post Mortems on Dien Bien Phu." *Far Eastern Survey,* October, 1958.

———. *Hell in a Very Small Place: The Siege of Dien Bien Phu.* New York: J. B. Lippincott, 1967.

———. *Street Without Joy.* 4th ed., rev. Harrisburg: Stackpole, 1964.

———. *The Two Viet-Nams: A Political and Military Analysis.* 2nd ed., rev. New York: Frederick A. Praeger, 1967.

————. *Viet-Nam Witness: 1953–1966.* New York: Frederick A. Praeger, 1966.

Fifield, Russell H. *The Diplomacy of Southeast Asia.* New York: Harper & Brothers, 1958.

Gavin, James M., with Arthur T. Hadley. *Crisis Now.* New York: Random House, 1968.

Gras, Yves. *Histoire de la Guerre d'Indochine.* Paris: Librairie Plon, 1959.

Gurtov, Melvin. *The First Vietnam Crisis: Chinese Communist Strategy and United States Involvement, 1953–1954.* New York: Columbia University Press, 1967.

Harrison, James Pinckney. *The Endless War: Fifty Years of Struggle in Vietnam.* New York: Free Press, 1982.

"Hit and Run." *Newsweek,* December 21, 1953, p. 42.

Jirika, Stephen, Jr., ed. *From Pearl Harbor to Vietnam: The Memoirs of Admiral Arthur W. Radford.* Stanford, Calif.: Stanford University, Hoover Institution Press, 1980.

"Jungle War: Turn of the Tide." *Newsweek,* December 14, 1953, p. 40.

Karnow, Stanley. *Vietnam: A History.* New York: Viking Press, 1983.

Keegan, John. *Dien Bien Phu.* New York: Ballantine Books, 1974.

Koch, Harlan G. "Terrain Tailors Tactics in Indochina." *United States Army Combat Forces Journal,* April, 1954.

Lancaster, Donald. *The Emancipation of French Indochina.* Published for the Royal Institute of International Affairs. London: Oxford University Press, 1961.

Langlais, Pierre. *Dien Bien Phu.* Paris: Éditions France–Empire, 1963.

Laniel, Joseph. *Le Drame Indochinois: De Dien-Bien-Phu au Pari de Genève.* Paris: Librairie Plon, 1957.

Maclear, Michael. *The Ten Thousand Day War: Vietnam, 1945–1975.* New York: Avon Books, 1981.

McCuen, John J. *The Art of Counter-Revolutionary War: The Strategy of Counter-Insurgency.* Harrisburg, Penn.: Stackpole Books, 1966.

Martin, H. G. "The War in Indo-China." In *Brassey's Annual: The Armed Forces Year-Book, 1954.* New York: Macmillan, 1954.

Martin, Norman E. "Dien Bien Phu and the Future of Airborne Operations." *Military Review,* vol. 36, no. 3 (June, 1956).

Navarre, Henri. *Agonie de l'Indochine, 1953–1954.* Paris: Librairie Plon, 1956.

————. *Le Temps des Vérités.* Paris: Librairie Plon, 1979.

O'Ballance, Edgar. *The Indo-China War, 1945–1954: A Study in Guerrilla Warfare.* London: Faber & Faber, 1964.

O'Neill, Robert J. *Indo China Tragedy, 1945–1954.* Melbourne, Australia: F. W. Cheshire, 1968.

Porter, Gareth, ed. *Vietnam: The Definitive Documentation of Human Decisions.* vol. 1. Stanfordville, N.Y.: Earl M. Coleman, 1979.

Prados, John. *The Sky Would Fall. Operation Vulture: The U.S. Bombing Mission in Indochina, 1954.* New York: Dial Press, 1983.

Randle, Robert F. *Geneva 1954: The Settlement of the Indochinese War.* Princeton, N.J.: Princeton University Press, 1969.

Rosson, William B. "Four Periods of American Involvement in Vietnam: Development and Implementation of Policy, Strategy and Programs, Described and

Analyzed on the Basis of Service Experience at Progressively Senior Levels." Ph.D. dissertation, University of Oxford, 1979.

Roy, Jules. *The Battle of Dienbienphu.* New York: Harper & Row, 1965.

Santoli, Al. *To Bear Any Burden: The Vietnam War and its Aftermath in the Words of Americans and Southeast Asians.* New York: E. P. Dutton, 1985.

"Seize and Hold." *Time,* November 30, 1953, p. 42.

Simcock, William. "Dien Bien Phu: Yesterday's Battlefield." *Canadian Army Journal* 12 (July, 1958).

Smith, Robert Ross. *United States Army in World War II. The War in the Pacific: Triumph in the Philippines.* Washington, D.C.: U.S. Army Center of Military History, 1984.

Snyder, Glenn H. "The New Look of 1953." In Warner R. Schilling, Paul Y. Hammond, and Glenn H. Snyder, *Strategy, Politics and Defense Budgets.* New York: Columbia University Press, 1962.

Spector, Ronald H. *United States Army in Vietnam; Advice and Support: The Early Years, 1941–1960.* Washington, D.C.: U.S. Army Center of Military History, 1983.

Stanley, George F. G. "Dien Bien in Retrospect." *International Journal,* vol. 10, no. 1 (Winter, 1954–55).

Tanham, George K. *Communist Revolutionary Warfare: From the Vietminh to the Vietcong.* Rev. ed. New York: Frederick A. Praeger, 1967.

"Three by the Sea." *Time,* December 14, 1953, p. 32.

Trinquier, Roger. *Modern Warfare: A French View of Counterinsurgency.* New York: Frederick A. Praeger, 1964.

Turner, Robert F. *Vietnamese Communism: Its Origins and Development.* Stanford, Calif.: Stanford University, Hoover Institution Press, 1975.

Vo Nguyen Giap. *Dien Bien Phu.* 2nd ed. Hanoi: Foreign Languages Publishing House, 1962.

Warner, Denis. *The Last Confucian.* New York: Macmillan, 1963.

"Without a Fight." *Time,* December 21, 1953, p. 30.

Zasloff, Joseph J. *The Role of Sanctuary in Insurgency: Communist China's Support to the Vietminh, 1946–1954.* Santa Monica, Calif.: The Rand Corp., Memorandum RM-4618-PR, May, 1967.

Official Documents and Histories

U.S. Congress, Senate Subcommittee on the Far East of the Committee on Foreign Relations, 83rd Congress, 2nd Session. *The Far East and South Asia: Report of Senator H. Alexander Smith, Chairman, Subcommittee on the Far East, Senate, Committee on Foreign Relations, on a Study Mission to the Far East* (Committee Print), January 25, 1954. Washington, D.C.: U.S. Government Printing Office, 1954.

U.S. Department of Defense. *United States–Vietnam Relations, 1945–1967* (The

Pentagon Papers), vol. 1, Washington, D.C.: U.S. Government Printing Office, 1971.

U.S. Department of State. *Department of State Bulletin.*

U.S. Department of State. *Foreign Relations of the United States, 1952–1954,* vol. 5, pt. 2. Washington, D.C.: U.S. Government Printing Office, 1983, 1982.

U.S. Department of State. *Foreign Relations of the United States, 1952–1954,* vol. 13, pt. 1. Washington, D.C.: U.S. Government Printing Office, 1982.

U.S. Joint Chiefs of Staff. *The History of the Joint Chiefs of Staff. The Joint Chiefs of Staff and the War in Vietnam: History of the Indochina Incident, 1940–1954,* vol. 1. Wilmington, Del.: Michael Glazier, 1982.

Index